Palgrave Studies in European Union Poli

Edited by: **Michelle Egan**, American Univ
College of Europe, Bruges and Honorary Pro
Paterson OBE, University of Aston, UK.

Editorial Board: **Christopher Hill**, Cambridge, UK, ...
Economics, UK, **Mark Pollack**, Temple University, USA, **Kalypso Nicolaïdis**, Oxford UK,
Morten Egeberg, University of Oslo, Norway, **Amy Verdun**, University of Victoria, Canada,
Claudio M. Radaelli, University of Exeter, UK, **Frank Schimmelfennig**, Swiss Federal
Institute of Technology, Switzerland.

Following on the sustained success of the acclaimed *European Union Series*, which essentially publishes research-based textbooks, *Palgrave Studies in European Union Politics* publishes cutting edge research-driven monographs.

The remit of the series is broadly defined, both in terms of subject and academic discipline.
All topics of significance concerning the nature and operation of the European Union
potentially fall within the scope of the series. The series is multidisciplinary to reflect the
growing importance of the EU as a political, economic and social phenomenon.

Titles include:

Jens Blom-Hansen
THE EU COMITOLOGY SYSTEM IN THEORY AND PRACTICE
Keeping an Eye on the Commission?

Oriol Costa and Knud Erik Jørgensen (*editors*)
THE INFLUENCE OF INTERNATIONAL INSTITUTIONS ON THE EU
When Multilateralism hits Brussels

Falk Daviter
POLICY FRAMING IN THE EUROPEAN UNION

Renaud Dehousse (*editor*)
THE 'COMMUNITY METHOD'
Obstinate or Obsolete?

Kenneth Dyson and Angelos Sepos (*editors*)
WHICH EUROPE?
The Politics of Differentiated Integration

Michelle Egan, Neill Nugent, and William E. Paterson (*editors*)
RESEARCH AGENDAS IN EU STUDIES
Stalking the Elephant

Theofanis Exadaktylos and Claudio M. Radaelli (*editors*)
RESEARCH DESIGN IN EUROPEAN STUDIES
Establishing Causality in Europeanizaion

David J. Galbreath and Joanne McEvoy
THE EUROPEAN MINORITY RIGHTS REGIME
Towards a Theory of Regime Effectiveness

Wolfram Kaiser, Brigitte Leucht, and Michael Gehler
TRANSNATIONAL NETWORKS IN REGIONAL INTEGRATION
Governing Europe 1945–83

Robert Kissack
PURSUING EFFECTIVE MULTILATERALISM
The European Union, International Organizations and the Politics of Decision Making

Palgrave Studies in European Union Politics
**Series Standing Order ISBN 978–1–4039–9511–7 (hardback) and ISBN 978–1–4039–9512–4
(paperback)**

You can receive future titles in this series as they are published by placing a standing order.
Please contact your bookseller or, in case of difficulty, write to us at the address below with
your name and address, the title of the series and one of the ISBNs quoted above.

Customer Services Department, Macmillan Distribution Ltd, Houndmills, Basingstoke,
Hampshire RG21 6XS, UK

The European Neighbourhood Policy in Perspective

Context, Implementation and Impact

Edited by

Richard G. Whitman
Professor of Politics, University of Kent, UK

and

Stefan Wolff
Professor of International Security, University of Birmingham, UK

First published in hardcover 2010
Published in paperback 2012
PALGRAVE MACMILLAN

Palgrave Macmillan in the UK is an imprint of Macmillan Publishers Limited, registered in England, company number 785998, of Houndmills, Basingstoke, Hampshire RG21 6XS.

Palgrave Macmillan in the US is a division of St Martin's Press LLC, 175 Fifth Avenue, New York, NY 10010.

Palgrave Macmillan is the global academic imprint of the above companies and has companies and representatives throughout the world.

Palgrave® and Macmillan® are registered trademarks in the United States, the United Kingdom, Europe and other countries

ISBN: 978–0–230–20385–3   hardback
ISBN: 978–1–137–03123–5   paperback

This book is printed on paper suitable for recycling and made from fully managed and sustained forest sources. Logging, pulping and manufacturing processes are expected to conform to the environmental regulations of the country of origin.

A catalogue record for this book is available from the British Library.

A catalog record for this book is available from the Library of Congress.

10 9 8 7 6 5 4 3 2 1
21 20 19 18 17 16 15 14 13 12

Printed and bound in Great Britain by
CPI Antony Rowe, Chippenham and Eastbourne

Contents

Illustrations

Table

Figures

Preface to the Paperback Edition

When the first edition of this volume was completed in 2010 the EU's neighbourhood was exhibiting a high degree of stability and stasis. This situation was to change dramatically in early 2011. The events in North Africa that were subsequently to be dubbed the 'Arab Spring' ushered in changes within the EU's southern neighbourhood that were akin to those in Eastern Europe in 1989.

The EU, alongside other external actors such as the United States, was unprepared for the events of the Arab Spring and struggled to formulate an appropriate policy response. In addressing the events in its southern neighbourhood the EU grappled with two issues. First, the new foreign policy innovations introduced by the Lisbon Treaty were not yet fully operational, and most particularly the new European External Action Service (EEAS) was still being constructed. This created a capacity deficit in the EU's mechanisms to respond to a foreign policy challenge. Further, it severely constrained the capacity of the High Representative to fully exploit the main innovation of the Lisbon Treaty: that is, the drawing together of the EU's Common Foreign and Security Policy (CFSP) and its external relations.

The second issue was that the EU's European Neighbourhood Policy (ENP) was not designed as a policy for crisis management but rather as a policy for the EU's medium- and long-term engagement with its neighbours. Consequently, the architecture of the ENP that we described in our previous edition of this book remained largely unchanged by the events across North Africa and the eastern Mediterranean in 2011 and 2012. Furthermore, the EU's objectives for the region have not changed substantially with the Arab Spring.

The EU's policy design for the region is primarily intended to maintain security for its member states and citizens. As this volume stresses this is primarily because the EU's policy towards its neighbourhood has been largely cast in security terms, defined as a 'low probability of damage to acquired values' (Baldwin 1997, 13). The EU prides itself in being a community founded on shared values among its members[1] and its ENP frequently refers to a 'vision [of] a ring of countries, sharing the EU's fundamental values and objectives', while realising that the 'degree of commitment to common values' may differ across the different partner countries (European Commission, 2004: 5, 8). This analysis and broad policy objective has not been altered by the regime changes in the EU's neighbourhood.

As early as 2003 the so-called 'Wider Europe' Communication from the European Commission noted that 'neighbouring countries are the EU's essential partners ... to create an enlarged area of political stability' (European Commission, 2003b: 3) and in 2004, the Commission's ENP Strategy Paper emphasised that an 'important priority will be the further development of a shared responsibility between the EU and partners for security and stability in the neighbourhood region' (European Commission, 2004: 13), reflecting a similar observation in the EU Security Strategy of December 2003 (Council of the European Union, 2003a: 7, 9, 11).

To comprehend why the EU's Neighbourhood Policy has not undergone a fundamental redesign as a consequence of the events in its southern neighbourhood requires an understanding of both how the policy has evolved and how its broad objectives are still maintained by the EU. This volume allows for such an understanding.

Our assertion is that to understand where the ENP currently is, its origins have to be understood as period of two sequential, partially overlapping phases as outlined in the introduction of this book. During the early phase, between 2002 and 2006, ENP was clearly a policy encapsulating the 'alternative to enlargement' more than anything else. During the following period, roughly between 2006 and 2010, the ENP began a transition towards the regional foreign and security policy that it arguably is now. In many ways 2011 presented a major juncture for the ENP: never before did the EU produce as many strategy documents on the ENP in one year as it did in 2011 (Council of the European Union, 2011c; European Commission, 2011a, 2011c, 2011e, 2011f), nor was the increase in the ENP budget ever as significant in relative and absolute terms, not to mention the fact that it comes at a time of profound economic crisis within the EU.[2] This was partly in response to the momentous developments in its southern neighbourhood, partly the result of a longer review process triggered by the implementation of the Lisbon Treaty.

The ground for the reinvigoration that the ENP has seen over the past 12 months was partially prepared in the years 2006–10. Two reviews of the ENP in 2006 and 2007, respectively entitled 'On Strengthening the ENP' and 'A Strong ENP' (European Commission, 2006, 2007) were followed by a flurry of activity in relation to the developing Eastern Partnership (EaP), which had been developed by the Commission following a request by the Council in June 2008 (Council of the European Union 2008) and gained additional significance following the Russia–Georgia war in August 2008. The EaP took concrete shape with a Communication from the Commission in December 2008 (European Commission, 2008a, 2008b) and was officially launched in May 2009 (Council of the European Union, 2011c). The importance that this particular element of differentiation within the ENP as a whole took on in the two years following the launch of the EaP is also evident from the two implementation reports in 2009 and 2010, respectively, and the relative progress that was made in relations especially with Moldova, including notably in relation to a more constructive and pro-active EU engagement on the conflict in Transnistria and Ukraine.

Yet, despite another Eastern Partnership Summit in Warsaw in September 2011 (Council of the European Union, 2011c), the focus of the ENP decidedly shifted to the southern neighbourhood as the Arab Spring began to engulf the region from early 2011 onwards in developments at least partly reminiscent to the events in Central and Eastern Europe after 1989. The relatively routine policy process of the ENP was thus suddenly presented with significant challenges and opportunities at a time when its place and role in the post-Lisbon environment was still being defined.

On 25 May 2011, the High Representative of the Union for Foreign Affairs and Security Policy and Commission Vice-President, Baroness Catherine Ashton, and the European Commissioner for Enlargement and Neighbourhood Policy, Štefan Füle, presented a new communication from the Commission to the European Parliament, the Council, the European Economic and Social Committee and the Committee of the Regions, underlining the new possibilities for close cooperation between the emerging EEAS and the Enlargement and ENP portfolio (in the Commission). Boldly entitled 'A new response to a changing neighbourhood', the document is the outcome of a review of the ENP that began in summer 2010 in response to the changes of the Union's new foreign affairs set-up under the Lisbon Treaty. The 'New Response' communication proclaims the need for a new approach 'to build and consolidate healthy democracies, pursue sustainable economic growth and manage cross-border links' and specifically mentions 'stronger political cooperation on ... security [and] conflict resolution matters' (European Commission, 2011e: 1, 3). Crucially, and thus reaffirming a persistent theme across a decade of EU strategy papers on the ENP, the communication insists that 'the new approach must be based on mutual accountability and a shared commitment to the universal values of human rights, democracy and the rule of law' (European Commission, 2011e: 2) and puts significant emphasis on both positive and negative conditionality (European Commission, 2011e: 4).

Comprising the countries on the southern and eastern Mediterranean shores – Morocco, Algeria, Tunisia, Libya, and Egypt; and the Palestinian Territories, Israel, Jordan, Lebanon, and Syria – the EU's southern neighbourhood faces no shortage of challenges that undermine the region's stability and threaten the EU's security. In order to assess how much impact the envisaged outcomes of the new ENP are likely to have in this respect, these challenges first need to be identified. They fall into two broad categories. The first of them is related to instability *in* the southern neighbourhood itself:

- Latent/unresolved conflicts between states, primarily evolving around borders in the Middle East between Israel and Syria and Lebanon;
- Communal/sectarian/secessionist civil wars, primarily the on/off power struggles in Lebanon and the Palestinian territories, as well as the self-determination struggle in Morocco/Western Sahara;
- The Israeli-Palestinian conflict which combines elements of inter-state and intra-state conflicts linked to the broader regional setting of the Arab-Israeli conflict;
- The 'Arab Spring', i.e., the popular uprisings against a widely per-ceived lack of economic opportunity, freedom and dignity in a num-ber of the authoritarian regimes in the Middle East and North Africa – with their largely unpredictable outcomes and consequences, including continuing violence in Egypt, Libya, and Syria.

All of these conflicts pose a serious humanitarian challenge (and have in many instances done so for years if not decades), but they also consti-tute a security challenge to the EU (and more broadly) in that they are an essential part of an environment that is conducive to the prolifera-tion of cross-border security threats. In this second category of security challenges, the issues are of more immediate and direct impact on the EU itself:

- Illegal (trans-) migration to EU member states;
- Transnational organised crime, especially related to smuggling of goods and trafficking in humans, arms, and drugs;
- International terrorism;
- Supply and transit dimensions of European energy security.

The new ENP mission statement recognises that addressing these threats is an interest that the EU shares with the countries of the southern neigh-bourhood, and at least implicitly, also makes a connection between the two categories in seeing problems *in* the neighbourhood among the causes of security threats *beyond* its geographical boundaries, including for the EU. More to the point organised crime, international terrorism, etc., are, to some extent, symptoms of underlying problems, such as the lack of civil and political liberties and economic opportunities, in the countries of the southern and eastern Mediterranean, which may be addressed by the breadth of policies that comprise the ENP, including institution building, economic cooperation, and cooperation on a range of security issues that fall into the areas of CSDP and JHA.

Looking back over close to a decade of ENP, the track record of these policies to achieve their strategic goals of strengthening the prosperity, stability and security of the EU and its neighbours is less than stellar. Among all the countries of the southern neighbourhood, only two–Morocco and Jordan–have fully implemented, and moved beyond, their original action plans. In recognition of this, the EU granted them 'advanced status' in 2008 and 2010, respectively. Yet, one might question, for example, how much Morocco really has advanced since the inauguration of the ENP in 2003: the conflict in the Western Sahara – after all, one of the security challenges in the southern neighbourhood constantly referred to in EU documents – is nowhere nearer a resolution than it was eight years ago.

Is this likely to change now? The 'New Response to a Changing Neighbourhood' signifies a certain degree of continuity in its commitment to democracy, economic development, sub-regional cooperation and regional differentiation that has characterised the ENP since 2003. What is if not new, so at least far more explicit, is a greater emphasis on conditionality and political and security cooperation. Thus, the EU seeks to 'enhance [its] involvement in solving protracted conflicts' (European Commission, 2011e: 5). However, rather than outlining concrete steps that go beyond the implementation of ENP (and CFSP/CSDP) to date, the emphasis is on continuing what already happens (and has arguably not been very effective): membership in the Middle East Quartet, opposition to violent border changes, using operational presence through existing missions to back reform efforts, and employing instruments that promote economic integration and sectoral reform to support confidence-building measures and conflict resolution objectives (European Commission, 2011e). The only, partially innovative new initiative is that the 'EU intends to enhance its support for confidence-building and outreach to breakaway territories, for international efforts and structures related to the conflicts, and, once that stage is reached, for the implementation of settlements' (European Commission, 2011e: 5).

Here is where the EU may be able to find (yet again) a niche for an effective contribution to stability in its neighbourhood through the instruments that the ENP offers. Consider, briefly, the case of Libya. While the UN-authorised military intervention was a NATO operation almost solely conducted and led by Europeans – first and foremost the UK and France–the EU has not so far played any significant role. Clearly constrained by its economic and financial crisis, the real blow to concerted and unified EU action was dealt by the German abstention during the vote on UN Security Council Resolution 1973 (2011).[3] Until then, the EU had been fully supportive of UN actions and contributed to enforcing sanctions against the Gadhafi regime. A joint statement by the President of the European Council, Herman Van Rompuy, and the EU High Representative, Catherine Ashton, on the day the crucial UN resolution was passed already indicated more lukewarm support of the EU, noting its readiness 'to implement this Resolution *within its mandate and competences'* (Rompuy and Ashton 2011) and the subsequent Council Conclusions three days later unsurprisingly offered no more than 'CSDP *support to humanitarian assistance* in response to a request from OCHA and under the coordinating role of the UN' (Council of the European Union 2011a). At that time, the NATO military operation, carried predominantly by military forces of EU members Britain and France, was already in full swing. A starker contrast could hardly be imagined.

The EU did follow up with a Council Decision on an EU military operation in support of humanitarian assistance operations in Libya, setting up operational headquarters in Rome and preparing various scenarios (Council of the European Union 2011b). Embarrassingly, a request for the activation of EU military assistance was never made. EU Military Staff and assets were, however, involved in the evacuation of EU citizens from Libya and third-country refugees via Tunisia.

While it is easy (and not wrong) to belittle the inability of the EU to offer any substantial military support during the Libyan crisis (even though it did, through its member states, clearly have the necessary capabilities), the EU has been an important player in a different way: by providing significant humanitarian assistance, worth over €150 million by October 2011. An additional €25 million are available for short-term stabilisation needs, as well as a further €60 million for assistance in the transition process. These will include measures decided together with the transitional government to build up state institutions, to support civil society, human rights and democratisation, to provide health services and assist with border management and security sector reform. (European Commission 2011b)

The statement by the High Representative following the fall of Sirte and the death of Gadhafi clearly indicates the EU's willingness to become a strong partner of the new Libya (Ashton 2011). The case of Libya demonstrates in an exemplary way that the countries of the Arab Spring in the southern neighbourhood, which go through a challenging, and at times violent, transition process now, and the EU need each other economically and politically (as did and do the Central and Eastern European countries that joined the EU in 2004 and 2007 or are now covered by the Eastern Partnership). These countries' successful transition to democracy is crucial to stability in the EU's southern neighbourhood, and thus to the EU's security, and it is here where the ENP will have to prove its mettle. An understanding as to whether the ENP is fit for this purpose remains of crucial importance and as a reviewer of the first edition noted '[the] volume is indisputably well-placed to offer a unique and coherent perspective on the nature and utility of EU relations with the "neighbours"' (Korosteleva-Polglase, 2011).

Notes

1. As per Article 2 of the Consolidated Version of the Treaty on European Union 'The Union is founded on the values of respect for human dignity, freedom, democracy, equality, the rule of law and respect for human rights, including the rights of persons belonging to minorities.'
2. The commission has proposed a total budget for the ENP for the period 2014–20 of €18.2 billion, reflecting a 40% increase on the current budget (European Commission 2011d).
3. For a record of the 6498th Meeting of the UN Security Council see (UN Security Council 2011).

References

Ashton, Catherine. 2011. Statement by High Representative Catherine Ashton on the fall of Sirte and reports of the death of Colonel Gaddafi. Brussels: European Union.

Baldwin, David A. 1997. The concept of security. *Review of International Studies* 23 (1): 5–26.

Council of the European Union. 2002. *Copenhagen European Council: Presidency Conclusions*. Brussels: Council of the European Union.

Council of the European Union. 2003a. *A Secure Europe in a Better World: European Security Strategy*. Brussels.

Council of the European Union. 2003b. *Thessaloniki European Council: Presidency Conclusions*. Brussels: Council of the European Union.

Council of the European Union. 2008. *Presidency Conclusions of the Brussels European Council, 19–20 June 2008*. Brussels: Council of the European Union.

Council of the European Union. 2010. *Draft Internal Security Strategy for the European Union: 'Towards a European Security Model'.* Brussels: Council of the European Union.

Council of the European Union. 2011a. *Council Conclusions on Libya (3076th Foreign Affairs Council meeting).* Brussels: Council of the European Union.

Council of the European Union. 2011b. *Council Decides on EU Military Operation in Support of Humanitarian Assistance Operations in Libya.* Brussels: Council of the European Union.

Council of the European Union. 2011c. *Joint Declaration of the Eastern Partnership Summit, Warsaw, 29–30 September 2011.* Brussels: Council of the European Union

European Commission. 2003a. *Paving the way for a New Neighbourhood Instrument.* Brussels: European Commission.

European Commission. 2003b. *Wider Europe – Neighbourhood: A New Framework for Relations with our Eastern and Southern Neighbours.* Brussels: European Commission

European Commission. 2004. *European Neighbourhood Policy Strategy Paper.* Brussels: European Commission.

European Commission. 2006. *Communication from the Commission to the Council and the European Parliament on Strengthening the European Neighbourhood Policy.* Brussels: European Commission.

European Commission. 2007. *Communication from the Commission: A Strong European Neighbourhood Policy.* Brussels: European Commission.

European Commission. 2008a. *Commission Staff Working Document Accompanying the Communication from the Commission to the European Parliament and the Council on Eastern Partnership.* Brussels: European Commission.

European Commission. 2008b. *Communication from the Commission to the European Parliament and the Council on Eastern Partnership.* Brussels: European Commission.

European Commission. 2011a. *Dialogue for Migration, Mobility and Security with the Southern Mediterranean Countries.* Brussels: European Commission.

European Commission. 2011b. *EU support to Libya.* Brussels: European Commission.

European Commission. 2011c. *A Medium Term Programme for a Renewed European Neighbourhood Policy (2011–2014).* Brussels: European Commission.

European Commission. 2011d. *The Multiannual Financial Framework: The Proposals on External Action Instruments.* Brussels: European Commission.

European Commission. 2011e. *A New Response to a Changing Neighbourhood.* Brussels: European Commission.

European Commission. 2011f. *Partnership for Democracy and Shared Prosperity in the Southern Mediterranean.* Brussels: European Commission.

Korosteleva-Polglase, Elena. (2011) 'Book Reviews' *Journal of Common Market Studies* 49 (2): 498.

Rompuy, Herman Van, and Ashton, Catherine. 2011. Joint statement on UN Security Council resolution on Libya. Brussels: European Union.

United Nations Security Council. 2011. *Security Council Approves 'No-Fly Zone' Over Libya, Authorizing 'All Necessary Measures' to Protect Civilians, by Vote of 10 in Favour with 5 Abstentions.* New York: United Nations Department of Public Information.

Acknowledgements

The editors would like to acknowledge the support of the British Academy through its Small Research Grants programme for financial assistance for the project on *The Study of the European Neighbourhood Policy: Methodological, Theoretical and Empirical Challenges*, of which this book is a direct product. We further acknowledge the support of the Economic and Social Research Council (ESRC Research Seminar Series award RES-451-26-0419: The European Union as a Global Conflict Manager: From Pragmatic Ad-hocism to Policy Coherence?) for providing additional financial assistance for a workshop that brought together the contributors to this volume.

Contributors

Federica Bicchi is Lecturer in International Relations of Europe at the Department of International Relations, London School of Economics. She is the author of *European foreign policy making toward the Mediterranean* (Palgrave Macmillan, 2007) and co-editor, with E. Adler, B. Crawford and R. Del Sarto, of *Convergence of Civilizations: Constructing the Mediterranean Region* (University of Toronto Press, 2006).

Sven Biscop is Director of the Security and Global Governance Programme at Egmont – The Royal Institute for International Relations in Brussels, and the editor-in-chief of its journal *Studia Diplomatica*. He is a Visiting Professor for European security at the College of Europe in Bruges and at Ghent University and a member of the Executive Academic Board of the European Security and Defence College. He is co-director of the Higher Studies in Security and Defence, co-organised by Egmont and Belgium's Royal High Institute for Defence.

Carlos Echeverría Jesús is Professor of International Relations at the Spanish National Open University-UNED in Madrid and Professor at the Spanish Armed Forces High School (ESFAS). Since 2002 he has been Deputy Director of the Research Unit on Security and International Cooperation (UNISCI), at the Complutense University in Madrid. Between 1998 and 1999 he was Visiting Scientist at the Institute for Prospective Technological Studies (IPTS) of the Joint Research Centre of the European Commission, in Seville, and between 1994 and 1997 Research Fellow at the Western European Union Institute for Security Studies, in Paris, in charge of Mediterranean security projects at both institutions. Between 1992 and 2000 he was Lecturer on North Africa and the Mediterranean at the NATO Defense College, Rome.

Carmen Gebhard is Postdoctoral Research Fellow at the Institute for Advanced Studies in Vienna, and Associate Fellow at the Institute for Peace Support and Conflict Management at the Austrian National Defence Academy. From 2005 to 2006, she was Researcher and Project Leader on EU Crisis Management at the Austrian Institute for European Security Policy. She was then awarded a Research Fellowship at the European Decision-Making Unit of the European Institute of Public Administration (EIPA) in Maastricht from 2006 to 2007. Carmen

Gebhard holds a Master of Arts in Political Science (Vienna/Stockholm), a diploma in History (Vienna), a doctorate in Comparative Politics (Vienna) and she is a doctoral candidate in Security Studies at the Military University in Budapest.

Narine Ghazaryan has been a Research Student at School of Law, University of Nottingham since 2006. Her research area involves various aspects of the external relations of the EU. It is currently focused on the effectiveness of the European Neighborhood Policy in transposing the democratic values of the EU into the legal order of the countries of Southern Caucasus. Her professional experience includes advising the Armenian government on the issues of European integration within the Armenian-European Policy and Legal Advice Centre funded by the EU.

Hiski Haukkala is a Special Adviser at the Unit for Policy Planning and Research at the Ministry for Foreign Affairs of Finland. Before joining the Ministry in 2009 he was a Researcher at the Finnish Institute of International Affairs in Helsinki (from 2000). Over the years he has also held several visiting positions, including the EU Institute for Security Studies in Paris, the International Institute for Strategic Studies in London and the Department of Politics at the University of Stirling, Scotland.

Christine Pihlkjær Jensen is currently working as a political consultant for the Danish Financial Services Union (Finansforbundet). She was a Research Assistant at the Department of Political Science at the University of Southern Denmark until December 2008.

Ian Manners is Professor at the Institute for Society and Globalisation, Roskilde University. He was formerly at the Danish Institute for International Studies, Copenhagen, Malmö University, Sweden and the University of Kent at Canterbury, England. He has published on De Danske Forbehold over for Den Europæiske Union [The Danish Opt Outs from the EU] (2008); 'Another Europe is Possible: Critical Perspectives on EU Politics' (2007); Values and Principles in EU Foreign Policy (with Sonia Lucarelli, 2006); 'Normative Power Europe: A Contradiction in Terms?' (2002); The Foreign Policies of European Union Member States (with Richard Whitman, 2000); and Substance and Symbolism: An Anatomy of Cooperation in the New Europe (2000).

Antonio Missiroli is Director of Studies at the European Policy Centre in Brussels. From 1998 to 2005 he was Research Fellow at the WEU

Institute for Security Studies in Paris. Previously, he was also a British Council Visiting Fellow at St Antony's College, Oxford (1996/97), a Lecturer in European Politics at Dickinson College (Carlisle, PA, and Bologna) and Head of European Studies at CeSPI (Rome).

Annemarie Peen Rodt is a research fellow at the Exeter Centre for Ethno-Political Studies. Her research appraises the role of regional security organisations in the regulation of violent conflict. Her PhD, which examined the success of EU military conflict management operations worldwide, was completed at the Centre for International Crisis Management and Conflict Resolution at the University of Nottingham in September 2009. Her professional experience in this field includes work for the chief civilian peace implementation agency in Bosnia-Herzegovina: the Office of the High Representative and the Royal Danish Embassy in Sarajevo.

Sten Rynning is Professor of International Relations at the Department of Political Science at the University of Southern Denmark. His main research areas are security studies, transatlantic security relations, NATO and the EU. He is the author of *NATO Renewed: The Power and Purpose of Transatlantic Cooperation* (Palgrave Macmillan, 2005). The Danish Social Science Research Council funds his 2008–2010 research project, *Whither the West? An Assessment of the Vitality of the Atlantic Alliance*.

Gwendolyn Sasse is a Professorial Fellow at Nuffield College and a University Reader in Comparative Politics in the Department of Politics and International Relations, University of Oxford. Prior to her arrival in Oxford in April 2007 she was Senior Lecturer at the European Institute and the Department of Government at the London School of Economics. Among her research interests are post-communist transitions, ethnic conflict, 'old' and 'new' minorities, EU conditionality and enlargement, the ENP and Ukrainian politics.

Ben Tonra is the Director of the UCD College of Human Sciences' Graduate School and Jean Monnet Professor of European Foreign, Security and Defence Policy at the UCD School of Politics and International Relations. Professor Tonra was previously a Lecturer at the Department of International Politics, University of Wales, Aberystwyth, at the Department of Political Science at Trinity College, University of Dublin and a Research Associate at the Center for Strategic and International Studies (CSIS), Washington, DC. His research interests and publications are concerned with EU security and defence, Irish foreign policy and International Relations theory. His latest book, *European*

Republic to Global Citizen, Irish Foreign Policy in Transition is published by Manchester University Press.

Richard G. Whitman is Professor of Politics and International Relations at the University of Kent and Associate Fellow at Chatham House. His current research interests include the external relations and foreign and security and defence policies of the EU, and the governance and future priorities of the EU. He has published in a variety of academic journals including *International Affairs, European Foreign Affairs Review, Contemporary Security Policy, Journal of European Public Policy,* and *Journal of Common Market Studies.* His recent books include *The European Neighbourhood Policy in Perspective: Context, Implementation and Impact* (Palgrave, 2010), co-edited with Stefan Wolff, and he is editor of *Normative Power Europe: Empirical and Theoretical Perspectives* (Palgrave, 2011).

Stefan Wolff is Professor of International Security at the University of Birmingham, UK. A political scientist by background, he specialises in the management of contemporary security challenges, especially in the prevention and settlement of ethnic conflicts and in post-conflict state-building in deeply divided and war-torn societies. Among Wolff's 16 books to date are *Conflict Management in Divided Societies: Theories and Practice* (Routledge 2012, with Christalla Yakinthou), *The Routledge Handbook of Ethnic Conflict* (Routledge 2011, with Karl Cordell), *Ethnic Conflict: Causes, Consequences, and Responses* (Polity 2009, with Karl Cordell), and *Ethnic Conflict: A Global Perspective* (Oxford University Press 2006). Bridging the divide between academia and policy-making, Wolff has been involved in various phases of conflict settlement processes, including in Iraq, Sudan, Moldova, Sri Lanka, and Kosovo. Currently, he works in an advisory capacity on the settlement of the status of Transnistria, Moldova, and on the National Dialogue in Yemen.

Introduction

1
Much Ado About Nothing? The European Neighbourhood Policy in Context

Richard G. Whitman and Stefan Wolff

Introduction

The European Union's European Neighbourhood Policy (ENP) is intended to offer a deeper political and economic relationship between the EU and its neighbours, without an accession perspective.[1] The ENP has been in existence since 2003. It was developed in the context of the prospective enlargement of the EU to include eight states in Central and Eastern Europe and two states in the Mediterranean. The 2004 enlargement to 25 states expanded the space occupied by the EU in the international relations of Europe, with membership now encompassing the majority of European nation states.

The ENP was developed as a strategic approach to the post-enlargement situation, with redrawn boundaries between the EU 'insiders' and the 'outsiders' on the EU's borders. The ENP draws a wider definition of the neighbourhood to embrace the Western Newly Independent States (NIS), the Caucasus and Southern and Eastern Mediterranean states. The ENP also dovetails with the key objective of the EU's first Security Strategy (approved in December 2003) of 'building security in our neighbourhood'. It is intended to advance the EU's interests in creating a stable regional environment for European integration, and to mitigate challenges to EU security and stability.

So, to what extent has the ENP achieved these objectives? What have been the strengths and weaknesses in the implementation of the ENP? And what are the future prospects for the policy?

This volume contends that the ENP represents a distinctive challenge for scholars studying the European Union. The development of a structured relationship that embraces states that neighbour the EU represents a 'coming of age' for the Union. The ENP also has a structuring function vis-à-vis the EU's neighbourhood: it is aimed at, and thereby designates, permanent non-members, while leaving aside potential members and candidate countries, as well as countries with which the EU has a special relationship, such as Russia. This volume seeks to highlight the methodological, theoretical and empirical challenges for scholars seeking to assess the rationale behind the development of such a policy. It identifies the sources of influence impinging on the development of the policy; investigates policy design and its rationale; assesses appropriate frameworks and explanations and understanding of the designation of the neighbourhood and considers methods for assessing the implementation of the policy to date and its impact on the states of the neighbourhood and their relations with the EU.

The contributions to this book offer methodological, theoretical and empirical exploration of the ENP. While the main emphasis is on the empirical assessment of the impact that it has had so far and on the factors that have shaped its implementation since 2003, we also aim to provide a theoretical and methodological perspective on how to study this relatively new policy area. Considerations of methodology and theory are of great significance in any emerging area of academic study and political practice as they determine to a large extent how meaningful academic debates will be, how effective they will be in describing and explaining a particular policy process and its outcomes and how influential they therefore can and ought to be in guiding future policy formulation, implementation and assessment.

In this introductory chapter we first provide an overview of the development of the ENP as a policy domain since its inception in 2003. We then introduce the component parts of this volume, providing both the rationale for their inclusion and an overview of each chapter and its contribution toward enhancing our knowledge and understanding of the ENP and, more widely, the EU.

The ENP since 2003: an overview

Defining the neighbourhood

When the EU enlarged to 25 member states in 2004 it met new countries on its borders to the east, most of which were unstable post-communist countries, grappling with low living standards, fragile political systems and widespread corruption and organised crime. Having such neighbours represented a significant risk of potential instability on the borders of the EU. In addition, there was the need to deal with the feelings of exclusion felt by several of these new neighbours, in particular Ukraine and Moldova, which were left out by the wave of enlargement and failed to understand why they were not considered to be potential candidates when their western neighbours had been.

The genesis of the ENP was in the recognition at the November 2002 General Affairs and External Relations Council (GAERC) of the need for a set of appropriate policies for the EU's soon-to-be new borders and neighbours, in response to a joint letter to the Council from High Representative Javier Solana and Commissioner Chris Patten in August 2002. This was then set as an objective for the Union at the December 2002 Copenhagen European Council. The European Commission's response in its Communication of March 2003 set the tone for what was eventually to result in a new policy for the neighbourhood.[2] The Communication made clear that the policy was to exclude explicitly all those states with a membership perspective (then Turkey, Romania, Bulgaria and the countries of the Western Balkans) and was envisioned as embracing the Western NIS of Moldova, Ukraine and Belarus; the Southern and Eastern Mediterranean (i.e. North Africa and the Middle East) and Russia. By excluding countries with a membership perspective, the intended policy equally explicitly *excluded* the prospect of EU membership for the states it would cover, while emphasising flexibility in bilateral relations with each prospective partner to allow for the continuation of the differential existing relationships with the EU. These relationships ranged from very limited bilateral relations (Belarus and Libya) to Partnership and Cooperation Agreements (PCAs) (for example Soviet successor states such as Armenia and Moldova) and to Association Agreements (with states such as Egypt, Morocco and Tunisia).

The rationale for these neighbours being drawn together within a wider policy becomes clear from the twofold objectives of the policy that the EU had set out:

- To work with the partners to reduce poverty and create an area of shared prosperity and values based on deeper economic integration, intensified political and cultural relations, enhanced cross-border cooperation and shared responsibility for conflict prevention between the EU and its neighbours.

- To anchor the EU's offer of concrete benefits and preferential relations within a differentiated framework which responds to progress made by the partner countries in political and economic reform.[3]

Central to achieving these objectives was that the all states would be offered the opportunity to move toward full access to the EU's internal market and to enjoy its four freedoms; a status 'as close to the Union as it can be without being a member'.[4] Throughout its Communication, the European Commission used examples drawn from the 1995 Euro-Mediterranean Partnership (EMP) – the Barcelona Process – to illustrate policy areas in which collaboration might be enhanced. These included border policing and visas, conflict prevention, crisis management and security policies, energy and the environment: 'The long-term goal … is to move towards an arrangement whereby the Union's relations with the neighbouring countries ultimately resemble the close political and economic links currently enjoyed with the European Economic Area.'[5] To realise these ambitions a set of benchmarks would be used for judging the progress of individual partner states within tailored Action Plans for each country.

The Commission's work on what was to become the ENP progressed throughout the rest of 2003 and early 2004 with the oversight and approval of the Council of Ministers and the European Council and with consultations with third countries on the notion of Action Plans. The summation of all of this work was brought together in a Commission Strategy Paper published in the immediate aftermath of the 2004 enlargement.[6]

The Strategy Paper confirmed the EU's desire to exert greater influence over the new neighbours in an attempt to mitigate potential instability, while making it clear that the Union was unwilling to consider offering the perspective of membership at that time. Consequently, as an alternative to membership, the ENP was designed to spread prosperity, stability and security in the EU's new neighbourhood:[7]

> The privileged relationship with neighbours will build on mutual commitment to common values principally within the fields of the rule of law, good governance, the respect for human rights, including minority rights, the promotion of good neighbourly relations, and the principles of market economy and sustainable development.[8]

The ENP was confirmed as an offer made by the EU to its new neighbours of deeper political and economic integration in exchange for progress in reforms in different fields supporting democracy, the rule of law and a market-oriented economy.[9] The policy aimed to build a special partnership between the EU and its neighbours based on shared values and common interests, and to create a ring of friends.[10]

The Action Plans were confirmed as the primary vehicle through which these ambitions would be realised. They would cover periods of three to five years, be formally approved through the Cooperation or Association Councils held with each partner (and thereby bring together representatives of the partner country, the member states, the Council Secretariat and the European Commission) and be 'defined by common consent and will thus vary from country to country.'[11]

The ENP was to be based on enlightened self-interest: 'by helping our neighbours, we help ourselves.'[12] In concrete terms, the ENP was explicitly intended to straddle all three of the EU's pillars and to further the objectives of the Security Strategy.[13] As a result, Action Plans, as conceived in the Commission Strategy, focused on the following priorities:

1. 'Commitment to Shared Values' (to ensure that partners complied with the international and regional conventions on democracy, human rights, the rule of law and cooperation with the ICC and of which they were already signatories);
2. 'A more effective political dialogue' (facilitating EU Common Foreign and Security Policy (CFSP) and European Security and Defence Policy (ESDP) objectives);
3. 'Economic and social development policy' (legislative and regulatory approximation to the Internal Market and accompanying policies to address poverty and inequality);
4. 'Trade and Internal Market' (approximation to the Internal Market, regulatory convergence and marketing opening to further the principles of the World Trade Organization);
5. 'Justice and Home Affairs' (border management and cooperation on JHA issues);
6. 'Connecting the neighbourhood' (safety and security of energy supply, transport links and the environment, information and communications technology, research and innovation); and
7. 'People-to-people, programmes and agencies' (a gradual opening of community programmes directed at individuals and their well-being).

Furthermore, the ENP was also intended to strengthen and develop existing regional and sub-regional cooperation.

A key change in the policy was that Russia was now not to be included within the ENP but rather bilateral relations were to be expanded by the development of four 'common spaces' agreed at the May 2003

St Petersburg Summit.[14] The development of the relationship with Belarus was put on hold pending regime change in Minsk, and for Libya pending its entry into the Barcelona Process. The implementation of the ENP for the states of the Mediterranean basin (except Turkey) was to be 'implemented through the Barcelona process and the Association Agreements with each partner country'.[15] The Commission also proposed the extension of the ENP to encompass the Southern Caucasus states of Armenia, Azerbaijan and Georgia. Financing for the ENP was to take place through a new financial mechanism – the European Neighbourhood and Partnership Instrument (ENPI) – introduced in 2007 and subsuming the existing financial arrangements through the Technical Aid to the Commonwealth of Independent States (TACIS), Measures Accompanying the Euro-Mediterranean Partnership (MEDA) and other smaller-scale financing arrangements.

Implementing the ENP

With such an ambitious set of objectives the question arises as to whether the ENP has been a success since its introduction? In theory, the ENP has the potential for being an effective policy framework. It is based on the EU's power of attraction and the instrumentalisation of conditionality – tools which the EU has used successfully in the past to influence its environment.

The EU's recent decade-long enlargement policy has most vividly illustrated the EU's ability to influence its environment through the offer of incentives. Through the extensive use of carrots and sticks the EU was able to motivate substantial political and economic reforms in the candidate countries, stabilising new democracies, fostering economic growth and solving regional disputes.[16] The policy successfully culminated in May 2004 in the accession of eight former communist states that were judged to have successfully completed the transition to democracy and a market economy, with Romania and Bulgaria following on 1 January 2007. As a consequence the enlargement toward Central and Eastern Europe is widely considered as the EU's most successful foreign policy.[17]

The ENP has, at its heart, a shared ethos with the EU's enlargement policy – a point addressed by Gebhard in Chapter 5. The ENP attempts, through the offer of incentives, to influence extensive reforms within the EU's neighbours. In addition, the ENP is based on a set of mechanisms which should strengthen its potential for success. It is a multilateral policy embracing all neighbours who are not candidates for accession to the EU, and the Action Plans developed for each individual partner country list extensively the different priorities for engagement and reforms the partner country should undertake. In this respect the

Action Plans are very similar to the Europe Agreements used within the enlargement policy in that they offer a road map and guidance for reform, comprehensively identifying the different areas which need to be tackled. Illustrative of the detail involved is the EU-Moldova Action Plan, which lists more than 300 reforms across a whole range of sectors from political institutions to the economy and highlighting the most important priorities in each of them.[18]

In addition, the EU offers expert advice, financial assistance programmes and tools such as TAIEX[19] and Twinning[20] (which proved their usefulness in the enlargement process) and evaluations on progress achieved (through progress reports or detailed annual scoreboards elaborated with the partner country) in order to help to achieve the listed aims.

While the ENP does not go as far as offering the prospect of membership in order to motivate the desired reforms, it does, in principle, offer the prospect of wide and substantial benefits to the partner countries through the possibility of 'an increasingly close relationship, going beyond cooperation to involve a significant measure of economic and political integration'.[21] In addition to a variety of short-term benefits such as an increase in financial assistance and visa facilitations, the ENP offers the prospect of far-reaching integration in the form of participation 'in key aspects of EU policies and programmes'[22] and 'a stake in the EU's Internal Market',[23] which is presented by the EU as the most novel and far-reaching offer within the ENP.[24] These gains are significant and could potentially allow for substantial leverage over the partner countries in order to motivate the desired reforms.

Over the last five years the ENP has developed a somewhat structured, or cyclical, set of processes. Implementation of the individual Action Plans is monitored by a set of sub-committees reviewing the progress across sectors or issues. The Commission has packaged together sets of progress reports on the individual countries periodically (in 2006, 2007 and 2008) and then drawn conclusions from these evaluations as to how the policy might be enhanced.[25]

Most recently the EU has differentiated between two groups of states participating in the ENP, through the creation of the Union for the Mediterranean and the Eastern Partnership. The ENP has thus become an umbrella, or perhaps more a shell, of two different neighbourhood policies – one for the countries of Eastern Europe (excluding Russia), and one for the countries of the Southern and Eastern Mediterranean, thus acknowledging the significant differences between these two sets of neighbours.

Union for the Mediterranean

The notion of a Mediterranean Union was first raised by Nicolas Sarkozy during his presidential election campaign in a speech on 7 February 2007. According to his original plan, the Mediterranean Union would bring together all the Mediterranean coastal states to revitalise and strengthen cooperation across the Mediterranean basin, but outside the EU framework. The initiative constituted a major attempt to reshape not only French foreign policy, but also European foreign policy. It openly recognised the fact that the Barcelona Process – itself subsumed within the wider ENP policy – had failed to further economic and democratic reforms in the EU's southern neighbours, and to close the widening gap between the northern and southern coasts of the Mediterranean. This initiative was also viewed in some quarters as an attempt to frustrate Turkey's membership aspirations.

By July 2008, a change of name to the 'Barcelona Process: Union for the Mediterranean' signalled a scaling back of ambitions and significant changes to the initial project. Sarkozy's initiative had to overcome severe opposition and criticisms from both its EU partners and Southern Mediterranean countries.[26] Fierce opposition to the original Mediterranean Union came from France's traditional ally, Germany. Chancellor Merkel rejected the idea of a Union restricted to Mediterranean coastal states, fearing that such a project would lead to the establishment of different spheres of influence in EU foreign policy. Spain and Italy were concerned about the impact of this initiative on the Euro-Mediterranean policy. Other member states were concerned about an unnecessary duplication of institutional arrangements. Turkey, for its part, rejected any suggestions that the Mediterranean Union would provide an alternative to EU membership. Libya was also very critical of the project, and while other Southern Mediterranean countries did not openly oppose the initiative, they were far from enthusiastic about it.

As a result of this opposition, particularly from Germany, the original French plan was watered down. A new Franco-German proposal in the form of a 'Barcelona Process plus' was presented to the European Council on 13 March 2008. The Commission was then entrusted with fleshing out the proposal. A Commission Communication of 20 May 2008 spelt out the main elements of this initiative.[27] The 'Barcelona Process: Union for the Mediterranean' aims to complement rather than replace existing EU policies (it is described by the Commission as a relaunch of the Barcelona Process[28]) and is open to all EU member states, the members and observers of the Barcelona Process and other Mediterranean states (Croatia, Bosnia and Herzegovina, Montenegro and Monaco). The new initiative is expected to give a new impetus to the Barcelona Process in three ways: 1) by upgrading political relations between the EU and its Mediterranean partners with a biannual summit of Heads of Government, 2) by increasing co-ownership of the process (a co-Presidency has been established with this end in mind) and 3) by launching regional and sub-regional projects relevant to the citizens of the region. A number of initiatives dealing with energy, environment, civil protection and transport are currently being discussed.

The Union for the Mediterranean was officially launched at the Paris Summit for the Mediterranean on 13 July 2008. In November 2008, Foreign Ministers decided that Barcelona would be the Union for the Mediterranean's Headquarters.[29]

Eastern Partnership

The proposal for an Eastern Partnership was presented jointly by Poland and Sweden at the GAERC on 26 May 2008. The Eastern Partnership was a well-prepared diplomatic initiative by the Polish government led by Donald Tusk, and represented a significant departure in substance and style from those of the preceding Law and Justice party government. As with the Union for the Mediterranean the initiative was intended to reinvigorate the relationship between the EU and a sub-group of countries covered by the ENP, in this instance Eastern Europe and the Southern Caucasus. The countries covered by the Eastern Partnership are Ukraine, Moldova, Armenia, Azerbaijan, Georgia and Belarus.[30] The latter's participation is conditional upon improved human rights and moves toward democracy. Belarus's formal inclusion was debated at length by the member states because of long-standing EU opposition to the governing regime and the leadership of its President Alexander Lukashenko.

That the Eastern Partnership was a counterbalancing and linked Eastern initiative to the southern-focused Mediterranean Union was illustrated by both proposals being debated at the 19–20 June 2008 meeting of the European Council. The Commission was invited to prepare a proposal on the Eastern Partnership for the spring of 2009 and then, at the 1 September 2008 Extraordinary European Council called in response to the war in Georgia, encouraged to accelerate its work and report by the end of the year.[31]

The Commission's proposals are to embed the Eastern Partnership within the wider ENP. They are also to give the Eastern Partnership a multilateral framework but with the bulk of its implementation pursued bilaterally with the participating states. The multilateral framework is for four 'policy platforms' on democracy, good governance and stability; economic integration and convergence with EU policies; energy security and contacts between people.

Bilaterally, each of the participants is offered the prospect of an Association Agreement with the EU but with no commitment that these agreements hold out any prospect of future full membership of the Union. The Association Agreements would provide for the creation of individual deep and comprehensive free trade areas (DCFTA) with each partnership country, which, in turn, could be joined together to form a Neighbourhood Economic Community. 'Mobility and Security Pacts' are also envisioned to ease cross-border movement and as part of a 'phased approach' via visa facilitation negotiations with partners and, 'in the longer term', opening dialogues on visa-free travel with all the partners.

No new institutions or secretariat or dedicated funding initiative is proposed for the Eastern Partnership. Activities are envisioned as being covered under the existing ENPI and the Neighbourhood Investment Facility (NIF). The formal launch of the Partnership took place at the Eastern Partnership Summit in May 2009.

The arrangements proposed for the Eastern Partnership by the Commission have faint echoes of the Stabilisation and Association Process for the Western Balkans and share the same intended benefit for the EU of creating a road map for development and deepening of relations. However, the significant difference is that the Eastern Partnership is not intended to hold out the prospect of EU accession as the final destination.

Assessing the ENP: a policy lacking credibility and leverage?

The contributors to this volume assess the success of the ENP to date, explore where the policy is not working effectively and seek to shed light on why that is and whether it has any potential for success. They analyse the strengths and flaws of the policy and consider what steps might have to be undertaken in order to give it a chance of having greater weight.

The problem with the ENP that is apparent from the contributions to Part III of this volume is that since its inception the far-reaching benefits on offer have remained in the realm of *possibilities*. In practice the ENP has offered only rather modest gains to the partner countries to date. The case studies in Part III illustrate that the benefits alluded to in the

Action Plans are vague and illusive, the EU has not stated which policies and programmes the partner countries can participate in, nor indicated when this participation might take place. Similarly, the prospect of a stake in the EU's internal market is not a guaranteed offer. External Relations Commissioner Ferrero-Waldner explicitly stated this lack of guarantee even as late as the summer of 2008 in a speech in which she said that 'to take full advantage of integration in the Single Market [...] takes significant time and effort. Indeed, there's no guarantee the goal will ever be reached'.[32]

This book thus contends that the ENP has the potential to be a successful policy framework, but that this potential is not currently being fulfilled as a result of several important structural problems. Most crucially, the policy lacks any substantial incentives – incentives which are necessary when resorting to the use of conditionality. As a result the policy has been deprived of any substantial leverage.

The ENP was designed to achieve two objectives: to spread stability, security and prosperity in the EU's neighbourhood as a way to minimise the risks of instability flowing across the EU's borders, and to prevent feelings of exclusion within the new neighbours. At the time of writing, the ENP seems to have failed in both these objectives. Despite some cooperation, the EU is still surrounded by unstable neighbours affected by low living standards, high levels of corruption and organised crime, volatile political systems and violent domestic conflicts. Several eastern neighbours feel very unhappy about being relegated to the neighbourhood and paradoxically most of the cooperation that does take place under the ENP is motivated by the hope of escaping the policy and receiving what the ENP was designed to exclude – a membership perspective.

Why has the ENP been apparently so ineffective in addressing challenges in the EU's neighbourhood? In the past the EU has proved very successful in instrumentalising its soft power in order to influence its neighbours and promote democracy, stability and prosperity (as best illustrated through its enlargement policy), yet in the case of the ENP the EU is proving unsuccessful.

The ENP has some short-term practical benefits to offer – including financial assistance and the prospect of visa facilitations – but these are too modest to encourage the extensive and often painful and costly reforms desired by the EU. It would seem that for a policy based on conditionality to function effectively it requires long-term substantial compensation – a benefit comparable to the offer of membership which was present in the case of the enlargement policy. Instead, however, the EU seems to have reversed the logic of conditionality: rather than offering a clear carrot from the outset, under the ENP the EU requires countries to undertake a variety of reforms, and only once reforms have been implemented will the EU *consider* offering the possibility of some form of deeper relations. The uncertain long-term benefits on offer through the ENP are a theme to which this volume returns in its final chapter.

One reason behind the absence of substantial gains within the ENP is a lack of political will among the member states and their reluctance to deal with the strategic finality of relations with the partner countries of the ENP. This is a theme that runs throughout this volume. Moreover, as the emergence of the Mediterranean Union and the Eastern Partnership illustrate, different member states have different opinions regarding the preferable state of relations with countries in the neighbourhood more generally, ranging from the prospect of membership, a form of substantial integration or even no integration at all. The ENP was designed to give the EU time to reflect upon the strategic finality of its relations with its neighbours, but over the last five years the EU has been reluctant to discuss the future of its relations with its neighbours and has been postponing this as much as possible.

This reluctance on the part of the EU to address the long-term state of relations with its neighbours is affecting the effectiveness of its policy. Refusing to give the ENP any strategic finality affects the credibility of the policy: it generates a short-term response, rather than the intended long-term perspective, by asking the partners to focus on cooperation in the present and not waste time on thinking what might possibly happen in the future. By failing to address the future, the EU is preventing the ENP from offering any substantial long-term incentives, weakening its potential for leverage.

The ENP's credibility is further weakened by flaws in its scope and nature. The most substantial of these is that the ENP is a 'catch-all' policy embracing a broad and diverse range of states. That there is this difference has been formally acknowledged with the creation of the Mediterranean Union and the Eastern Partnership. 'European' neighbours with membership aspirations such as Ukraine and Moldova are grouped under the same overarching ENP umbrella as countries like Israel and Algeria, whose relations with, and aspirations toward, the EU are of a very different nature. The absence of Russia as a participant within the ENP or the Eastern Partnership creates the impression that Russia is considered to be too important for the ENP and deserving of a separate policy, thus signalling that the ENP is not the most politically significant relationship that the EU could have with a country on its borders.

Second, serious doubts remain about whether the relationship between a third country and the EU under the ENP is really one of partnership. In particular, the joint ownership of the Action Plans can be questioned. According to the Commission, joint ownership of the Action Plans is a cornerstone of the ENP,[33] but various tasks within the Action Plans are clearly biased toward EU interests.[34] For example, many political objectives in the Action Planss relate to the EU's internal security agenda; the Action Plans for Moldova, Morocco, Tunisia and Ukraine all insist that neighbours must conclude readmission agreements with the EU and there is an important emphasis on nuclear safety in the Ukraine Action Plan.

Finally, because the ENP is a supplement to the existing contractual frameworks with the partner countries and currently offers no substantial gains, it has the appearance of merely recycling previous policies.

These issues, in particular the absence of substantial benefits, result in a serious credibility problem for the ENP and in turn deprive it of effective leverage. This view – to which the contributors in this volume frequently return – is at variance with the perspective held by the EU, which has been arguing that over the last five years the ENP has seen a modest set of successes.

Structure of the volume

Our collective assessment of the development and impact of the ENP is divided into three parts, framed by this introduction and a conclusion. In Part I, the focus is on the methodological, theoretical and empirical challenges posed by the study of the policy. Contributors identify the challenges that the ENP represents for analysts of the EU's regional and international role and discuss the location of the ENP in the wider frame of EU foreign policy and whether existing frameworks of analysis are adequate for the analysis of the ENP.

In Chapter 2 Manners argues that analysing the ENP presents a wide variety of challenges for scholars of the EU's relations with its near neighbours, in particular the question of theoretical presuppositions. He argues that the challenges of studying the ENP are least well served by traditional approaches to political science, and might be better advanced by rethinking these presumptions. Thus, conventional presumptions of 'much ado about nothing' in the ENP may benefit from a reflection on the extent to which these presuppositions are determinate in analysing whether the ENP is 'as you like it'. The chapter suggests that one way of overcoming some of the analytical challenges of studying the ENP might be to pursue a normative power approach. For Manners, such an approach would have the advantage of getting away from discourses of force (e.g., transatlanticist discourses of the EU as a 'force for good') and the utilitarian emphasis placed on conditionality (e.g., the lack of the 'golden carrot' of EU membership). The analytical challenges identified in the first section of the chapter suggest that a non-traditional method of analysis appropriate to the subject of study should be found. The chapter further suggests that critical social theory may provide a means to critique, advocate and change EU politics and policy. The chapter concludes by setting out how an emphasis on ideational aspects including the legitimation of principles, persuasiveness of actions and impact of socialisation in the normative power approach may be appropriate in the study of ENP.

Tonra's Chapter 3 complements that of Manners in that he sets out the basic conceptual argument for looking at the ENP through the prism of identity construction. Tonra argues that this approach offers a unique frame of reference that is potentially capable of providing a more profound understanding of the EU, both as an international actor and as source of foreign policy in the international system. Tonra makes a case for looking at the ENP through the prism of identity construction.

From this standpoint he argues that the definition of 'European' has always been a contested one, that it has undergone repeated revisions, and that it has never been definitively resolved, and iterates this point by a focus on Europe's 'identity borders'. Tonra highlights the construction of the ENP's 'borders' – tracing the relevant elite-level discourses and addressing the critical junctures which have contributed to the solidification of this particular border set at this particular time. In particular he offers an answer to the question 'Why this ENP and why now?'

The attention that Tonra devotes to the definition of borders in terms of the 'non-prospective EU membership criteria' dovetails with Gebhard's Chapter 5.

Biscop's Chapter 4 connects the ENP to the wider constellation of EU policies, locating it against the European Security Strategy (ESS) agreed in 2003. As Biscop notes in quoting from the ESS: '[e]ven in an era of globalisation, geography is still important', thus the definition of 'building security in [the EU's] neighbourhood' is one of three strategic objectives for EU foreign policy. The ENP is seen by Biscop as the operationalisation of this objective. For Biscop there is a read-across between the Action Plans with each of the neighbours linking political, economic and social reforms and security cooperation through conditionality mechanisms. However, he argues that a number of fundamental, strategic-level choices have yet to be made, revealing that the EU is an emergent, but not yet a fully fledged strategic actor. These questions arise both as a result of the great difficulties experienced in implementing the ENP and as a consequence of important gaps in the ESS itself.

Biscop establishes a number of themes that are taken up by the chapters in Part III of this volume: that it has proved difficult to reconcile the objective to promote democracy and human rights and the desire to operate in partnership with the existing regimes, notably in the more authoritarian neighbours. As a result, the EU is often seen by both public opinion and reformist actors in the neighbouring countries as a status quo actor, which prioritises good relations over fundamental reform. Furthermore, the ENP, although emphasising permanent prevention and stabilisation, cannot be seen separately from the 'hard' security or politico-military dimension. For Biscop, the Action Planss will not lead to many results in a country involved in conflict with its neighbours or in internal strife – and as borne out by the events of 2008 in Georgia. Instead, he asks whether the definition of the neighbourhood implies the objective of maintaining peace in that area, including through military means if necessary. Moreover to what extent is this question confined to the neighbourhood beyond the ENP (and does the neighbourhood need redefinition)?

In Gebhard's Chapter 5 the key relationship between the ENP and the EU's enlargement process is explored. She looks at the strategic foundations of the ENP and seeks to locate the policy in the broader context of previous EU policies directed toward the Union's neighbourhood. Her chapter investigates the policy solutions developed in the ENP framework, assesses their structural design and relates them to institutional models and policy instruments that the EU has employed in the past to achieve governance impact and compliance in its neighbouring regions, most importantly in the context of enlargement and in the course of the pre-accession processes. This is intended to help to answer the question of whether the ENP's overall strategic conception actually constitutes a policy departure that suitably accounts for the unprecedented challenges posed in the post-enlargement context, and thus, whether and to what extent the policy indeed has the potential of being effective and successful in the long run. In order to contextualise the ENP along these lines, the chapter employs a historical institutionalist perspective, mainly building on the theoretical argument of path dependency and structural 'stickiness' in institutional development. The chapter is divided into three sections: an outline of the analytical framework, an empirical study and a concluding section. It ends on a critical note, pointing at the inherent ambivalence of a policy conception that is intended to achieve 'integration without accession' while relying on the conditionality formula of enlargement.

Part I of this volume thus explores a range of methodological, theoretical and empirical challenges posed by the study of the ENP. Part II goes further, in particular connecting with the themes raised by Biscop, in examining the context of the EU's wider strategic relationships and policies which provide the background against which the ENP was originally formulated and has been developed and implemented ever since. Three dimensions are of particular significance here: the transatlantic relationship, the EU's relations with Russia, and, given the vast numbers of conflicts in the EU's neighbourhood, the EU's 'Balkan experience'.

In Chapter 6 Rodt and Wolff argue that the EU's approach to violent conflicts was born and developed in the Balkans, and that the Union's experience in this region is therefore an important aspect of any debate on the EU's potential future global role as a conflict manager. They examine the EU's capabilities and recent track record in dealing with the conflicts in the Western Balkans in order to assess what, if any, lessons can be learnt from the Balkan experience and to consider whether the ENP could potentially serve as a tool for the management of violent conflict in the rest of Union's 'new neighbourhood' and beyond.

Rynning and Jensen note in Chapter 7 that it is common to portray the ENP as a reasonable and indeed functional response to a gap in the EU's panoply of external relations tools. But they assert that the ENP should also be seen as a geopolitical event, which illuminates the EU's growing presence in its near abroad and its inevitable involvement in conflicts on its periphery. As such, the ENP is seen as highlighting both strengths and weaknesses in the EU's external presence, and this is where transatlantic relations are important for them. For Rynning and Jensen, as the ENP lumps together disparate countries, the challenge is to address the regional level that falls between the individual (country) and collective (ENP) levels. Furthermore, as the ENP has moved into the Russian sphere of influence it challenges Russian policy in several contexts. For them, most fundamentally, the ENP overlaps with American interests in Europe and its peripheries. They argue that geopolitically speaking, the US has an interest in influencing events in the Eurasian rim areas – particularly Europe and South-East Asia – and organising relationships with local partners that enable this influence. For them the ENP may signal that the EU is more ready and able to engage in this type of partnership, but this remains to be seen.

Haukkala's Chapter 8 turns to another key actor and discusses and analyses Russian reactions to the ENP. It seeks to explain Russia's rejection of the ENP with a reference to a wider domestic context in the country. The essential finding of his analysis is that the ENP was rejected because its very logic – the Union's regional normative hegemony and the imposition of European norms and values in the process – was seen as incompatible with the Russian ideas concerning the legitimate course of action internationally. In addition, Russia's growing weariness toward the idea of normative convergence in the context of wider EU-Russia 'strategic partnership' indicates for Haukkala that we are dealing with a more profound and growing rejection of the Union's normative hegemony than 'just' the rejection of one of its policy templates. In fact, the very logic of interaction based on certain shared ideals ('European values') that the EU has sought to promote and cultivate during the post-Cold War era in Europe is being increasingly questioned by Russia.

Given the variety of different conflicts across the European neighbourhood, EU foreign policy-makers have in recent developments of the CFSP and the ESDPolicy stressed the importance of managing violent conflicts as a contribution to achieving the ENP's aims of creating a secure, stable, democratic and prosperous neighbourhood for the EU. The 2004 and 2007 enlargements moved the EU closer – geographically, politically and security-wise – to a number of latent ('frozen') and active conflicts in its so-called 'new neighbourhood'. These conflicts included ongoing disputes in Israel/Palestine, the Lebanon, Algeria, Moldova (Transnistria), Armenia/Azerbaijan (Nagorno-Karabakh), Georgia (Abkhazia and South Ossetia), Morocco/Western Sahara, Egypt, Ukraine, Jordan and Syria. With the ESS in 2003 and the launch of the ENP in 2004, the Union explicitly reiterated its intention to take a more active stance in the management of violent conflicts in the ENP area (and beyond).

Part III of this book turns to evaluation of the ENP in practice to assess its implementation and impact through case study analysis of four distinct regions: the Middle East, North Africa, Eastern Europe and the Southern Caucasus.

Each of these chapters considers the strengths and weaknesses of the ENP to date. For Sasse in Chapter 9, the Eastern neighbours of the enlarged EU have provided an important impetus for the conception and ongoing formulation of the ENP. Ukraine and Moldova are putting not only the overall scope of the policy to the test, but also the procedural similarity between the ENP dynamics and the accession process. This chapter asks whether the ENP shapes the domestic politics of ENP countries, and, if so, how the is ENP framed, articulated and channelled. The inclusion of Ukrainian and Moldovan perspectives into the analysis underlines the importance of the domestic political context.

For Sasse the main interrelated functions of the ENP are twofold: mobilisation and socialisation. The ENP provides an external reference point which domestic actors in the ENP countries can choose to mobilise – as part of either a pro- or anti-EU agenda. Ukraine and Moldova demonstrate how the openness of the ENP allows Eurosceptic actors to ease themselves and their supporters into a new line of argument. Over time, the predominant perceptions of the ENP appear to be moving through cycles of engagement and disengagement: in Ukraine, the foreign policy elite initially saw the ENP as a disappointment but chose to adopt an increasingly pragmatic approach, hoping to redefine the relationship over time. In Moldova, the ENP initially helped Moldovan politicians to gain Western attention, but there is also evidence that the vagueness of the ENP stores up dissatisfaction and potential disengagement.

Furthermore, for Sasse, Ukraine and Moldova point to underexplored dimensions of the concept of socialisation. The first of these is that socialisation is not a uni-directional process: it can weaken as much as strengthen EU-oriented foreign and domestic policies. Second, socialisation and mobilisation effects reach beyond the narrow circle of visible top-level politicians, but the links between the different layers of the political and administrative system, or between governmental and non-governmental actors, can be hard to institutionalise. Third, socialisation can produce unintended consequences: the functionalist logic underpinning the ENP, in particular with regard to Ukraine and Moldova (and potentially, Belarus), is such that in the case of consistent domestic reforms the EU will find it hard to deny these countries a membership perspective. Fourth, the ENP socialises the EU into a more visible role in foreign policy and conflict management and requires the mobilisation of adequate resources and political will.

For Bicchi in Chapter 10, the ENP's main innovation in North Africa has been to allow third countries to affect the pace and the agenda for cooperation with the EU. This chapter shows that, as a consequence, Morocco, Algeria and Tunisia have developed in very different directions. Bicchi summarises the position with the title of a Western movie, 'The good, the bad and the ugly'. Relations between the EU and Morocco (the 'good') have thrived since the introduction of the ENP, and as a reflection of the progress made Morocco was granted 'advanced status' in October 2008. Tunisia (the 'bad') has consolidated its success-ful economic cooperation with the EU but it has remained closed to any attempt to turn economic successes into political openings. Relations with Algeria (the 'ugly') have experienced a series of ups and downs, and several aspects of cooperation lag behind the track record of its neigh-bours. As this chapter demonstrates, therefore, the ENP has not only emphasised bilateralism over region-building, but it has increased the distance between partners, as the 'regatta approach' was introduced.

Ghazaryan's Chapter 11 focuses on the Southern Caucasus, comprising Georgia, Armenia and Azerbaijan. Although the Southern Caucasus was initially excluded from the ENP, the strategic location of the region and its vicinity to the Union, which became immediate after the accession of Romania and Bulgaria in 2007, influenced the decision to include the three countries in the policy. The chapter explores the development of relations between the EU and the region as breaking down into two stages. The first stage was marked by general reluctance on the part of the Union to engage in the problems of the region and the conclusion of identical PCAs with each of the countries with a focus on trade-related issues. The second stage of relations is concerned primarily with the enhanced interest of the EU in the region stemming from geopolitical and security-related considerations and is framed within the ENP. Ultimately, the chapter focuses on whether the ENP and the Eastern Partnership, as its latest development, provide a sufficient framework to pursue the interests of the EU in the region and at the same time meet the expectations of the countries concerned.

In Echeverría's Chapter 12 on the Middle East he asserts that the ENP represents a new approach in the EU's relations with a number of Middle Eastern countries, in particular because the region as a whole is not included in its framework. A number of conflicts in the area in the current decade have obliged the ENP to be limited to a country-by-country level. Because of this, and because actors such as Iran, Iraq, Saudi Arabia and other Gulf countries are not eligible for membership, the ENP does not permit the EU to have a comprehensive approach to the Middle East. Connecting to Rynning and Jensen's Chapter 7, he asserts that in strategic terms, if the EU and the US are able to craft common Middle Eastern policies, then the ENP stands a good chance of success. Echeverría draws a distinction between present practice and future possibilities. At the present time, the ENP is viewed as facilitating a bilateral framework in which each country can adapt the level of ambition of its relations with the EU with the rhythm of the implementation of agreed domestic reforms. In the near future, the ENP could use these reinforced bilateral relations with Middle Eastern actors to bolster the EU's role, providing it is able to solve two problems that are emerging with ENP implementation. First, without the membership perspective a number of partners are not motivated to undertake domestic reforms, and second, the ENP is providing the EU with an enlarged vision (including Eastern European countries) in which the Mediterranean-specific approach has disappeared and the Middle East will never be included as a single region in terms of external relations and/or foreign, security and defence policies.

The volume concludes with Missiroli's Chapter 13 that reflects on the ENP since its inception to offer a perspective on its future. As Missiroli notes, since the start the ENP has been conditioned by a number of factors. The first is that there have been competing visions for it. The Commission wanted to adopt a single 'template' to deal with the (old and new) EU 'neighbours', following the example of the 2004 enlargement. For their part, member states advanced the notion that the ENP should 'cover' both the Eastern and the Southern 'neighbourhoods' of the enlarged Union – and later on also the Southern Caucasus – thus bringing into the new policy framework very different (and ultimately incomparable) countries and issues.

Second, there is the mode of operation of the ENP. Over time, the Commission has tried to focus more on the individual Action Plans, but has remained constrained by the existence of two main 'clubs' among the EU-27, competing over resources and priorities. Most recently, the launch of the Mediterranean Union and then that of the Eastern Partnership have further highlighted this structural rift.

For Missiroli, conversely, the ENP has also been conditioned by the fact that, in essence, it is neither enlargement nor foreign policy proper, and cannot bring to bear fully the tools of either. It cannot exercise conditionality like the former (the rewards for compliance are not attractive enough to the 'neighbours') nor complement and mainstream national approaches like the latter. As a result, its actual impact is very low and hard to assess even in those countries that are considered success stories (Ukraine, Morocco, Jordan and of course Israel).

Missiroli's chapter – and the volume – concludes with the assertion that the ENP would therefore benefit by its reconstruction: by splitting up at least the Eastern and the Southern neighbourhoods (as already accomplished, in part, with the creation of the Mediterranean Union and the Eastern Partnership) and by joining up Community and CFSP tools. The Lisbon Treaty, if and when ratified, could make connection to the wider EU agenda possible: furthermore the formation of the new Commission in the autumn of 2009, alongside the implementation of the Treaty provisions on foreign policy and external relations, would represent an opportunity to improve both the formulation and the delivery of the Union's policies vis-à-vis its immediate neighbours.

Notes

1. Commission of the European Communities (2004), Communication from the Commission, *European Neighbourhood Policy: Strategy Paper* COM(2004) 373 final, Brussels, 12 May 2004, available at http://ec.europa.eu/world/enp/pdf/strategy/strategy_paper_en.pdf, last accessed 21 July 2008.
2. Commission of the European Communities (2003), Communication from the Commission, *Wider Europe – Neighbourhood: A New Framework for Relations with our Eastern and Southern Neighbours* COM(2003) 104 final, Brussels, 11 March 2003.
3. Ibid. p. 9.
4. Ibid. p. 10.
5. Ibid. p. 15.
6. Commission of the European Communities (2004), Communication from the Commission, *European Neighbourhood Policy, Strategy Paper* COM(2004) 373 final, Brussels, 12 May 2004, available at http://ec.europa.eu/world/enp/pdf/strategy/strategy_paper_en.pdf, last accessed 21 July 2008.
7. Benita Ferrero-Waldner, European Commissioner for External Relations and European Neighbourhood Policy, speech 'European Neighbourhood Policy', Stockholm, 7 March 2006, available at http://europa.eu.int/rapid/pressReleasesAction.do?reference=SPEECH/06/149&format=HTML&aged=0&language=EN&guiLanguage=en, last accessed 19 December 2006.
8. Commission of the European Commission (2004), Communication from the Commission, *European Neighbourhood Policy, Strategy Paper*, COM(2004) 373 final, p. 3, Brussels, 12 May 2004, available at http://ec.europa.eu/world/enp/pdf/strategy/strategy_paper_en.pdf, last accessed 21 July 2008.
9. Landaburu Eneko, Director General in the DG External Relations of the European Commission (2006), 'From Neighbourhood to Integration Policy: are there concrete alternatives to enlargement?', *CEPS Policy Brief*, 95 (March), p. 10, available at http://shop.ceps.be/BookDetail.php?item_id=1305, last accessed 7 July 2006.
10. Commission of the European Communities (2004), Communication from the Commission, *European Neighbourhood Policy: Strategy Paper* COM(2004) 373 final, p. 6, Brussels, 12 May 2004, available at http://ec.europa.eu/world/enp/pdf/strategy/strategy_paper_en.pdf, last accessed 21 July 2008.
11. Commission of the European Communities (2004), Communication from the Commission, *European Neighbourhood Policy: Strategy Paper* COM(2004)

373 final, p. 8, Brussels, 12 May 2004, available at http://ec.europa.eu/world/enp/pdf/strategy/strategy_paper_en.pdf, last accessed 21 July 2008.

12. Landaburu Eneko, Director General in the DG External Relations of the European Commission (2006), 'From Neighbourhood to Integration Policy: are there concrete alternatives to enlargement?', *CEPS Policy Brief*, 95 (March), p. 9, available at http://shop.ceps.be/BookDetail.php?item_id=1305, last accessed 7 July 2006.

13. Landaburu Eneko, Director General in the DG External Relations of the European Commission (2006), 'From Neighbourhood to Integration Policy: are there concrete alternatives to enlargement?', *CEPS Policy Brief*, 95 (March), p. 6, available at http://shop.ceps.be/BookDetail.php?item_id=1305, last accessed 7 July 2006.

14. Common economic space (including and with specific reference to environment and energy); a common space of freedom, security and justice; a space of cooperation in the field of external security and a space of research and education, including cultural aspects.

15. Commission of the European Communities (2004), Communication from the Commission, *European Neighbourhood Policy: Strategy Paper* COM(2004) 373 final, p. 6, Brussels, 12 May 2004, available at http://ec.europa.eu/world/enp/pdf/strategy/strategy_paper_en.pdf, last accessed 21 July 2008.

16. Karen E. Smith (2005), 'Enlargement and European Order', in Christopher Hill and Michael Smith (eds), *International Relations and the European Union*. Oxford: Oxford University Press, p. 271.

17. See for example: Christopher Hill (2002), 'The geopolitical implications of enlargement', in Jan Zielonka (ed.), *Europe Unbound, Enlarging and reshaping the boundaries of the European Union*. London: Routledge, p. 95; Roy H. Ginsberg (1998), 'The Impact of Enlargement on the Role of the European Union in the World', in John Redmond and Glenda Rosenthal (eds), *The Expanding European Union*. Boulder, CO: Lynne Rienner, p. 197; Karen E. Smith (2005), 'Enlargement and European Order', in Christopher Hill and Michael Smith (eds), *International Relations and the European Union*. Oxford: Oxford University Press , p. 271.

18. EU-Moldova Cooperation Council (2005), 'EU/Moldova Action Plan', 22 February, p. 5, available at http://ec.europa.eu/world/enp/pdf/action_plans/moldova_enp_ap_final_en.pdf, last accessed 15 December 2006.

19. TAIEX is a form of targeted expert assistance. 'The Policy: Funding, The European Neighbourhood Policy', Website of the European Commission.

20. Twinning provides the framework for administrations and semi-public organisations in the beneficiary countries to work with their counterparts in member states towards institution-building. 'Pre-Accession Assistance for Institution Building – Twinning', Enlargement, Website of the European Commission, http://ec.europa.eu/comm/enlargement/institution_building/twinning_en.htm, last accessed 7 July 2006.

21. Commission of the European Communities (2004), Communication from the Commission, *European Neighbourhood Policy: Strategy Paper* COM(2004) 373 final, p. 4, Brussels, 12 May 2004, available at http://ec.europa.eu/world/enp/pdf/strategy/strategy_paper_en.pdf, last accessed 21 July 2008.

22. EU-Ukraine Cooperation Council (2005), 'EU/Ukraine Action Plan', 21 February, p. 2, available at http://ec.europa.eu/world/enp/pdf/action_plans/ukraine_enp_ap_final_en.pdf, last accessed 15 December 2006.
23. Ibid.
24. Landaburu Eneko, Director General in the DG External Relations of the European Commission (2006), 'From Neighbourhood to Integration Policy: are there concrete alternatives to enlargement?', *CEPS Policy Brief*, 95 (March), p. 10, available at http://shop.ceps.be/BookDetail.php?item_id=1305, last accessed 7 July 2006.
25. Commission Staff Working Document accompanying the Communication from the Commission On Strengthening the European Neighbourhood Policy Overall Assessment COM(2006) 726 final, Brussels, 4 December 2006 SEC(2006) 1504/2. Commission of the European Communities (2006), Communication from the Commission, *Strengthening the European Neighbourhood Policy* SEC(2006) 1504; SEC(2006) 1505; SEC(2006) 1506; SEC(2006) 1507; SEC(2006) 1508; SEC(2006) 1509; SEC(2006) 1510; SEC(2006) 1511; SEC(2006) 1512. COM(2006)726 final, Brussels, 4 December 2006; 5 December 2007 COM(2007) 774 final, Brussels, 5 December 2007. Commission of the European Communities (2008a), *A Strong European Neighbourhood Policy*, COM(2008) 164 Brussels, 3 April 2008. Commission of the European Communities (2008b, 2009a), Communication from the Commission *Implementation of the European Neighbourhood Policy in 2007*, SEC(2008) xx01–xx13.COM(2009) 188/3 Brussels, 23 April 2009. Commission of the European Communities (2009b) Communication from the Commission, *Implementation of the European Neighbourhood Policy in 2008* SEC(2009) pp. 511–523, Brussels, 23 April 2009.
26. *International Herald Tribune*, 6 July 2008.
27. Commission of the European Communities (2008c), Communication from the Commission, *Barcelona Process: Union for the Mediterranean* COM(2008) 319 final, Brussels, 20 May 2008.
28. http://ec.europa.eu/external_relations/euromed/index_en.htm.
29. Joint Declaration of the Paris Summit for the Mediterranean (2008), Paris, 13 July 2008 Under the co-presidency of the President of the French Republic and the President of the Arab Republic of Egypt, available at http://www.ue2008.fr/webdav/site/PFUE/shared/import/07/0713_declaration_de_paris/Joint_declaration_of_the_Paris_summit_for_the_Mediterranean-EN.pdf.
30. Commission of the European Communities (2008d), Communication from the Commission, *Eastern Partnership* COM(2008) 823 final, Brussels, 3 December 2008.
31. European Council (2008a), 'Presidency Conclusions', Brussels European Council, 19/20 June 2008, Brussels. European Council (2008b), 'Presidency Conclusions', Brussels European Council, 1 September 2008, Brussels.
32. Benita Ferrero-Waldner, 'Giving the Neighbours a stake in the EU internal market', speech, Brussels, 6 June 2006, http://europa.eu/rapid/pressReleasesAction.do?reference=SPEECH/06/346&format=HTML&aged=0&language=EN&guiLanguage=en, last accessed 6 July 2006.

33. Commission of the European Communities (2004), Communication from the Commission, *European Neighbourhood Policy: Strategy Paper* COM(2004) 373 final, p. 8, Brussels, 12 May 2004, available at http://ec.europa.eu/world/ enp/pdf/strategy/strategy_paper_en.pdf, last accessed 21 July 2008.
34. Karen E. Smith (2005), 'The outsiders: the European neighbourhood policy', *International Affairs*, 81 (4), p. 765.

Part I

The Study of the European Neighbourhood Policy: Methodological, Theoretical and Empirical Challenges

2
As You Like It: European Union Normative Power in the European Neighbourhood Policy

Ian Manners

Introduction

This chapter addresses some of the methodological, theoretical and empirical challenges of studying the European Neighbourhood Policy (ENP). It will argue that analysing the youthful ENP presents a wide variety of challenges for scholars of the EU's relations with its near neighbours, in particular the question of theoretical presuppositions. The chapter will discuss these challenges in four parts involving the methodological location of the ENP, the theoretical framing of the ENP, a 'normative power' approach to the ENP and concluding with a brief analytical reflection. The chapter also carries an argument – that the challenges of studying the ENP are least well served by traditional approaches to political science, and might be better advanced by rethinking these presumptions. Thus, conventional presumptions of 'much ado about nothing' in the ENP may benefit from a reflection on the extent to which these presumptions are determinate in analysing whether the ENP is 'as you like it'.

The rest of the chapter is as follows. First, the challenges of methodological location and analytical frameworks are discussed in the rest of this section. Second, the chapter will reflect on the theoretical framing of the ENP by comparing and contrasting conventional causal theories of EU policies with those of more constitutive theories. This section will also seek to locate some of the other contributors to this book in this theoretical framing. Third, the chapter will advocate a 'normative power' approach to the study of the ENP in order to better understand and judge the practices of EU engagement with its nearest neighbours. Finally, the chapter will conclude with a brief analytical reflection on the relative merits of 'much ado about the ENP' versus an 'as you like it ENP'.

The analytical challenges of the ENP

The study of the ENP presents a wide variety of challenges for scholars, not least because the policy area is relatively new and different. With most scholars of the ENP migrating to the subject in the mid-2000s from the study of EU enlargement, EU-conflict policy and area/national studies (such as the Euro-Mediterranean Policy – EMP), it is unsurprising that ENP means many things to many people.[1] This mixture of backgrounds of scholars working on the ENP is further complicated by the two defining features of the area of study. First, ENP is a particularly diverse and thus difficult empirical field of study characterised by large geographical and linguistic differences. So it is not unfair to say that ENP scholars are either Eastern (Eastern Europe or the Caucasus) or Southern (North Africa or the Middle East) specialists. There are few, if any, ENP scholars who genuinely straddle this East-South divide and bring knowledge of both the post-Soviet space as well as the Mashreq/ Maghreb regions. Second, the ENP is neither strictly EU enlargement policy nor strictly EU foreign policy. Instead, the ENP is best characterised as a mass of contradictory impulses, led by an EU desire to improve relations with its nearest neighbours in the aftermath of its most recent enlargements.[2] Its location within the wider frame of EU foreign policy is therefore contested as the ENP remains caught in 'conflicts between practice and principle, security and democracy, interest and values'.[3] These two defining features mean that the study and analysis of the ENP almost requires differentiation between East and South – that one size cannot fit all.[4]

Such analytical contestation is further complicated by the agencies, instruments and states involved the ENP. The polycentric polity of the EU ensures that a variety of agencies, such as DG Relex and the High Representative, are involved in aspects of ENP relations. Furthermore, the ENP involves a mixture of states who participate in a variety of existing instruments, such as the Barcelona Process, Association Agreements, and Partnership and Cooperation Agreements (PCAs). In addition a number of ENP states seek membership of the EU (such as Ukraine and Georgia), while other ENP states have little formal participation (Belarus, Libya). As well as this variety of agencies, instruments and states there is the observation that the EU is by no means the only actor in the ENP region, with national (e.g. Russia and the US), international (e.g. the Organization for Security and Co-operation in Europe (OSCE), Council of Europe and African Union), and transnational (e.g. oil and gas companies and civil society) actors playing important roles. As the 2008 conflict in Georgia illustrated, the variety of agencies (Presidents of Council and Commission, High Representative) and instruments (the European Neighbourhood and Partnership Instrument (ENPI), European Community Humanitarian Assistance (ECHO), European Security and Defence Policy (ESDP)), as well as actors (Russia, the US and EU) make the analysis of ENP particularly challenging.

While questions of locating the ENP and its actors are analytically problematic, there are also wider issues of *climate, sovereignty* and *time* associated with studying the ENP in the 2003–2008 period.[5] First, the changed international *climate* of the Bush/Bin Laden world since 11 September 2001 raises the question of whether the EU emphasis on counter-terrorism and traditional security promotion in the period 2001–2008 will prove representative of the much longer timescales going into the ENP funding period 2007–2013.[6] Second, the resistance of the 'axis of ego' to the sharing of *sovereignty* in international law has made the promotion of multilateral treaty commitments, and their acceptance by ENP partners, particularly difficult. The 'axis of ego' refers to the permanent members of the UN Security Council (here the US, Russia and China) when they consider themselves exceptional or superpowers, and thus above international norms and law.[7] Finally, the important question is that of *time* – in the case of an open-ended policy field such as the ENP, it may be simply too early to assess the EU's role in any meaningful way. As Barbara Lippert has argued, the ENP is 'neither conceptually complete nor operationally stable', and is likely to remain this way for some time.[8]

Compounding these analytical questions are the methodological difficulties regarding *how* to study ENP. For example, is it only appropriate to study the whole of the ENP region, or is it possible to study just one region (East/South), or one country? Furthermore, *what* exactly is it appropriate to study in the ENP – shared values, political dialogue, economic and social development policy, trade and the Internal Market, justice and home affairs, neighbourhood connections, human resource development or all of the above? All of these areas are identified as important in the 2004 ENP Strategy Paper, but clearly it is improbable that all of them could be promoted at the same time, to the same extent, in all the partner countries. Last, what should be the *focus* of empirical study of the ENP – data, documents, discourses, public opinion, press opinion or researcher opinion? All of these have been and are the focus of current ENP studies, raising the suggestion that it is problematic to make 'much ado about nothing', when the 'something' is relatively uncertain.

This observation regarding the uncertainty of the 'something' ensures that the object of study is largely constituted by study itself – that the ENP as a field of study is in the process of being created by scholarship in the field. Thus analysis of the ENP, which is neither conceptually complete nor operationally stable, at the same time as the field is being continuously reconstituted by study itself, produces more analytical challenges than agreements. As the rest of the contributions to this volume illustrate, the mixture of scholarly backgrounds and presumptions, analytical locational contestation, variety of agents and instruments, wider analytical questions and methodological difficulties make studying the ENP both challenging and potentially interesting. One of the most important challenges is the role of theory, or means of understanding the ENP, as the next section will now explore.

'Much ado about nothing' or 'as you like it'?

'Given the topicality of its theme, the play [*As You Like It*] may well indeed have been written at speed. Yet it is actually well constructed, with no major discrepancies or loose ends. It is a good deal more watertight, as a narrative, than *Much Ado About Nothing*, written a year or two earlier.'[9] In the short time since the ENP was proposed a number of commentators have deployed the idiom of 'much ado about nothing' to capture the EU's relations with its nearest neighbours.[10] While this analytical emphasis on the 'something' in neighbourhood relations is interesting, understanding the EU as a regional actor requires that we think about its ENP both causally and constitutively. The emphasis on theory in this chapter is driven by the argument that 'theory is a guide to empirical exploration, a means of reflecting…upon complex processes of [political] evolution and transformation in order to highlight key periods or phases of change which warrant closer empirical scrutiny'.[11] But theories of the ENP do more than simply guide exploration and scrutiny; they also represent the realities of it, for as Catherine Hoskyns observed, 'theory constitutes as well as explains the questions it asks (and those it does not ask)'.[12] In the study of the ENP it is useful to contrast causal with constitutive approaches in order to understand how differing theories lead to differing understandings of the 'nothing' or 'something' that EU policy makes possible.

Causal theory argues that the object of study can be explained as a causal relationship between one factor and another.[13] Hence a causal expectation would be for the ENP to be 'some ado about something' analytically. In contrast, constitutive theory contends that the subject of study is constituted or created within the context of a specific social relationship.[14] Thus a constitutive expectation would be for the ENP to constitute, and to reconstitute, its subjects through their relations. In other words the focus of a constitutive approach is on how the practices and experiences of the participants are changed by the ENP – is the ENP 'as you like it'? rather than asking if there is 'much ado about nothing'? To stretch the idiom into a metaphor, following Duncan Jones it may be suggested that an understanding of the ENP 'as you like it' might be a good deal more water-tight as a narrative than the ENP as 'much ado about nothing'. By keeping in mind that causal and constitutive explanations are not looking for the same thing in their social science, we can reflect on differing existing theories of the EU's ENP.

Causal theories of the ENP – 'much ado about nothing'?

From the perspective of causal theory, the evolution of the EU's ENP can be explained as the result of three determining factors suggested 30 years ago by Carole Webb in her tripartite analysis of intergovernmental cooperation, supranational community and transnational processes.[15]

The first factor is the role of member states primarily seen in intergovernmental bargaining in the Council of Ministers and at the European Council. The role of states, their governments and ministries has long been an important factor in explaining the policies of the EU, as Helen Wallace's work on national governments in the study of the communities has made clear since the early 1970s.[16] Wholly state-based, or intergovernmentalist, explanations for European integration reached their peak in the 1990s with the publication of Andrew Moravcsik's widely repudiated *Choice for Europe*.[17] Despite this, Moravcsik and Milada Anna Vachudova have argued 'the EU enlargement process and its consequences are decisively influenced by material national interests and state power'.[18] The widespread criticism that the ENP has primarily been articulated within the framework of security concerns may well be attributable to member state preferences in the post-11 September world. Within this volume the contributions by Sten Rynning and Christine Pihlkjær Jensen, and to a lesser extent Narine Ghazaryan, serve as examples of state-based casual explanations for the ENP. For example, Rynning and Jensen describe the ENP in terms of competing geopolitical spheres of interest between the US and Russia, while

Ghazaryan writes of the competing alliances in the Caucuses between US and Russian interests.

The second factor is the role of the supranational institutions of the EU, in particular the Commission and Court, as a central factor in explaining the policies of the EU. Writing in the 1950s and 1960s, Miriam Camps stressed the importance of understanding a 'European Community' that was a 'living experiment in creating new relationships among states and between peoples'.[19] Wholly supranationalist explanations for European integration have mutated over the decades, but have been advocated by neo-functionalists, political system theorists and supranational governance approaches. Supranationalist explanations for the ENP are advanced in varieties of institutionalist theories, for example in the emphasis placed on historical institutionalism and path dependency in the work of Judith Kelley, as well as Sandra Lavenex's governance perspective on the ENP's macro-institutional set-up.[20] Within this volume, Carmen Gebhard's chapter serves as a good example of a supranational, historical institutionalist, causal explanation for the ENP with her discussion of 'path-dependent stickiness' in the strategic conception and structural design of the ENP.

The third factor is the role of transnational actors and institutions inside and outside the EU, such as transnational capital, social movements/groups and transnational institutions. EU transnational institutions include the European Parliament, the Economic and Social Committee and the Committee of the Regions, all of which represent local and transnational civil society, rather than the member states or the supranational EU. The role of transnational factors has been of increasing importance in explaining the policies of the EU since the 1970s, with Susan Strange's emphasis on transnational firms and economic interdependence and Carole Webb's focus on transnational activities within the EU.[21] Wholly transnational explanations for European integration have emerged as important in the post-Cold-War world with emphasis placed on the role of transnational firms and business, transnational parties and networking and transnational trade unions and non-governmental organisations (NGOs).[22] Transnational explanations for the ENP are to be found in work emphasising the role of cross-border, transnational and regional cooperation in the ENP programmes and instruments, as well as approaches focused on NGOs and civil society. For example, Rosa Balfour and Antonio Missiroli look at how the EU focuses support on civil society by directing the 'bulk of its aid...towards NGOs dedicated to human rights training and awareness-raising in civil and military services', while others emphasise the role of NGOs and civil society actors within both EU member states and ENP partner countries.[23] In this volume, the discussion of 'global public goods' by Sven Biscop illustrates the role of transnational factors in shaping the ENP through a method of 'positive conditionality'.

Constitutive theories of the ENP – 'as you like it'?

In contrast to causal theories of the ENP, from the perspective of constitutive theory the evolution of the ENP can be best understood via three approaches – social constructivism, post-structural theory and critical social theory.[24]

Social constructivist perspectives on the EU emphasise the role of norms, identity and socialisation in European integration. First becoming influential in the 1990s, following the collapse of Cold War theoretical rationalisations, social constructivist approaches flourished as edited volumes brought together new scholarship using 'reflective' or 'constructivist' theories.[25] Social constructivist approaches to enlargement and the ENP have become widespread in the 2000s, with volumes edited by Frank Schimmelfennig, Ulrich Sedelmeier and Rachel Epstein proving particularly important in theorising enlargement, Europeanisation and conditionality in the EU neighbourhood.[26] Scholars in this volume have made some important contributions to the study of the ENP from a constructivist perspective such as Federica Bicchi's work on the ideational processes and definition of ideas in EU-Mediterranean policy, Hiski Haukkala's study of international institutionalisation and Wendtian thin constructivism in EU-Russian relations and Gwen Sasse's argument regarding 'conditionality as a process rather than a clear-cut causal or intervening variable'.[27] Within this volume the chapters by Haukkala, Bicchi and Sasse all illustrate some of the insights gained from a constructivist understanding of the ENP, in particular the discussions of 'international society' (Haukkala) and the ENP as a framework for socialisation (Sasse).

Post-structural theoretical perspectives on the EU go beyond social construction toward discursive deconstruction and genealogical excavation as a means of revealing EU structures of knowledge. Similar to constructivism, post-structural scholarship began to engage with EU politics in the 1990s with the work of Thomas Diez being particularly influential.[28] Post-structural approaches to the ENP have been advanced by Pertti Joenniemi, Christopher Browning and Michelle Pace, all placing theoretical emphasis on the construction of EU policies and identity in opposition to a neighbouring 'other'.[29] Within this volume, Ben Tonra's contribution on identity construction in the ENP serves as a good example of post-structuralist theory with its emphasis on the role of borders and boundaries in constructing the identities of insiders and outsiders.

The final perspective considered here is that of critical social theory, which seeks to both critique and change society at the same time. Critical social theory perspectives on the EU are relatively rare, but can be found in the work of Gerald Delanty, Chris Rumford and Craig Calhoun and their emphasis on the need to understand European integration in the context of more general changes represented by globalisation.[30] Critical social theory approaches to the ENP suggest that the policy represents attempts to organise (non-)European space that blurs external borders and creates governable spaces.[31] Within this volume there are no other contributions which seek to use critical social theory to understand the ENP, so the rest of this chapter will set out how a 'normative power' approach might be used to study the ENP.

EU normative power in the ENP

Critical social theorists such as Craig Calhoun and Seyla Benhabib critique aspects of universalism and relativism inherent in much normative theory. As Calhoun comments '[t]he very scientistic attempt to severe empirical theory from normative theory has contributed to normative theory's problematic over-commitment to a culturally insensitive Enlightenment universalism', while Benhabib argues 'against attempts in normative political theory that reify cultural groups and their struggles for recognition'.[32] The normative power approach attempts to strike a critical path between culturally insensitive universalism and the reification of cultural relativism in order both to critique and change the EU in world politics. It does this by seeking to study the ideational aspects of the EU, and by seeking both to advocate and critique such aspects in order to change EU policy.[33]

In order to study the EU's normative power in the ENP, it is useful to analyse and judge the ideational aspects found in EU principles, actions and impact in this policy field.[34] Although the normative power approach is aimed at analysing single policies, rather than an entire policy field such as the ENP, this section suggests how the approach might be used.

EU principles in the ENP – legitimacy, coherence and consistency

'The Union's neighbours have pledged adherence to fundamental human rights and freedoms, through their adherence to a number of multilateral treaties as well as through their bilateral agreements with the EU. All the EU's neighbours are signatories of UN human rights conventions.'[35] The passage from the 2004 Communication from the Commission 'European Neighbourhood Policy: Strategy Paper' illustrates the way in which the principles promoted in the ENP gain their legitimacy from previously established treaties, agreements and conventions. For eastern neighbours the passage continues with reference to further sources of legitimacy:

> Some are members of the Council of Europe and OSCE and have ratified the European Convention for the Protection of Human Rights and Fundamental Freedoms and committed themselves to adhere to relevant conventions and bodies setting high democratic and human rights standards as well as to accept strong and legally binding mechanisms to ensure that they comply with human rights obligations.

Here the Communication refers to the pre-existing commitments given by the five eastern participants (Armenia, Azerbaijan, Georgia, Moldova and Ukraine) as part of their memberships of the Council of Europe and the OSCE. For southern neighbours the passage continues with reference to other sources of legitimacy:

> Signatories to the Barcelona declaration have accepted inter alia a declaration of principles to act in accordance with the United Nations Charter and the Universal Declaration of Human Rights, and to develop the rule of law and democracy in their political systems, respect human rights and fundamental freedoms and guarantee the effective legitimate exercise of such rights and freedoms.

This part of the Communication refers to the ten southern participants (Algeria, Egypt, Israel, Jordan, Lebanon, Libya, Palestine, Morocco, Syria and Tunisia) as signatories to the Barcelona Declaration and members of the UN. Finally, the passage ends with reference to broader international sources of legitimacy within the UN system: 'Partner countries are committed to respecting core labour standards and to promoting fundamental social rights, as parties to relevant ILO conventions; they are also committed to the pursuit of a sustainable mode of development, as defined at the Johannesburg world summit.' This final part of the passage on 'commitment to shared values' refers to the fact that all ENP partners, both non-EU and EU, have committed themselves to core labour standards and sustainable development. Such references to pre-existing commitments to non-EU organisations, treaties, conventions and agreements can act as important sources of legitimacy for the promotion of principles that are external to the EU.[36] These external sources of legitimacy have at least four effects on this promotion through EU normative power. First, the external sources of legitimacy act as 'clear and public objectives and benchmarks…. key benchmarks should include the ratification and implementation of international commitments which demonstrate respect for shared values, in particular the values codified in the UN Human Rights Declaration, the OSCE and Council of Europe standards'.[37] Such benchmarks are set out in the Annex to the 2004 Strategy Paper and include UN core human rights conventions, fundamental International Labour Organization (ILO) conventions on core labour standards, Council of Europe 'core' conventions on human rights, the Rome Statute of the International Criminal Court, the UN Framework Convention on Climate Change and the Barcelona Convention for the protection of the marine environment and the coastal region of the Mediterranean.[38] These benchmarks are referred to in the discussions of 'political dialogue and reform', including 'democracy and the rule of law', 'human rights and fundamental freedoms' and 'fundamental social rights and core labour standards', as well as 'sustainable development' under 'economic and social reform and development' in the processes and dialogues on country reporting, action planning and progress reporting.

Second, the use of external sources of legitimacy encourages such organisations to engage more directly with ENP partner countries as seen, for example, in the Council of Europe's 2006 initiatives to encourage the incorporation of its standards and values into the ENP and its programme on human rights, democratic governance and development through dialogue between Europe, the southern Mediterranean and Africa, as well as the renewing the OSCE's 'Mediterranean Partnership'.[39] Both the use of benchmarking and the engagement of other organisations can act as reference points in debates within ENP countries regarding such principles, as Soha Bayoumi illustrates in her discussion of Egyptian civil society: 'governmental stances towards the EU … differ from those of civil society, which sometimes seem more attracted by the 'normative power' of the EU as a (potential) promoter of human rights, democracy and the rule of law in the world'.[40]

Finally, external sources of legitimacy for principles promoted by the EU can contribute to their coherence and consistency. The importance of claims to legitimacy for such principles involves ensuring that the EU is both normatively coherent and consistent in its policies. Coherence involves ensuring that the EU is not simply pragmatically promoting its own norms, but that the principles are part of more international commitments. The coherence of EU principles is improved by the fact that democracy, human rights, rule of law, social solidarity (core labour standards and social rights) and sustainable development are all part of the UN system. In this context, the EU may better exercise normative power if 'a neighbourhood policy for a European Union acting coherently and efficiently in the world' is aware that 'in the implementation of the ENP it is of the utmost importance that the Institutions and the Member States act in a consistent and coherent way'.[41]

Thus, in addition to legitimacy and coherence, consistency is important in ensuring that the EU is not promoting norms with which it does itself not comply. In the case of the Euro-Mediterranean Partnership (EMP) Kalypso Nicolaïdis and Dimitri Nicolaïdis have put this clearly when they conclude that:

> Fundamentally, normative power can only be applied credibly under a key condition: consistency between internal policies and external prescriptions and actions.... Nevertheless, at least initially, the democratic peace argument won the day in the design of the EMP simply because this is the narrative at the core of the EU construct itself, and one increasingly applied to its relations with the rest of the world.[42]

Roland Dannreuther has argued that 'the ENP seeks to promote a greater coherence and consistency in its neighbourhood policy' by the introduction in 2007 of the ENPI, which seeks to simplify the existing and complex financial relations, replacing the Interregional Cooperation (INTERREG), Poland and Hungary: Assistance for Restructuring their Economies (PHARE), Community Assistance for Reconstruction, Development and Stabilisation (CARDS), Technical Assistance for the Commonwealth of Independent States (TACIS) and MEDA instruments.[43] However, despite these two previous discussions of coherence and consistency, a critical question remains regarding the consistent application of the freedom of movement of people within the EU to ENP citizens.[44] Problems of consistency are clearly greatest in the ENP-South which was an 'add-on' to the original aim of improving EU relations with its Eastern neighbours. This problem was further compounded by the later development of strategic partnerships with Russia (as well as China, Canada, Japan, India, and the US). The creation of the ENP in the context of so many compromises between the aims and practices of the Barcelona Process, EMP, Association Agreements, PCAs and the perceived advantages of strategic partnerships, means that consistency is very difficult to achieve – which badly undermines the images of the EU in the eyes of partners.

From a critical perspective, the extent to which the ENP constantly refers to external sources of legitimacy suggests that there is a tension here in the post-colonial context of EU-Mediterranean relations. This tension is between the perceived 'imposition' of EU values in the ENP process and the lack of imposition implicit in the notion on 'ownership' discussed below. Therefore a normative power approach to the study of ENP would begin by analysing the legitimacy, coherence and consistency of the principles the EU seeks to promote, and it would then turn to looking at the actions taken by the EU in the neighbourhood. However, it would need to be critically aware of the tensions between imposition and ownership in post-colonial relations within the Mediterranean.

EU actions in ENP – persuasion, engagement and differentiation

The second stage of analysis involves studying the means through which EU normative power is enacted in ENP, in particular by looking at the processes of persuasion, engagement and differentiation. If normative power has importance as a concept it is through the powers of persuasion, argumentat and ability to shame or confer prestige.[45] As Rosemary Foot has argued, persuasion is important because 'norms are expressed through language and the process of argumentation and debate can shape what is said subsequently in both domestic and international venues'.[46] But persuasion has little meaning in the ENP without fora for engagement and an ability to differentiate in the attribution of shame or prestige.

Thus, engagement involves ensuring that the EU encourages dialogue and participation in the conduct of its relations with others, including public discussions both within the EU and with EU partners. Historically, the EMP has been about engagement – between institutions, governments, ministers, parties, social groups, NGOs and civil society – in order to allow many more voices to be heard. In contrast to these EMP multilateral (if not plurilateral) practices, the ENP was designed more as bilateral relations with an aim to encouraging reform. However, the sheer growth of voices being heard in and on ENP relations since 2003 does provide some illustration of the importance of engagement. Examples of this growth of voices in and on the ENP can be seen in the increase in venues for argument and debate between participants.[47] Scholarly dialogue and participation increasingly includes ENP voices and expertise from the Mediterranean and Eastern Europe.

It is clear, as Raffaella Del Sarto and Tobias Schumacher (as well as Dannreuther) have shown, that the ENP has abandoned the one-speed regionality of the EMP for 'differentiated bilateralism' based on Action Plans and benchmarking.[48] As the ENP puts it:

> the drawing up of an Action Plan and the priorities agreed with each partner will depend on its particular circumstances. These differ with respect to geographic location, the political and economic situation, relations with the European Union and with neighbouring countries, reform programmes, where applicable, needs and capacities, as well as perceived interests in the context of the ENP. Thus the Action Plans with each partner will be differentiated. Differentiation should at the same time be based on a clear commitment to shared values and be compatible with a coherent regional approach, especially where further regional cooperation can bring clear benefits.[49]

ENP Commissioner Benita Ferrero-Waldner added in 2006 that 'we agree Action Plans with our partners which set out the path to a closer relationship. Differentiation is the key – each country's Action Plan responds to its particular needs and benefits'.[50] This differentiation in approach provides a greater opportunity for partners to participate in the drawing up, reviewing, and completion of the content of Action Plans. The intention is that the ENP offers participants a 'privileged form of partnership' which 'increases the opportunity of voicing their particular concerns'.[51] The first example of such a form of partnership was announced by Benita Ferrero-Waldner in October 2008 as an 'advanced status' for Morocco involving a range of measures strengthening political, economic and social relations.[52]

As discussed here, a normative power approach to the study of ENP would proceed by analysing the persuasion, engagement and differentiation in the actions the EU takes to promote the principles discussed previously, and then it would finally look at the impact of the EU in the neighbourhood.

EU impact in the ENP – socialisation, ownership and conditionality

The final stage of analysis looks at the impact of EU normative power in the ENP by studying the processes of socialisation, ownership and conditionality. To a remarkable degree, much of the recent ENP literature argues that traditional, rationalist incentive-based explanations for EU conditionality needs rethinking. Gwen Sasse argues that 'a more flexible conceptualisation … frames conditionality as a process rather than a clear-cut causal or intervening variable'.[53] Sandra Lavenex suggests that 'traditional rationalist, actor-based foreign policy approaches to the ENP that stress its weakness owing to the absence of accession conditionality may miss an essential part of EU external influence'.[54] Rachel Epstein and Ulrich Sedelmeier have called into question the 'dominant incentive-based explanation for EU conditionality', arguing instead that 'only the long-term perspective of the post-accession phase will allow researchers to identify and appreciate the full importance of socialization processes that accompanied the use of conditionality'.[55] What this scholarship argues is that the ENP must be seen as a longer-term process of socialisation rather than the application of shorter-term utilitarian calculation.

This longer-term process of socialisation should to be reflected on in the context of the EU's open-ended institutionalisation of the ENP. Open-ended institutionalisation of the ENP includes the creation of a Commission-based responsibility within DG Relex; the commitment to promoting good governance in neighbouring countries set out in the 2003 European Security Strategy (ESS); and the aim of developing special relationships with neighbouring countries set out in the Lisbon Treaty. Such bureaucratic, strategic and treaty-based institutionalisation illustrates the extent to which the ENP is seen within the EU as an open-ended process continuing beyond the foreseeable future.

Thus, in this context, socialisation should be seen as being a part of an open-ended process where the EU reflects on the impact of its policies with the partner countries, in particular through encouraging local ownership and practising positive conditionality. Local ownership is crucial in ensuring that the ENP relationship is one that is 'other-empowering' rather than replicating some of the self-empowering motivations of much foreign, development and humanitarian policy. The 2004 ENP Strategy Paper suggests this might be possible:

> The ENP is an offer made by the EU to its partners to which they have responded with considerable interest and engagement. Joint ownership of the process, based on the awareness of shared values and common interests, is essential. The EU does not seek to impose priorities or conditions on its partners. The Action Plans depend, for their success, on the clear recognition of mutual interests in addressing a set of priority issues. There can be no question of asking partners to accept a pre-determined set of priorities. These will be

defined by common consent and will thus vary from country to country.[56]

Del Sarto and Schumacher suggest that 'the introduction of the principle of 'joint ownership' is certainly a positive development' in encouraging partner involvement and consultation in the formulation of priorities.[57] Dannreuther also argues that 'local ownership...fits in with the increasing recognition that economic reform and democracy cannot be imposed from outside but must be nurtured from within'.[58]

Positive conditionality is also important in ensuring that 'progress is rewarded with greater incentives and benefits [and] an even deeper relationship'.[59] The move from the negative conditionality of sanctions to the positive conditionality of the ENP reflects lessons learnt from other policy fields over the past ten years. Del Sarto and Schumacher observe that positive conditionality involves a 'benchmarking approach' and moves the EU from 'passive engagement' to 'active engagement'.[60] There is, however, one major dilemma to the aims of partnership and local empowerment expressed here, as Nicolaïdis and Nicolaïdis make clear:

> when normative power aims at changing deep-seated patterns of governance, framing the one-way imposition of certain norms as an exercise in 'partnership' raises major dilemmas of disempowerment in partner societies. While one may argue that normative power is not neo-colonial if it is meant to empower local actors, it may in fact rob them of their autonomy in defining the substance of empowerment; for example, activists do not share with Europeans the same appreciation of pluralism and point to a European secular bias...The EU's failure to apply principles of democracy promotion consistently over time is the result in part of the lack of government agreement between member states over the desirable trade-offs they are willing to make among different goals and the values underpinning these goals (e.g. political reform versus stability or poverty reduction).[61]

From a critical perspective, two questions can be asked of the EU's impact regarding socialisation and ownership. The difficulty with seeing the ENP as a longer-term process of socialisation is that so far all the evidence and examples appear to come from ENP-East, rather than ENP-South. There is a parallel to this differentiation in the question of ownership, where civil society/pro-democracy movements in ENP-East partners have tended to be more empowered through processes of ownership. In contrast, it is likely to be the case in the ENP-South that partner governments will never take ownership of a process which might challenge their grip on power.[62] As almost 15 years of EMP illustrate, in a climate of non-coercion it appears too easy for participants to avoid a process that challenges their power base, assuming that base remains solid. Thus, the last stage illustrates how a normative power approach to the study of the ENP would finish by analysing the socialisation, ownership and conditionality in the impact of the EUs promotion of the principles introduced at the beginning of the analysis. But it would also seek to identify critical concerns in these processes and whether they live up to principles identified in the earlier stages of the analysis.

Conclusion: 'much ado about...you'?

This chapter has suggested one way of overcoming some of the analytical challenges of studying the ENP might be to pursue a normative power approach. Such an approach would have the advantage of getting away from discourses of force (e.g., transatlanticist discourses of the EU as a 'force for good') and from the utilitarian emphasis placed on conditionality (e.g., the lack of the 'golden carrot' of membership).[63] The analytical challenges identified in the first section suggest that non-traditional methods of analysis appropriate to the subject of study should be found. The chapter has further suggested, in the second section, that critical social theory may provide a means to critique, advocate and change EU politics and policy. In the third section, the chapter set out how an emphasis on ideational aspects, including the legitimisation of principles, persuasiveness of actions and impact of socialisation in the normative power approach may be appropriate in the study of the ENP. A brief overview of ENP literature provided in this chapter indicates that rather than prematurely concluding that the lack of material leverage in, for example conditionality, leads to 'much ado about nothing', the ENP might be seen as an open-ended process of socialisation, changing whether the ENP is 'as you like it' for both the EU and neighbours. A normative power approach might shift an objective focus on the 'ado' to a more subjective focus on the 'you', asking instead whether ENP is 'much ado about...you'?

Notes

I am very grateful to Helle Malmvig, as well as Stefano Bartolini, Benoît Challand, May Chartouni-Dubarry, Marise Cremona, Raffaella Del Sarto, Hanaa

Ebeid, Abdellah Labdaoui, Sonia Lucarelli, Leonardo Morlino, Baskan Oran, Daniela Pioppi, Nadim Shehadi, Nathalie Tocci and Ben Tonra, together with the Nottingham workshop participants for their helpful comments on earlier drafts.

1. On the study of EU enlargement see: Frank Schimmelfennig and Ulrich Sedelmeier (eds) (2005), *The Politics of European Union Enlargement: Theoretical Approaches*. London: Routledge; Frank Schimmelfennig and Ulrich Sedelmeier (eds) (2006), *The Europeanization of Central and Eastern Europe*. Ithaca: Cornell University Press. On the study of EU-Mediterranean relations see: Emanuel Adler, Beverly Crawford, Federica Bicchi and Raffaella Del Sarto (eds) (2006), *The Convergence of Civilizations: Constructing a Mediterranean Region*. Toronto: University of Toronto Press; Raffaella Del Sarto, *Contested State Identities and Regional Security in the Euro-Mediterranean*. Basingstoke: Palgrave Macmillan. On the study of EU-conflict policy in the region see: Helle Malmvig (2006), *State Sovereignty and Intervention*. London: Routledge; Thomas Diez, Mathias Albert and Stephan Stetter (eds) (2008), *The European Union and Border Conflicts: The Power of Integration and Association*. Cambridge: Cambridge University Press.
2. For first discussions of these impulses see: Iris Kempe (1998), *Direct Neighbourhood: Relations between the Enlarged EU and the Russian Federation, Ukraine, Belarus and Moldova*. Gutersloh: Bertelsmann Foundation; Lucia Padure, Andrew Williams and Ian Manners (1999), *The Republic of Moldova: Time for a New EU Strategy?* Brussels: SWP-CPN Selected Contributions, 5.
3. Helle Malmvig was referring to explanations for EU democracy and human rights promotion in the Mediterranean/Middle East, but this characterisation might also be stretched to many of the discussions of ENP, see: Helle Malmvig (2006), 'Caught between cooperation and democratization: the Barcelona Process and the EU's double-discursive approach', *Journal of International Relations and Development*, 9, pp. 343–70.
4. Commission of the European Communities (2003), Communication from the Commission to the Council, *Wider Europe – Neighbourhood: A New Framework for Relations with our Eastern and Southern Neighbours*, COM(2003) 104 final, Brussels, 11 March 2003. Commission of the European Communities (2004), Communication from the Commission, *European Neighbourhood Policy, Strategy Paper*, COM(2004) 373 final, p. 6, Brussels, 12 May 2004.
5. Ian Manners (2008a), 'The normative power of the European Union in a globalised world', in Zaki Laïdi (ed.), *European Union Foreign Policy in a Globalised World: Normative Power and Social Preferences*. London: Routledge, p. 37.
6. Malmvig argues that 'the EU's Mediterranean policies are caught between two security discourses' contrasting cooperative security and liberal security. Helle Malmvig (2006), 'Caught between cooperation and democratization: the Barcelona Process and the EU's double-discursive approach', *Journal of International Relations and Development*, 9, p. 364.
7. Ian Manners (2006a), 'European Union 'Normative Power' and the Security Challenge', in Cathleen Kantner, Angela Liberatore and Raffaella Del Sarto (eds), 'Security and Democracy in the European Union', Special Issue of *European Security*, 15, p. 410.

8. Barbara Lippert (2007), 'The EU Neighbourhood Policy – Profile, Potential, Perspective', *Intereconomics* (July/August) 180.
9. Katherine Duncan-Jones (2005), 'Introduction' to William Shakespeare, *As You Like It*. London: Penguin, 2005, p. xlix.
10. Elena Aoun (2003), 'European Foreign Policy and the Arab-Israeli Dispute: Much Ado About Nothing?', *European Foreign Affairs Review*, 8 (3), pp. 289–312; Stelios Stavridis (2004), 'From Parliamentary Forum to Parliamentary Assembly in the EMP: Does it all Amount to Much Ado About Nothing?', *Observatori de politítiques mediterrànies*, working paper 2; Nathalie Tocci (2004), 'The European Neighbourhood Policy: Much Ado about Nothing?', unpublished manuscript, European University Institute.
11. Colin Hay (2002), *Political Analysis: A Critical Introduction*. Basingstoke: Palgrave Macmillan, p. 47.
12. Catherine Hoskyns (2004), 'Gender perspectives', in Antje Wiener and Thomas Diez (eds), *European Integration Theory*. Oxford: Oxford University Press, 224.
13. Colin Hay (2002), *Political Analysis: A Critical Introduction*. Basingstoke: Palgrave Macmillan, p. 32; Peter Burnham, Karin Gilland, Wyn Grant and Zig Layton-Henry (2004), *Research Methods in Politics*. Basingstoke: Palgrave Macmillan, p. 27.
14. Mervyn Frost (1996), *Ethics in International Relations: A Constitutive Theory*. Cambridge: Cambridge University Press, p. 138. See also Alexander Wendt (1999), *Social Theory of International Politics*. Cambridge: Cambridge University Press.
15. Carole Webb (1977), 'Introduction: Variations on a Theoretical Theme', in Helen Wallace, William Wallace and Carole Webb (eds), *Policy-making in the European Communities*. Chichester: John Wiley, pp. 1–31.
16. Helen Wallace (1971), 'The Impact of the European Communities on National Policy-making', *Government and Opposition*, 6, pp. 520–38.
17. Andrew Moravcsik (1998), *The Choice for Europe: Social Purpose and State Power from Messina to Maastricht*. London: University College London Press. See discussion in Robert Lieshout, Mathieu Segers and Anna van der Vleuten (2004), 'De Gaulle, Moravcsik, and The Choice for Europe, Soft Sources, Weak Evidence', *Journal of Cold War Studies*, 6 (4), pp. 89–139.
18. Andrew Moravcsik, Andrew and Milada Anna Vachudova (2003), 'National Interests, State Power, and EU Enlargement', *East European Politics and Societies*, 17, pp. 42–57.
19. Miriam Camps (1971), 'European Unification in the Seventies', *International Affairs*, 47 (4), p. 678.
20. Judith Kelley (2006), 'New Wine in Old Wineskins: Promoting Political Reforms through the New European Neighbourhood Policy', *Journal of Common Market Studies*, 44 (1), pp. 29–55; Sandra Lavenex (2008), 'A Governance Perspective on the European Neighbourhood Policy: Integration Beyond Conditionality', *Journal of European Public Policy*, 15 (6), pp. 938–55.
21. Susan Strange (1971), 'International Economic and International Relations: A Case of Mutual Neglect', *International Affairs*, 46 (2), pp. 304–15; Carole Webb (1977), 'Introduction: Variations on a Theoretical Theme', in Helen Wallace, William Wallace and Carole Webb (eds), *Policy-making in the European Communities*. Chichester: John Wiley, pp. 22–24.

22. Susan Strange (1996), *The Retreat of the State: The Diffusion of Power in the World Economy*. Cambridge: Cambridge University Press, pp. 171–79; Susan Strange (1998), 'Who are EU? Ambiguities on the Concept of Competitiveness', *Journal of Common Market Studies*, 36 (1), pp. 101–14; and Wolfram Kaiser and Peter Starie (eds) (2005), *Transnational European Union: Towards a Common Political Space*. London: Routledge.

23. Rosa Balfour and Antonio Missiroli (2007), 'Reassessing the European Neighbourhood Policy', European Policy Centre Issue Paper 54 (June), p. 11.

24. For broad discussions of these approaches see: Ian Manners (2006b), 'Another Europe is Possible: Critical Perspectives on European Union Politics', in Knud Erik Jørgensen, Mark Pollack and Ben Rosamond (eds), *Handbook of European Union Politics*. London: Sage, pp. 77–95.

25. Thomas Christiansen, Knud Erik Jørgensen, and Antje Wiener (eds) (1999), 'The Social Construction of Europe', Special Issue of *Journal of European Public Policy*, , 6 (4), pp. 527–720.

26. Frank Schimmelfennig and Ulrich Sedelmeier (eds) (2005), *The Politics of European Union Enlargement: Theoretical Approaches*. London: Routledge; Frank Schimmelfennig and Ulrich Sedelmeier (eds) (2006), *The Europeanization of Central and Eastern Europe*. Ithaca: Cornell University Press; Rachel Epstein and Ulrich Sedelmeier (eds) (2008), 'International Influence Beyond Conditionality', Special Issue of *Journal of European Public Policy*, 15 (6), pp. 795–955.

27. Federica Bicchi (2007), *European Foreign Policy Making toward the Mediterranean*. Basingstoke: Palgrave, pp. 2–4; Hiski Haukkala (2008), *Multi-causal Social Mechanisms and the Study of International Institutionalisation: The Case of EU-Russia Strategic Partnership*. Turku: Turun Yliopisto; Gwendolyn Sasse (2008), 'The European Neighbourhood Policy: Conditionality Revisited for the EU's Eastern Neighbours', *Europe-Asia Studies*, 60 (2), pp. 296 and 300.

28. Thomas Diez (1999), 'Speaking "Europe": the politics of integration discourse', in Thomas Christiansen, Knud Erik Jørgensen and Antje Wiener (eds), 'The Social Construction of Europe', Special Issue of *Journal of European Public Policy*, 6 (4), pp. 598–613; Thomas Diez (2002), *The European Union and the Cyprus Conflict: Modern Conflict, Postmodern Union*. Manchester: Manchester University Press.

29. Christopher Browning and Pertti Joenniemi (2008), 'Geostrategies of the European Neighbourhood Policy', *European Journal of International Relations*, 14 (3), 519–51; Michelle Pace (2007), *The Politics of Regional Identity: Meddling with the Mediterranean*. London: Routledge. See also Helle Malmvig (2006), 'Caught between cooperation and democratization: the Barcelona Process and the EU's double-discursive approach', *Journal of International Relations and Development*, 9, pp. 343–70.

30. Gerard Delanty and Chris Rumford (2005), *Rethinking Europe: Social Theory and the Implications for Europeanization*. London: Routledge; Craig Calhoun (2010), *Cosmopolitanism and Belonging: From European Integration to Global Hopes and Fears*. London: Routledge.

31. Gerard Delanty and Chris Rumford (2005), *Rethinking Europe: Social Theory and the Implications for Europeanization*. London: Routledge, pp. 120–35. See also Chris Rumford (ed.) (2006a), 'Theorizing Borders', special issue of *European Journal of Social Theory*, 9 (2), pp. 155–287; and Chris Rumford (ed.)

(2006b), 'Rethinking European Spaces', special issue of *Comparative European Politics*, 4 (2/3), pp. 127–308.

32. Craig Calhoun (1995), *Critical Social Theory: Culture, History and the Challenge of Difference*. Oxford: Blackwell, p. 73; Seyla Benhabib (2002), *The Claims of Culture: Equality and Diversity in the Global Era*. Oxford: Princeton University Press, p. 5.

33. See discussions of the ideational nature and impact of the EU in Ian Manners (2002), 'Normative Power Europe: A Contradiction in Terms', *Journal of Common Market Studies*, 40 (2), pp. 238–39.

34. For an introduction to this tripartite analytical method see Ian Manners (2008b), 'The Normative Ethics of the European Union', *International Affairs*, 84 (1), pp. 55–59.

35. Commission of the European Communities (2004), Communication from the Commission, *European Neighbourhood Policy, Strategy Paper*, COM(2004) 373 final, Brussels, 12 May 2004.

36. Judith Kelley (2006), 'New Wine in Old Wineskins: Promoting Political Reforms through the New European Neighbourhood Policy', *Journal of Common Market Studies*, 44 (1), pp. 29–55; Rosa Balfour and Antonio Missiroli (2007), 'Reassessing the European Neighbourhood Policy', European Policy Centre Issue Paper 54 (June), p. 18.

37. Commission of the European Communities (2003), Communication from the Commission, *Wider Europe- Neighbourhood: A New Framework for Relations with our Eastern and Southern Neighbours* COM(2003) 104 final, Brussels, 11 March 2003.

38. Commission of the European Communities (2004), Communication from the Commission, *European Neighbourhood Policy, Strategy Paper*, COM(2004) 373 final, pp. 32–35, Brussels, 12 May 2004.

39. Parliamentary Assembly of the Council of Europe (2006), 'Memorandum of Understanding between the Council of Europe and the European Union, Doc. 10892, Strasbourg, 11 April 2006; North-South Centre of the Council of Europe (2007), 'Report of the 47th Meeting of the Committee of Representatives of the Member States', NSC/MS (2007) 1, Council of Europe, Strasbourg, 25.4.2007; Organization for Security and Co-operation in Europe (2006), 'The OSCE Mediterranean Partnership: From Recommendation to Implementation', Consolidated Summary of 2006 Mediterranean Seminar, Sharm El-Sheikh, SEC.GAL/215/06, 30 November 2006.

40. Soha Bayoumi (2007), 'Egyptian Views of the EU: Pragmatic, Paternalistic and Partnership Concerns', *European Foreign Affairs Review*, 12, pp. 346–47.

41. Commission of the European Communities (2004), Communication from the Commission, *European Neighbourhood Policy, Strategy Paper*, COM(2004) 373 final, p. 6, Brussels, 12 May 2004.

42. Kalypso Nicolaïdis and Dimitri Nicolaïdis (2006), 'The EuroMed beyond Civilisational Paradigms', in Emanuel Adler, Federica Bicchi, Beverly Crawford and Raffaella Del Sarto (eds), *The Convergence of Civilisations: Constructing a Mediterranean Region*. Toronto: University of Toronto Press, pp. 348–49.

43. Roland Dannreuther (2006), 'Developing the Alternative to Enlargement: The European Neighbourhood Policy', *European Foreign Affairs Review*, 11, p. 195.

44. Raffaella Del Sarto and Tobias Schumacher (2005), 'From EMP to ENP: What's at Stake with the European Neighbourhood Policy towards the Southern Mediterranean?' *European Foreign Affairs Review*, 10, pp. 30–33.
45. See discussion in Ian Manners (2008b), 'The Normative Ethics of the European Union', *International Affairs*, 84 (1), p. 57.
46. Rosemary Foot (2000), *Rights beyond Borders: the Global Community and the Struggle over Human Rights*. Oxford: Oxford University Press, p. 9.
47. Examples include fora such as EuroMeSCo, the Anna Lindh Foundation and the StrataGen programme at the Centre for European Policy Studies.
48. Raffaella Del Sarto and Tobias Schumacher (2005), 'From EMP to ENP: What's at Stake with the European Neighbourhood Policy towards the Southern Mediterranean?' *European Foreign Affairs Review*, 10, pp. 21–22; Roland Dannreuther (2006), 'Developing the Alternative to Enlargement: The European Neighbourhood Policy', *European Foreign Affairs Review*, 11, pp. 191–92.
49. Commission of the European Communities (2004), Communication from the Commission, *European Neighbourhood Policy, Strategy Paper*, COM(2004) 373 final, p. 8, Brussels, 12 May 2004.
50. Benita Ferrero-Waldner (2006), 'The European Neighbourhood Policy: the EU's Newest Foreign Policy Instrument', *European Foreign Affairs Review*, 11, p. 140.
51. Ibid.; Raffaella Del Sarto and Tobias Schumacher (2005), 'From EMP to ENP: What's at Stake with the European Neighbourhood Policy towards the Southern Mediterranean?' *European Foreign Affairs Review*, 10, p. 29.
52. These measures include 'political and security matters, the preparation of a comprehensive and deeper free trade agreement, the gradual integration of Morocco into a number of EU sectoral policies, and the development of people-to-people exchanges'. See European Commission, 'The European Union and Morocco strengthen their partnership', press release IP/08/1488, Brussels, 13 October 2008; and European Commission, 'Document conjoint UE-Maroc sur le renforcement des relations bilatérales/ Statut Avancé', doc. no. 13653/08, Brussels, 28 October 2008.
53. Gwendolyn Sasse (2008), 'The European Neighbourhood Policy: Conditionality Revisited for the EU's Eastern Neighbours', *Europe-Asia Studies*, 60 (2), p. 296. See also: James Hughes, Gwendolyn Sasse and Claire Gordon (2004), *Europeanization and Regionalization in the EU's Enlargement to Central and Eastern Europe: The Myth of Conditionality*. Basingstoke: Palgrave Macmillan.
54. Sandra Lavenex (2008), 'A Governance Perspective on the European Neighbourhood Policy: Integration Beyond Conditionality', *Journal of European Public Policy*, 15 (6), p. 951.
55. Rachel Epstein and Ulrich Sedelmeier (2008), 'Beyond Conditionality: International Institutions in Postcommunist Europe after Enlargment', *Journal of European Public Policy*, 15 (6), pp. 795 and 803.
56. Commission of the European Communities (2004), Communication from the Commission, *European Neighbourhood Policy, Strategy Paper*, COM(2004) 373 final, p. 8, Brussels, 12 May 2004.
57. Raffaella Del Sarto and Tobias Schumacher (2005), 'From EMP to ENP: What's at Stake with the European Neighbourhood Policy towards the Southern Mediterranean?' *European Foreign Affairs Review*, 10, p. 29.

58. Roland Dannreuther (2006), 'Developing the Alternative to Enlargement: The European Neighbourhood Policy', *European Foreign Affairs Review*, 11, p. 192.
59. Benita Ferrero-Waldner (2006), 'The European Neighbourhood Policy: the EU's Newest Foreign Policy Instrument', *European Foreign Affairs Review*, 11, p. 140.
60. Raffaella Del Sarto and Tobias Schumacher (2005), 'From EMP to ENP: What's at Stake with the European Neighbourhood Policy towards the Southern Mediterranean?' *European Foreign Affairs Review*, 10, pp. 22–23 and 29–30.
61. Kalypso Nicolaïdis and Dimitri Nicolaïdis (2006), 'The EuroMed beyond Civilisational Paradigms', in Emanuel Adler, Federica Bicchi, Beverly Crawford and Raffaella Del Sarto (eds), *The Convergence of Civilisations: Constructing a Mediterranean Region*. Toronto: University of Toronto Press, pp. 349–50.
62. Helle Malmvig (2006), 'Caught between cooperation and democratization: the Barcelona Process and the EU's double-discursive approach', *Journal of International Relations and Development*, 9, pp. 346–47.
63. On 'force for good' see: Michelle Pace (2008), 'The EU as a "force for good" in border conflict cases?', in Thomas Diez, Mathias Albert and Stephan Stetter (eds), *European Union and Border Conflicts*, pp. 203–19; Ester Barbé (2008), 'The EU as a modest "force for good": the European Neighbourhood Policy', *International Affairs*, 84 (1), pp. 81–96.

3
Identity Construction through the ENP: Borders and Boundaries, Insiders and Outsiders

Ben Tonra

Introduction

The basic conceptual argument for looking at the European Neighbourhood Policy (ENP) through the prism of identity construction is that this offers a unique frame of reference that is potentially capable of providing a more profound understanding of the European Union – both as an international actor and as source of foreign policy in the international system.

This chapter begins by laying out the basic conceptual arguments for looking at the ENP through the prism of identity construction, introducing readers to this theoretical approach, highlighting its assumptions and laying bare both its strengths and weaknesses as an analytical approach.

The second section opens with an argument that the definition of 'European' has always been a contested one, that it has undergone repeated revisions and that it has never been definitively resolved. This section also traces the roots and the movement of Europe's identity borders – underlining the contingent nature of these borders and how critical their political and cultural context is.

The third section addresses itself directly to the construction of the ENP's 'borders'. It traces the relevant elite-level discourses and highlights the critical junctures which have contributed to the solidification of this particular border set at this particular time, and offers an answer to the question 'Why this ENP and why now?' Special attention is given to the contested nature of ENP's definition of borders in terms of the 'non-prospective EU membership criterion'. The solidity of that criterion is tested, as is its prima facie rationale. In the final section we return to the contingent nature of borders and the 'fuzziness' of the Union's existing borders, and we make the argument for further Eastward and Southward enlargement of the Union in the medium- to long-term.

EU identity and international actorness[1]

There are three core post-structuralist claims on identity: that it is relational, that it is malleable and that it is socially constructed.[2] First, identity is as often constructed on the basis of what the subject is not as what the subject is. Within International Relations this means that declarations of a state's 'Europeanness' – by politicians, academics, pollsters, journalists, artists, etc. – are at least partly a signifier that these actors are rejecting counter-claims that the state might be better defined as Asian, American or African. Change and evolution in identity are also a sine qua non in that identities are under a constant barrage of discursive acts (speech acts) that serve to challenge any hegemonic or dominant definition of identity. Finally, it is through this process of social construction that identities are created, that they jostle for prominence, sometimes attain dominance – even hegemony – and are subsequently overthrown, redefined or otherwise adapted as the narrative chain of discursive acts moves on to the next historical chapter.[3]

There is certainly a long – if disparate – record of attempts to characterise the European Union's identity as an international actor. One of the earliest, dating back to the 1970s, was François Duchêne's conceptualisation of the then European Communities, as being a 'civilian power'.[4] This was swiftly contested first by Galtung's proposition[5] that in fact the Communities were a 'superpower' in the making and later Hedley Bull's insistence that the term 'civilian power' was an oxymoron and that Europe had to aspire to becoming a military power if it was successfully to pursue its international ambitions.[6]

More recently, the threads of Duchêne's approach have been reconsidered by a new generation of scholars who insist that the Union's uniqueness is grounded in its normative foundations and its efforts to pursue these normative ambitions outside the Union's borders in a manner that has the potential to be transformative of the international system itself.[7] The Union may also be presented as a new kind of hybrid structure that is neither domestic nor international – an entity that challenges our traditional Westphalian understanding of sovereignty, statehood and the international system.[8]

These analysts focus on the uniqueness of the Union as an international actor, contrasting it most frequently with the US – almost always to the latter's disadvantage. The Union, it is argued, has a very unique institutional structure, an approach to international affairs that is firmly rooted in multilateralism and, in sum, developed an alternative approach to international politics, turning away from old fashioned power politics and instead drawing upon the wells of international law, norms, rules, cooperation and integration. It is this 'normative' power that the Union now exerts. The impact of this is – in the minds of some – to create a vision of the Union as a 'post-modern'[9] entity or, in a less sympathetic light, a rather smug and self-satisfied Kantian island of perpetual peace shielded from international realities by a more traditionally power-oriented ally.[10]

While extending this post-modern condition and/or enlarging this island of peace to encompass much of Central and Eastern Europe has arguably been successful to date, the Union's effort to export its normative condition beyond its immediate neighbourhood has been more problematic.[11]

Moreover, the set of evolving norms also has internal implications – arguably contributing to the creation of a collective identity. This has the subsequent internal implication of 'Europeanising' the foreign policies of the member states through shared experience and the instantiation of common procedures and a convergence of values.[12] This has been represented as member states having '... created a notion of belonging to a community within a particular (international) order'.[13] Ian Manners cites the Union's own dedication to '... certain principles that are common to the member states'.[14] These norms have then been institutionalised into the very structures and policies of the Union which, in turn, have a constitutive effect that defines the Union's international identity.[15]

One of these core norms – based in part upon the Union's own 'story' of its roots, construction and even purpose – is that of 'peace'. The Union's own official narrative is that it was established to provide for an historic reconciliation of France and Germany, founded upon the withdrawal of national control over two key components of twentieth-century warfare: steel and coal. That founding bargain, which successfully domesticated security, was subsequently extended to European states struggling toward democracy following periods of dictatorship (Spain, Portugal and Greece) and has now been applied on a continental scale to the countries of Central and Eastern Europe as well as the Mediterranean. Indeed, in Turkey's application for membership the Union might be seen as seeking to apply this historic 'peace' model to a civilisational reconciliation between the worlds of Christendom and Islam. This 'peace' project has, over time, been increasingly defined in Kantian terms of a particular kind of 'democratic peace' in which values such as human rights, a dedication to the rule of law, liberal democracy and a broadly multilateral approach to interstate problem-solving have come to the fore.

These values have been specified and expanded in subsequent itera-tions of EU treaty change. The Maastricht Treaty, for example, stated that the objectives of the Common Foreign and Security Policy (CFSP) included the pursuit of 'democracy and the rule of law, and respect for human rights and fundamental freedoms',[16] which was itself echoed in another reference to policy which '...shall contribute to the general objective of developing and consolidating democracy and the rule of law and to that of respecting human rights and fundamental freedoms'.[17] Later, the Treaty of Amsterdam insisted that the European Union was '...founded on the principles of liberty, democracy, respect for human rights and fundamental freedoms, the rule of law, principles which are common to the Member States'.[18] Similarly, the Lisbon Treaty declared that 'In its relations with the wider world, the Union shall uphold and promote its values'.[19] Javier Solana, speaking about 'Europe's place in the world' specifies these values as being those of '...solidarity, of tolerance, of inclusiveness, (and) of compassion...We cannot give up on them, especially now that ugly racist pulsions (sic) are surfacing again; and that fighting against poverty is becoming critically important to prevent whole societies falling prey to radical and terrorist tensions.'[20]

To take our analysis further, we must assume that the Union's CFSP is more than an expression of lowest common denominator politics. There are then at least three scenarios one might envisage arising from a study of the ENP. First, one might find that EU policy is a function of 'complex interdependence', where an institutional regime has been established by self-regarding and rational states through which national interests are pursued.[21] The role of the state in the first instance is to aggregate competing domestic interests, to establish a hierarchy of those interests and then to set about – alongside its European partners – to maximise its relative gains through a complex system of collective bargaining. This process of negotiation – which in the European context is highly institutionalised – thereby establishes the norms of the result-ing EU regime vis-à-vis the ENP. A review of the ENP should therefore underline the conditional nature of EU policy 'bargains' and should illustrate policy difficulty and delay when faced with sudden shifts or challenges from other policy actors, and we should be able to identify clear member state policy leaders or even consortia of such leaders, who drive and direct the EU policy process.

Alternatively, one might instead find that while national governments remain key actors they do not exclusively monopolise the decision- or policy-making processes of the Union. First, it is argued that decision-making is a shared competence of actors at different levels of the Union; second, that collective decision-making entails an inevitable loss of control on the part of member state governments and third, that the arena of political debate is not the sum total of 'nested' national debates but must accommodate transnational actors and sub-national actors working across member state boundaries. Here, our analysis of the ENP should identify a range of key policy actors beyond the member states, including the Commission, the European Parliament and other transnational or even sub-national policy groups. There should also be some clear evidence of effective policy flexibility and a rapid response to external policy challenges as well as a clearly developed sense of collective interests.

Finally, one might find that the key dynamic within policy development is not one of bargains and balancing expressed 'interests' but one of evolving beliefs and norms. Here, a process of Europeanisation is understood to be in part a process of transformation in which the self-regard and beliefs of the state actors evolve and have an impact upon the construction of the 'interests' that they pursue. In any event, policy actors are in the business of constructing, pursuing and implementing policy norms and collective values deriving from this evolving political system.

This latter model would underscore much of the agenda of those seeing the Union as a normative power. A study of the ENP should, therefore, offer evidence of new norms deriving from collective action at the EU level. These would be expected to be both regulative[22] and constitutive.[23] The power of such norms would underline the extent to which – even without explicit regulatory mechanisms – they were observed in both day-to-day practice and in conditions of crisis. These norms would in turn suggest that EU policy toward the ENP was at least in part founded upon a normative base of shared mission and identity.

There should also be evidence that national 'interests' had undergone some evolution. Rather than such interests being seen as being chips in a poker game, they would change through participation in the game itself. Interests would therefore be developed/constructed endogenously within the collective policy process rather than being established exogenously – that is to say formulated within the domestic sphere and then brought to the negotiating table. This would also suggest the creation of common European norms driving the conduct and execution of EU foreign policy in this area.

Most documents and declarations underline the strategic relevance of the ENP, and it also emerges quite clearly from such a review that the ENP has indeed moved beyond the narrow interpretation of 'strategic relevance' – with its associated zero-sum games – toward comprehensive cooperation and even expressions of solidarity. This goes beyond the 'liberal' understanding and belief in multilateralism to take the founding values of the EU as the supreme norms that need to be propagated – not so as to defend the cause of the EU – but to recast the Union's borderlands in the normative mould of Europe. The identity acquired by the EU through its process of integration is then the driving force behind its foreign policy in the region.

Two challenges emerge with this approach. One is the 'misplaced' idealisation of how Europe and a European identity emerge. What is important to underline is that EU policy-makers have created an idealised account of their own identity that they believe in and attempt to export. What follows is that the policies directed toward ENP partners that derive from this idealised account may not work precisely because some crucial factors have been left out from the official report of the identity-building process.

The second challenge is the existence of competing 'interests' within the EU. While EU officials may have internalised norms, the EU is also constituted by member states pursuing their own, sometimes distinct, policies. This indicates that there may be two games taking place at the same time and that the contradictions generated by these conflicting actions may undermine the EU's credibility and norm-exporting power.

A cognitive approach to 'our Europe'

By employing a cognitive or identity-driven approach, this chapter already assumes that the Union is an incomplete political construction. What is of interest is not the *finalité politique* per se, rather it is the very construction of the Union's identity, most especially its contingency and fluidity and the implications of this for the Union's relations with other international actors – and, in particular, spatially proximate actors. The focus of attention is therefore given to a better understanding of the Union as a discursive construction and the processes which underpin the same. Moreover, these are rooted in their iterative performance by policy actors resulting in a boundary producing process.[24]

The lack of certainty in the Union's own boundaries and borders has to be another starting point in our analysis. The May 2004 enlargement of the Union to include the then ten applicant states of Central Europe and the Mediterranean was transformative of the Union's identity – up to that point an essentially 'Western' European and Cold War construct. The 'balance' struck on enlargement, which ultimately included applications from both Central Europe and the Mediterranean, was itself reflective of an internal and often difficult discourse surrounding the next phase of enlargement and the extent to which certain member states privileged an enlargement process directed toward the South as opposed to those that privileged enlargement to the East.[25] The new lines ultimately drawn, however, only exacerbated the next phase of that debate – with the Union now extending in membership toward the 'far' East of the European continent and as far South as the 'non-European' states of Northern Africa. Europe's 'neighbourhood' policy would necessarily have to deal with both 'European' and 'non-European' states.

Even when these new boundary lines were drawn, they were not clear, well defined and precise. Indeed, EU 'membership' boundaries remain problematic even when spatially specific. In some areas of policy, the set of participating states is actually a subset of EU members (such as in the case of Monetary Union) whereas in other areas those participating include a subset of EU members alongside non-members (e.g., the Schengen Group). Although it should not be overstated, this does give rise to a certain degree of 'fuzziness' in the very idea of EU insiders and outsiders, centre and periphery, which extends beyond debates about who and who does not potentially qualify for actual membership of the Union.[26]

Even the very definitions of what is 'European' and 'Europe' remain contested.[27] We can trace conceptions of the European back as far as the ancient world and even more contemporary-sounding discussions of European unity as far back as the writings of Grotius, Sully, Comenius, Penn, Saint-Pierre, Montesquieu and Rousseau. Europe itself has been characterised as resting upon a number of different foundations. Geographic Europe is perhaps the most obvious.[28] A Europe whole and free from the Atlantic to the Urals defines a political aspiration for this geographic representation of Europe. Yet, at one and the same time, that definition gives rise to difficulties – not least of which is that the Eastern border to this construction does not coincide with any political boundary, which has instead ebbed and flowed across the great Eastern plains of continental Europe. Moreover, while the north of this geographic construction might be successfully implied, its southern boundaries are especially problematic. In geographical terms the Mediterranean is an internal European lake, while its southern shores remain defined as being both within and without the European heartland. Geography, then, has its own limitations in defining – with any precision – the extent of the European.

Cultural Europe further complicates matters. The parameters of language, religion and ethnicity are layered in only the most complex patterns that overlay, underpin and intersect across innumerable axes. These then are the cleavages around which many European conflicts have centred, but these patterns do not, in turn, neatly define Europe's external borders. They reify few, if any, great cultural borders between 'Europe' and its neighbours. Indeed many, if not most, such conflicts have occurred within the 'European' heartland on precisely the grounds of religion (Protestant, Catholic and Orthodox) and language (Romance, Slavic and Germanic). Thus, a cultural definition of 'Europe' does not effectively serve as a clear border-producing realm.

A third foundation for the definition of the European is that of history. Shared sets of mythologies, symbols, critical events and epochs have served well in the past to create solid and well-founded political communities in the form of modern European states. At a pan-European level there are many which might serve a similar function – such as the Roman and Holy Roman Empires, Crusades, Renaissance, Reformation and Enlightenment. Each, however, has had an asymmetric impact in different regions of Europe and among different peoples within the broader European area and it is difficult to draw these strings together into a tightly woven cloth. At best, one creates a complex and differentiated story that is only partially recognisable to all segments of a pan-European audience – and which, at critical moments, draws widely differentiated responses.

A fourth foundation is that of shared values and norms. While many of these may be said to have a particular historic and/or cultural base, these are certainly the foundations that the Union endorses as defining itself. Among those that are often enumerated are the principles of natural justice and law, Judaeo-Christian ethics, humanism, rationalism and empiricism and the sociopolitical outcomes of this normative base in terms of democratic and juridical institutions linked to the vindication of human rights and freedoms. In sum, this amounts to a shared political identity rooted in values and principles which Europeans claim as being recognisably 'ours'. The difficulty, of course, rests in the fact that while Europe (read 'EU and its member states') and Europeans may indeed claim this political identity as being recognisably 'European' it is also claimed that these norms are, in fact, universal in both their origins and in their execution and pursuit. It would be difficult to read the core expressions of any liberal democratic constitution anywhere in the world and not see a reflection – and indeed even some claim to ownership – over the principles and norms that we have just identified as being quintessentially 'European'. Moreover, the Union is itself engaged in a rhetoric that claims these values to be of such a universal nature and that it is a central ambition of the Union to disseminate and sustain such values internationally.

In order to surmount the obvious inconsistency of basing a European identity upon a set of universal values, it is then possible to seek to align these values to a specific set of institutions and thereby define a unique subset as European – through a kind of constitutional patriotism.[29] That linkage of universal values of justice, solidarity, democracy, human rights, etc. to the institutions, law and founding treaties of the European Union raises its own challenges. At this point, the definition of Europe and of the European has become almost arbitrary – it has become a set of universal values linked to a particular set of European-denominated institutions. However, access to and membership of that set of institutions still have to be restricted – this is not a 'Global Union' after all but a 'European Union'. Here again, we are forced to fall back on some exclusionary framework which will allow the 'European' to exist in contradistinction to the 'Other'. At the same time, as we have seen, geography, history and culture do not provide us with the sharp profile required to provide an explicit reflection in terms of state membership of the EU. What if, instead of such sharp delineation, the Union embraced the concept of the contextual, the ambivalent and the negotiated? At least two options are then open. The first is to accept that a decision on who is 'in or out' of Europe is not a function of ticking appropriate geographic, historical or cultural boxes, but is instead necessarily a political choice, one which is framed by the circumstances of the time and the will of the peoples so engaged in making that decision. This approach was illustrated in the contribution of the German President-in-Office at the conclusion of a tense 2006 European Parliamentary debate on enlargement. She argued that '... neither geographers nor historians nor rulers will be of any use to us in the political decisions that we have to take, what will decide the issue will be...the people themselves'.[30] More formally, this is also echoed in the 1992 Lisbon Council Declaration:

> The term European has not been officially defined. It combines geographical, historical and cultural elements which all contribute to the European identity. The shared experience of proximity, ideas, values, and historical interaction cannot be condensed into a simple formula, and *is subject to review by each succeeding generation* [emphasis added].[31]

The second option, rather than take an ad hoc case-by-case approach such as that above, is to move further toward a condition in which the very contingency of EU borders is embraced so that instead of definitions specifying a status of being 'in or out' of Europe, they would privilege the condition of being 'more or less' European. Here, the multiple overlay of various policy borders – Monetary Europe, Schengen Europe, Defence Europe, Single Market Europe, etc. – grow to create a broad and wide network of policy communities. While 'membership' of the core institutional superstructure will remain significant, the associated softening of EU policy 'borders' will make the case that being 'in' Europe is a matter of degree rather than an absolute condition. These intersecting policy circles can also be supplemented in spatial terms through the construction of institutionalised regional geographic frameworks such as the 2008 initiatives to create the Eastern Partnership and the Union for the Mediterranean.

This is by no means a neat and simple solution, and it entails its own contradictions and inconsistencies. However, if we interrogate our contemporary – and necessarily ambiguous – understanding of Europe's 'border' then perhaps we can get a better grip on the implications of these borders for our understanding of European identity itself and membership of the associated – but by no means contiguous – European Union.

Eastern Europe's ebb and flow

Following Mayer and Palmowski it is indeed 'highly misleading to use the binary terms of 'self and other' because not every other has the same significance'.[32] In the case of Europe's 2004 and 2007 Eastern enlargements there were no general claims that on the basis of geography, culture, history, ethnicity or any other criterion, that the states of Central and Eastern Europe were in any way barred from membership of the Union, although it did open a debate surrounding a prospective 'Eastern' border of the Union.[33] Indeed, in most official and mass discourse the arguments centred on the pace of change and the terms and conditions under which these states would most certainly become members of the Union. At the same time, the undercurrent of the elite discourse certainly prefigured a particular reading of the 'East' which was redolent of a much earlier Enlightenment-era divide between a modern 'West' and a pre-modern 'East'.[34] This clearly differentiated the 'new' European states from the existing Union's membership, and it sought to address the associated fears of what might transpire following their membership. As a result, the Union anticipated enlargement by embedding and further reifying certain existing political and institutional understandings within the Union which might otherwise have had to be rebalanced after enlargement, while at the same time setting clear entry preconditions for the accession states to achieve.

Following an initial debate as to whether relations with the prospective applicant states should be preconditioned on an accession strategy or whether the goal of EU membership should be left an open question, relations with all these states were established on a clear path toward membership. That path was then constructed on the achievement of certain targets (the Copenhagen criteria), regular reporting and assessment of these and the simultaneous negotiation of each treaty chapter with each applicant.

Socialisation, learning, emulation and 'becoming' more European were the leitmotifs within this exercise – and in none of the several hundred treaty chapters negotiated, was there ever the suggestion that the Union might be socialised into, learn from or otherwise emulate the accession states. Becoming European was obviously a one-way process.[35] Central Europe was 'less Europe-like' than its Western cousins and had to serve its apprenticeship.[36]

With the 2004 and 2007 enlargements, the EU had to redefine and rediscover the essential Europeaness of its own new members while at the same time coming to terms with the new geopolitical neighbourhood into which it has been thrust. Now, regardless of the doubts about the nature or inadequacies of the 'new' EU member states, the Union today faces states about whom the very characterisation of European is at issue. How now to formulate a relationship where EU membership is ruled out by either one or both neighbouring partners? More significantly, how to formulate a relationship where the very possibility of such membership is contested and thus ambiguous? Furthermore, in the absence of that essential membership carrot, what is the incentive structure for the Union to spread the values, norms and beliefs that it holds to be both universal in nature and a 'gift' to be bestowed by the Union upon its neighbours in their joint quest for security, stability and mutual prosperity?

Southern rising tides

If the Union's border strategy is problematic on Europe's own continental shelf – how much more problematic is it with respect to its southern neighbours? Here Europe faces a contradiction of its own construction. If the values, norms and beliefs upon which it is constructed are universal, how then can an application for accession from Morocco be dismissed without consideration of the country's adherence to those common values? Conversely, if these values, norms and beliefs are culturally specific and/or rooted to a particular geographic land mass, then how can the Union aspire to the export and dissemination of such values etc. without being accused of a gross form of cultural imperialism?[37]

Throughout the Union's dealings with the states of the southern Mediterranean coast, another basic contradiction rests. This is that while the Mediterranean is characterised as the cradle of much of European civilisation and is, in the Latin, simply 'Our Sea' – the Mediterranean simultaneously serves as a critical and threatening 'Other' – as either a source of general strife and instability from which specific security threats (mass migration, human and other trafficking, etc.) may arise or the fault line of a major civilisational rift between Christendom and Islam. Holm reminds us that we have even to be conscious of the fact that the very construction of the region itself is open to interrogation and analysis. In earlier EU policy, distinction was made between the 'Maghreb' and 'Mashreq' – these being French colonial terms relating the rest of the region to Egypt's strategic position – with the region West of Egypt being the Maghreb while that to the East was the Mashreq.[38] Nor can it be disregarded that Europe's interests in the Southern Mediterranean are at least partly credited as being a function of French, Spanish, Italian and British post-colonialism.

These interests had coalesced to create an early prototype of the ENP in the signature of the November 1995 Barcelona Process and its associated Euro-Mediterranean Partnership. Structured very much on a multilateral and region-to-region basis, the Barcelona Process and its associated infrastructure was unilaterally absorbed within the ENP in 2003 and created thereby the Euro-Mediterranean Neighbourhood Space. The perceived inadequacies and lack of focus within this framework were then addressed in French proposals to create a distinct 'Mediterranean Union' limited to coastal states. In response to EU partners' concerns, this was modified to the 2008 creation of a broader 'Union for the Mediterranean' incorporating all EU member states with a number of North African partners.

The ENP and its borders

The means by which identity is constructed is, of course, a matter of contemporary contestation but it does centre on the differentiation of the self from the other. This does not necessarily entail the creation of a negative antithesis or of similarly obnoxious stereotypes. The 'other' can also be a negative temporal conceptualisation of the historic self – as with, it has been argued, the European Union. As noted above, the dominant narrative traditionally presented of the Union is as a successful European peace process. It might then be argued that a substantial part of the Union's difficulty today is that the salience of this identity narrative has substantially lessened. The prospect of European war – except at its extremities – is not seen as a realistic prospect and thus the historic gain delivered by the European project is no longer of contemporary relevance.

Thus, Waever's argument that the Union's identity rests on the twin pillars of a fear of its violent past and its potential for a violent future is only germane in so far as that past is recalled and that dangerous future is deemed to be possible.[39] The Union's very success as an identity-building project becomes its Achilles heel. As the peace which the Union delivers becomes normalised, the very rationale and spirit of the Union are open to greater contestation. Anthony Smith's warning that a European collective identity must then be constructed 'through opposition to the identities of significant others' becomes more salient.[40] If the Union is no longer unique as a peace process (in either historic or future terms) and is thus normalised as an international political actor, then like other international actors, its identity may rest upon other foundations. If, as is briefly noted above and very extensively within the literature on European identity, the Union cannot rely on the normal identity proxies of history, language, culture, geography, etc. it is thus – to an even greater degree than other actors – open to the very great danger of finding itself defined in terms of 'cultural and racial exclusion'.[41] This is perhaps why the Union goes to such extraordinary – and inconsistent – lengths to define itself in terms of positive contemporary, and universal, values.

As a policy tool, the ENP was driven in part by the perceived inadequacies of the Union's existing capacity for managing third country relations. These essentially fell into two large categories; partnership and membership. Membership strategies were driven by an expectation of ultimate accession to the European Union and, while never linked to any predetermined timing, did set out a process which was designed to culminate in membership. Usually underpinned by a framework of technical aid and financial assistance, that process also involved monitoring of progress to a set of specified accession targets. The second category of relationships – that of 'partnership' – was designed for states that could not aspire to membership but who sought some privileged relationship with the Union. By and large, EU policy-makers preferred to conduct such partner relationships on a region-to-region basis through multilateral processes.

This simple dyadic construction of membership versus partnership became increasingly problematic as pressures built for a more variegated framework within which the Union's prospective new neighbours might be drawn into a close and abiding relationship with it based upon a bespoke institutional and policy framework. In 1998 – even though from an accession country– the Polish government called upon the EU to begin thinking of a new strategy and set of relationships with the Union's 'new' neighbours in Eastern Europe. Similarly, in 2002 British Foreign Secretary Jack Straw wrote to the Spanish Presidency calling for a new relationship with specific countries in Eastern Europe with whom the Union would be sharing a new border, post-EU enlargement. Just six weeks later, the Swedish Trade and Foreign Ministers addressed a joint letter to the Commission seeking the extension of any new model to both Russia and the Mediterranean states. Other member mtate governments joined the chorus.[42] They also sought an in-between strategy which could draw existing or prospective neighbours much closer to the European core without writing open cheques for membership to every state that might ever border the Union. In sum, they sought something more tailored and more substantial than simple partnership but falling short of membership.

In March 2003 'Wider Europe – Neighbourhood: A New Framework for Relations with our Eastern and Southern Neighbours' was published by the Commission and addressed to the Council and Parliament.[43] The document specified the achievement of stability and security through the promotion of political and economic development and regional cooperation and, significantly, added the Mediterranean to the category of EU 'neighbourhood' – to the disappointment of at least some of the policy's initial advocates.[44] While the possibility of member-ship accruing to a 'neighbourhood' country was not explicitly ruled out, no 'accession perspective' was mentioned in the ENP.[45] The Greek European Council Summit in June 2003 agreed a further iteration of what was now dubbed a 'neighbourhood policy' and the final draft of the 'European Neighbourhood Policy' was published in May 2004 – with a further geographic extension (to include states of the Southern Caucasus).

The ENP is structured around the four 'common spaces' of economics; freedom, security and justice; external security and research and education. Its goals are pursued on multiple bilateral axes within a collective framework rather than on the traditional region-to-region interface which had been the preferred European model to date. This new 'differentiated bilateralism' was designed to address the particular and contextualised needs of each bilateral relationship, approaching something like a hub and spoke model.[46] Individual Action Plans are to be '...tailored to reflect the specific state of relations with each country, its needs and capacities, as well as the interests of the EU and the part-ner country concerned'.[47] From 2007 the new financing mechanism can accommodate intra- and extra-EU projects that are either bilateral and cross/border or multilateral, and thus eliminates the dyadic character of so much traditional EU 'partnership' spending. Interestingly, the ENP itself, in its gestation, structures and methods is much more reminiscent of the old Accession Agreements and Strategies, even if the addition of North African and other 'Mediterranean' states to the ENP was viewed in some quarters as a calculated rebuff to those who would have pre-ferred to see the ENP as part of a long-term enlargement strategy.[48]

Old geo-regional tensions related to European balances resurfaced once more with the Union for the Mediterranean. Several EU member states – most particularly Sweden and Poland – insisted by implica-tion that the new Southern initiative be at least shadowed by a similar regional framework to the East. The Union's Eastern Partnership resulted in 2008. Under-specified, lacking an intuitional underpinning and without much of the policy substance of its southern counterpart, the Eastern Partnership is nonetheless another vehicle linked into the ENP but providing an explicit multilateral regional focus.

The tensions underpinning the ENP are visible at a number of differ-ent levels. First there is a tension with respect to the ENP's asymmetrical egalitarianism. In its reference to 'joint ownership' the relationship is formally characterised as being one of equals with a set of shared interests,[49] but the ENP is clearly structured in such a way as to entail the adaptation by 'the neighbours' of the aims and means determined by one (albeit large!) European household.[50] Thus, while the documentation goes to extraordinary lengths to invoke the commonality and shared nature of its goals, interests and underpinning values – these are already predetermined within the ENP. There is no means or mechanism by which the 'neighbours' might formally interrogate or amend the agenda of the ENP better to reflect their assessment of the 'shared and common' interests that are held between the partners.[51] Instead, the ENP is very much more the creature of the Union's own proximate interests – and, particularly, its security interests.[52]

Moreover, when one begins to look in detail at some of the core provisions, it would appear as though one of the key motivations is to extend the Union's border controls beyond its own frontiers and to engage the ENP states and their associated regional frameworks in a joint effort directed to the defence of the Union's borders against unauthorised migration, transborder crime, terrorism, etc. On the initial face of it, this builds very neatly upon the 'shared values and norms' concept, that is 'our conflict is your conflict', but it is structured in such a way as to make the ENP states the subjects of EU policy – rather than engaging them as co-equal objects.

This asymmetry is further illustrated in the Union's use of a 'soft' conditionality (as opposed to the 'hard' conditionality predicated on membership). Access to EU policy fields – the Single Market, etc. – is determined by the accredited achievement of EU-set targets by the neighbouring states. While the ENP is also replete with the promise of 'everything but the institutions (of membership)'[53] it nonetheless appears to reflect little more than the 'progressive integration into certain policies' (Ferrero-Waldner, 2004) creating a cumulative effect that is directed 'at' the transformation of the neighbouring states as opposed to being one that was developed 'with' neighbours to an agreed agenda.[54]

As an incentive for domestically controversial root and branch socio-economic and legal reforms which have the ultimate effect of internalising the Union's *acquis* this soft conditionality is certainly a modest offer on the part of the Union. At the same time, the rhetoric of shared and common interests and values remains, reiterating the query that if even some of the neighbourhood parties share the same set of 'European' values, on what basis is the prospect of membership being withheld?

On this basis, there is an argument that what remains to be achieved is for the Union to determine on an explicit footing, the nature of its own identity. On that basis, many of the remaining ambiguities within the ENP could be eliminated. In a reading of the ENP source documentation, debates and surrounding elite-level discourse, there would be appear to be two contending identity narratives at play – Europe as a 'Common Home' and Europe as a 'Citadel'

The Union as *'Common Home'* implies a destination based on effort, the achievement of something, the possibility to join – even by adoption – or even to return to a common, shared home place. It implies the instantiation of a common set of values and expectations while also being inclusive. That inclusion, however, is specified against a very explicit set of norms and expectations – but is open to the logic of its own universality. If you share these European norms – you become, so to speak, European.

By contrast, the Union as *'Citadel'* offers a very different kind of model, one that plays strongly to a greater sense of geographic space in which 'soft power' predominates. The Union is a beacon of its own values, norms, etc. and is helpfully willing to facilitate its emulation through extensive bilateral cooperation with other regional organisations (c.f. the African Union). Moreover, the Union is not averse to espousing its normative aspirations and actively seeking to instantiate these in the international community generally and in specific sets of bilateral relations. It offers the 'the operation of EU norms without formal membership.'[55]

The Union's choice of Citadel or Common Home has potentially far-reaching implications for our understanding of it as an international actor. The paradigm of Citadel sits very neatly within very traditional understandings and ontological assumptions about the international system. However unique its norms and values may be (or be declared to be), these are expressed through a geographically fixed entity which, through the exercise of both soft and hard power interacts with similarly defined international actors. Clearly, within such a model there is plenty of scope for innovation and dynamism relying more heavily on soft power for example, tempering the use of hard economic and military power within the ambit of a strong multilateral commitment, etc. Nonetheless, this model is one which can find its place on the floor of the ancient Westphalian dance of states.

The choice of Common Home is, perhaps, the more intriguing, and for that the more challenging option. Here the Union would be embracing its own ambivalence and contingency, and exploiting to the greatest extent possible its transformatory potential. It would rest on three key choices: first, to acknowledge and espouse the universal nature and applicability of its core values and norms; second, to model its relationships with its neighbours along a graduated sense of what it is to be European ('more or less' rather than 'in or out') and third, consciously to leave open the question of full membership. Taken together, these three choices – mutually reinforcing and logically consistent – would open a path toward the transformation of the international system and become the beginning of a new history. The evolution of the ENP through its new Mediterranean and Eastern regional frameworks may be telling in that regard. To conclude in the words of Derida:

> What if Europe was nothing but the opening, the beginning of a history, for which the change of course, the change of the heading, the relation to the other heading or to the other of the heading, would become a continuously existing possibility? Could Europe in some sense carry the responsibility for this opening, which is the opposite of exclusion? Could Europe in a constitutive way *be* the responsibility for this opening? [emphasis in original] Derrida translated and cited by Diez.[56]

Notes

1. This section builds upon an argument presented earlier in Francesco Cavatorta and Ben Tonra (2007), 'Normative Foundations in the EU Foreign, Security and Defence Policy. The Case of the Middle East Peace Process: A View from the Field', *Contemporary Politics*, 13 (4), pp. 347–61.
2. Colin Wight (1999), 'They Shoot Dead Horses Don't They? Locating Agency in the Agent-Structure Problematique' *European Journal of International Relations*, 1, pp. 109–142.
3. Ernesto, Laclau and Chantal Mouffe (1985), *Hegemony & Socialist Strategy: Towards a Radical Democratic Politics*. London and New York: Verso. David Campbell (1998), *Writing Security: United States Foreign Policy and the Politics of Identity*. Minneapolis, MN/Manchester: University of Minnesota Press/ Manchester University Press.
4. François Duchêne, (1972), 'Europe's Role in World Peace' in Richard Mayne (ed.), *Europe Tomorrow: Sixteen Europeans Look Ahead*, London: Fontana.
5. Johan Galtung (1973), *The European Community. A Superpower in the Making*. Oslo: Norwegian Universities Press, London: Allen & Unwin, 1973.
6. Hedley Bull (1982), 'Civilian Power Europe: A Contradiction in terms?' *Journal of Common Market Studies*, 21 (2), p. 151.
7. Ian Manners, (2002), 'Normative Power Europe: A contradiction in terms', *Journal of Common Market Studies*, 40 (2); Richard Rosecrance (1998), 'The European Union: A New Type of International Actor', in Jan Zielonka, *Paradoxes of European Foreign Policy*. The Hague, London and Boston: Kluwer Law International; Karen Smith (2003) 'The European Union: A Distinctive Actor in International Relations', *The Brown Journal of International Affairs*, 9 (2).

8. Andrew Linklater, (1998), *The Transformation of Political Community.* Cambridge: Polity Press; Barry Buzan and Richard Little (2000), 'One World or Two?' *International Studies Review* 2 (1)., pp. 17–21; Philippe Schmitter (2000), *How to Democratize the European Union...And Why Bother?* Lanham, MD: Rowman and Littlefield; Rey Koslowski (2001), 'Understanding the European Union as a Federal Polity,' in Thomas Christiansen, Knud Erik Jorgensen and Antje Wiener, *The Social Construction of Europe* London: Sage; Cooper, Robert (2003) *The Breaking of Nations: Order and Chaos in the Twenty-first Century.* LondonL Atlantic Books.
9. Ibid.
10. Robert Kagan, (2002). 'Power and Weakness', *Policy Review*, 113.
11. Johan P. Olsen (2002), 'The Many Faces of Europeanisation' *Journal of Common Market Studies*, 40 (5); Roland Dannreuther, (2004), *European Union Foreign and Security Policy. Towards a Neighbourhood Strategy.* London: Routledge.
12. Reuben Wong (2005), 'The Europeanization of Foreign Policy' in Christopher Hill and Michael Smith (eds), *International Relations and the European Union,* Oxford: Oxford University Press; K. Pomorska (2007) 'The Impact of Enlargement: Europeanisation of Polish Foreign Policy? Tracking adaptation and change in the Ministry of Foreign Affairs', *The Hague Journal of Diplomacy*, 2 (1); Tonra, Ben (2001), *The Europeanisation of national foreign policy: Dutch, Danish and Irish foreign policy in the European Union.* Aldershot: Ashgate.
13. Karin Fierke and Antje Weiner (1999), 'Constructing Institutional Interests: The EU and NATO', *Journal of European Public Policy* 6 (5), p. 726.
14. Ian Manners, (2002), 'Normative Power Europe: A contradiction in terms', *Journal of Common Market Studies,* 40 (2), p. 240.
15. Ibid., p. 241.
16. Article J1 of the Treaty on European Union (Treaty of Maastricht) *Official Journal* C 191 of 29 July 1992.
17. Ibid.
18. Treaty Of Amsterdam Amending The Treaty On European Union, The Treaties Establishing The European Communities And Related Acts, *Official Journal* C 340, 10 November 1997.
19. Article 1. Treaty of Lisbon amending the Treaty on European Union and the Treaty establishing the European Community, signed at Lisbon, 13 December 2007 *Official Journal* C 306, 17 December 2007.
20. Javier Solana (2002), *Europe's Place In The World: The Role Of The High Representative.* Stockholm, 25 April 2002, S0078/02.
21. Robert Keohane and Joseph Nye (1977), *Power and Interdependence: World Politics in Transition.* Boston, Mass: Little Brown.
22. Robert Keohane (1984), *After Hegemony: Cooperation And Discord In The World Political Economy.* Princeton: Princeton University Press; Martha Finnemore and Kathyryn Sikkink (1998), 'International Norms and Political Change', *International Organisation,* p. 891; Hendryk Spruyt (2000), 'The End of Empire and the Extension of the Westphalian System: The Normative Basis of the Modern State Order,' *International Studies Review*, 2, p. 69.
23. Ronald L. Jepperson, Alexander Wendt and Peter J. Katzenstein (1996) 'Norms, Identity, and Culture in National Security', in Peter J. Katzenstein

(ed.), *The Culture of National Security: Norms and Identity in World Politics*, New York: Columbia University Press; Hendryk Spruyt (2000), 'The End of Empire and the Extension of the Westphalian System: The Normative Basis of the Modern State Order,' *International Studies Review*, 2, p. 68.

24. Judith Butler (1990), *Gender Trouble*. London: Routledge; Cynthia Weber (1995) *Simulating Sovereignty*. Cambridge: Cambridge University Press; and David Campbell (1998), *Writing Security*. Manchester: Manchester University Press.
25. Barbara Lippert (2007), 'The Discussion on EU Neighbourhood Policy – Concepts, Reform Proposals and National Positions', in *International Policy Analysis*. Berlin: Friedrich-Ebert-Stiftung, http://library.fes.de/pdf-files/id/04737.pdf , accessed 24 March 2008.
26. T.F. Christiansen, F. Petito and B. Tonra (2000), 'Fuzzy Politics Around Fuzzy Borders:The European Union's "Near Abroad"', *Cooperation and Conflict*, 35 (4), pp. 389–415.
27. Denis de Rougemont (1965), *The Meaning of Europe*. New York: Stein and Day; Victoria Goddard, Josep R. Llobera and Cris Shore, *The Anthropology of Europe. Identities and Boundaries in Conflict*, Oxford: Berg.
28. Anthony Smith (1991), *National Identity*. London: Penguin Books.
29. Jurgen Habermas (2002), 'Toward a European Political Community', *Society*, 39 (5).
30. Beatrix Futák-Campbell (2007), 'Is there a common institutional discourse on the ENP: rhetoric during debates and during Question Time at the European Parliament on the Eastern neighbours', Paper presented at the EUSA conference Montreal, May 17–20, 2007.
31. European Council Presidency Conclusions, Lisbon Summit, 26–27 June, *Bulletin*, 29 June 1992.
32. Franz Mayer and Jan Palmowski (2004), 'European Identities and the EU – The Ties that Bind the Peoples of Europe', *Journal of Common Market Studies*, 42 (3), pp. 573–598.
33. Sami Moisio (2002), 'EU eligibility, Central Europe, and the invention of applicant state narrative', *Geopolitics*, 7 (3).
34. L. Wolff (1994), *Inventing Eastern Europe: The Map of Civilization on the Mind of the Enlightenment*. Palo Alto, CA: Stanford University Press; Pim den Boer (1995), 'Europe to 1914: The Making of an Idea', in Kevin Wilson and Jan van der Dussen (eds), *The History of the Idea of Europe*. London: Routledge; Peter Bugge (1999), 'The Use of the Middle *Mitteleuropa vs. Stedn' Evropa'*, *European Review of History*, 6 (1).
35. Frank Schimmelfennig (2001), 'The Community Trap: Liberal Norms, Rhetorical Action, and the Eastern Enlargement of the European Union,' *International Organization*, 55 (1).
36. Merje Kuus (2007), 'Love, Peace and Nato: Imperial Subject-Making in Central Europe', *Antipode*, 39 (2).
37. Ulla Holm (2005), 'EU's Neighbourhood Policy. A Question of Space and Security', DIIS Working Paper, 2005/22.
38. Ibid.
39. Ole Wæver (1998), 'Insecurity, security, and asecurity in the West European non-war community', in E. Adler and M. Barnett (eds), *Security Communities*.

Cambridge: Cambridge University Press. Thomas Diez (2004), 'Europe's Other and the Return of Geopolitics', *Review of International Affairs*, 17 (2).
40. Anthony Smith (1991), *National Identity*. London: Penguin Books, p. 67.
41. Ibid., pp. 75–6.
42. Judy Batt, Dov Lynch, Antonio Missirroli, Martin Ortega and Dimitrios Triantaphyllou (2003), 'Partners and Neighbours: A CFSP for a wider Europe', Chaillot Paper 64, p. 48.
43. Commission of the European Communities (2003), Communication from the Commission, *Wider Europe – Neighbourhood: A New Framework for Relations with our Eastern and Southern Neighbours* COM(2003) 104 final, Brussels, 11 March 2003. These 'neighbours' were defined as Algeria, Armenia, Azerbaijan, Belarus, Egypt, Georgia, Israel, Jordan, Lebanon, Libya, Moldova, Morocco, Palestinian Authority, Syria, Tunisia and Ukraine.
44. See Karen E. Smith (2005), 'The Outsiders: The European Neighbourhood Policy', *International Affairs*, 81 (4).
45. Karen E. Smith (2005), 'The Outsiders: The European Neighbourhood Policy', *International Affairs*, 81 (4) p. 758.
46. Raffaella Del Sarto and Tobias Schumacher (2005), 'From EMP to ENP: What's at Stake with the European Neighbourhood Policy towards the Southern Mediterranean?' *European Foreign Affairs Review*, 10 (1), p. 5.
47. Commission of the European Communities (2004), Communication from the Commission, *European Neighbourhood Policy: Strategy Paper*, COM(2004) 373 final, p. 3, Brussels 12 May 2004.
48. See Raffaella Del Sarto and Tobias Schumacher (2005), 'From EMP to ENP: What's at Stake with the European Neighbourhood Policy towards the Southern Mediterranean?' *European Foreign Affairs Review*, 10 (1), p. 5; Karen E. Smith (2005), 'The Outsiders: The European Neighbourhood Policy', *International Affairs*, 81 (4) p.759; Judith Kelley (2006), 'New Wine in Old Wineskins: Promoting Political Reforms through the New European Neighbourhood Policy', *Journal of Common Market Studies*, 44 (1).
49. Commission of the European Communities (2004), Communication from the Commission, *European Neighbourhood Policy, Strategy Paper*, COM(2004) 373 final, p. 5, Brussels, 12 May 2004.
50. Ulla Holm (2005), 'EU's Neighbourhood Policy. A Question of Space and Security', DIIS Working Paper, 2005/22.
51. Ruben Zaiotti (2007), 'Of Friends and Fences: Europe's Neighbourhood Policy and the "Gated Community Syndrome"', *Journal of European Integration*, 29 (2), p. 150.
52. Ibid.; Barbara Lippert (2007), 'The Discussion on EU Neighbourhood Policy – Concepts, Reform Proposals and National Positions', in *International Policy Analysis*. Berlin: Friedrich-Ebert-Stiftung, http://library.fes.de/pdf-files/id/04737.pdf , accessed 24 March 2008.
53. Romano Prodi (2003), 'A Wider Europe – A Proximity Policy as the key to stability' Speech by Romano Prodi, President of the European Commission, 'Peace, Security And Stability International Dialogue and the Role of the EU' Sixth ECSA-World Conference. Jean Monnet Project, Brussels, 5–6 December 2002, SPEECH/02/619.

54. Benita Ferrero-Waldner (2004), Press Conference to launch first seven Action Plans under the European Neighbourhood Policy, Brussels, 9 December 2004 – Speech/04/529.
55. Merje Kuus (2007), 'Love, Peace and Nato: Imperial Subject-Making in Central Europe', *Antipode*, 39 (2), p. 161.
56. Thomas Diez (2004), 'Europe's Other and the Return of Geopolitics', *Review of International Affairs*, 17 (2), p. 324.

4
The ENP, Security, and Democracy in the Context of the European Security Strategy

Sven Biscop

Introduction

'Even in an era of globalisation, geography is still important', the 2003 European Security Strategy (ESS) states. 'It is in the European interest that countries on our own borders are well-governed. Neighbours who are engaged in violent conflict, weak states where organised crime flourishes, dysfunctional societies or exploding population growth on its borders all pose problems for Europe', hence the definition of 'building security in [the EU's] neighbourhood' as one of three strategic objectives for EU foreign policy.

The European Neighbourhood Policy (ENP), which was elaborated in the same period as the ESS itself, can be regarded as the operationalisation of this objective, translating the holistic approach to foreign policy advocated by the ESS into a concrete policy framework for relations with the Union's periphery. Bilateral ENP Action Plans (APs) with each of the neighbours are to link together political, economic and social reforms and security cooperation through conditionality mechanisms. The ENP thus fits in perfectly with the strategic orientation described. Nonetheless, a number of fundamental, strategic-level choices have yet to be made, revealing that the EU is an emergent, but not yet a fully fledged strategic actor. These questions arise both as a result of the great difficulties experienced in implementing the ENP and as a consequence of important gaps in the EU's security thinking itself. The debate about the future of the ESS, mandated by the European Council in December 2007 and culminating in the adoption of a report on the implementation of the ESS in December 2008, did not really fill those gaps. Two major issues will be addressed in this chapter.

First, it has proved difficult to reconcile the objective of promoting democracy and human rights with the desire to operate in partnership with the existing regimes, notably as regards the more authoritarian neighbours. As a result, the EU is often seen by public opinion and reformist actors in the neighbouring countries as a status quo actor which prioritises good relations with the regimes over fundamental reform. This will always be a difficult balancing act, but it appears that the EU has not yet earnestly confronted the stability versus democracy dilemma. What is the desired end-state of the ENP? Are the EU's instruments sufficient or is there an upper limit to what can be achieved through the consensual ENP?

Second, the ENP, although emphasising permanent prevention and stabilisation, cannot be seen separately from the 'hard' security or politico-military dimension. The APs will not lead to many results in a country involved in conflict with its neighbours or in internal strife. Yet the EU's neighbourhood contains numerous areas of tension, dispute and even regular full-blown conflict, notably in the Caucasus and the Middle East. Does the definition of the neighbourhood imply the objective of maintaining peace in that area, including through military means if necessary? Are the EU and its member states able and willing to commit forces to that end?

Positive power

The ESS certainly outlines a very ambitious agenda. The emphasis is on a holistic approach, putting to use the full range of instruments, through partnerships and multilateral institutions, for a permanent policy of prevention and stabilisation: 'The best protection for our security is a world of well-governed democratic states. Spreading good governance, supporting social and political reform, dealing with corruption and abuse of power, establishing the rule of law and protecting human rights are the best means of strengthening the international order'.

This approach can be conceptualised through the notion of global public goods (GPG). Physical security or freedom from fear; economic prosperity or freedom from want; political freedom or democracy, human rights and the rule of law and social wellbeing or education, health services, a clean environment, etc. are global or universal 'goods' because – at least in the EU view – everybody is entitled to them and they are public because it is the responsibility of public authorities at all levels of government to provide citizens with access to them. The gap between haves and have-nots in terms of access to these core GPG is at the heart of economic instability, mass migration, frustration, extremism and conflict, from the negative effects of which Europe cannot be insulated. Ultimately therefore, in today's globalised world, Europe can only be secure if everybody is secure, as expressed by the subtitle of the ESS: *A Secure Europe in a Better World*. The four core GPG are inextricably related – one needs access to all four in order to enjoy any one – and they are present in every foreign policy issue, hence the need for a holistic approach: all policies must address the four dimensions simultaneously in order to achieve durable results rather than just combat the symptoms of underlying issues. Working proactively to diminish inequality and increase access to GPG is the basis of prevention and stabilisation, and, because the EU does not want to impose, it does so through partnerships with other states and regions and through rule-based multilateral institutions.

The ESS thus has a very positive, indeed progressive, tone to it. Rather than being threat-based, it is aimed at achieving positive objectives, which are of course in the enlightened self-interest of the EU – that is what the policy is about and, as the opening quote makes clear, the ESS does not hesitate to state so explicitly. But these objectives at the same time directly benefit others and thus express a feeling of responsibility[1] for, and solidarity with, the have-nots in, in this case, Europe's neighbourhood. In that sense, the EU could be described as a positive power.[2]

Democracy versus stability

The EU is very active in prevention and stabilisation, notably in its bilateral relations with third countries, via the method of 'positive conditionality'. The ENP is undoubtedly one of the policies in which the translation of the strategic choices of the ESS into concrete actions is the most advanced. By linking them to market access and economic and financial support, the EU aims to stimulate economic, political and social reforms as well as security cooperation, so as to address the root causes and durably change the environment that leads to extremism, crisis and conflict.

Yet, if 'positive conditionality' as a theory seems sound enough, practice is often lagging behind, certainly in countries that do not – immediately – qualify for EU membership. The proverbial carrots that would potentially be most effective in stimulating reform, such as opening up the European agricultural market or setting up a system for legal economic migration, are those that the EU is not willing to consider – in spite of imperative arguments suggesting that Europe would actually benefit from such measures. At the same time, conditionality is seldom applied very strictly, which means that even if potentially more effective carrots were to be offered, the EU's influence on policy-making would remain limited. One reason why increased benefits are not more explicitly linked to the neighbours' performance is the absence of sufficiently specific objectives and clearly defined benchmarks in the APs. It is also a question of leadership and political courage, though – it is easier to maintain cordial relations than to adopt a critical stance.

The impression created is that the EU favours stability and economic – and energy – interests over reform, to the detriment of Europe's soft or normative power. Surprisingly perhaps, in for example the Mediterranean neighbours public opinion mostly views the EU as a status quo actor, working with the current regimes rather than promoting fundamental change, whereas, perhaps even more surprisingly after the invasion of Iraq, the US is seen as caring more sincerely about democracy and human rights.

This lack of EU soft power should not be underestimated. Rather than as the benign, multilateralist actor which the EU considers itself – 'the one that did not invade Iraq' – in many southern countries it is first and foremost seen as a very aggressive economic actor. In fact, in the economic sphere the EU is often a very 'traditional' power. For many countries, the negative economic consequences of dumping and protectionism – which often cancel out the positive effects of development aid – are far more important and threatening than the challenges of terrorism and proliferation that dominate the Western foreign policy agenda, and therefore far more determining for the image of the EU. In the current difficult international climate, the EU model's legitimacy is in urgent need of enhancement.

The EU must therefore muster the courage to apply conditionality effectively. Admittedly, 'positive conditionality' requires an extremely difficult balancing act, especially vis-à-vis countries with authoritarian regimes – and vis-à-vis great powers like Russia and China: maintaining partnerships and being sufficiently critical at the same time. But in that difficult context, the EU could notably show more consistency and resolve in reacting to human rights abuses, which should visibly impact on the relationship with any regime. A much enhanced image and increased legitimacy will follow, notably in the eyes of public opinion, which is a prerequisite for the gradual pursuit of further-reaching political, economic and social reforms.

Even then, however, the question remains whether there is not an upper limit to what can be achieved through the partnership approach of the ENP, particularly in the area of political freedom. An AP can be considered a contract; even if one of the contracting parties, the EU, carries more weight than the other, the neighbouring state, the latter in the end voluntarily agrees – or not – to subscribe to a number of reforms in return for the benefits offered by the EU. Through this method, incremental progress can certainly be achieved in the field of human rights, including in authoritarian regimes, because measures can be taken that improve the condition of citizens without fundamentally affecting the power base of the regime: prison reform, abolition of torture, etc. Democratisation, however, is much more difficult to achieve – in many states, this would effectively amount to regime change. The existing regimes therefore have no interest at all in promoting democratic reforms, a situation which no degree of economic carrots is likely to change. In recent years relatively peaceful transformations towards democracy have been possible in Georgia and Ukraine; to a significant extent these 'coloured revolutions' have been engineered from the outside. Yet the potential of replicating such peaceful transitions in other neighbouring states seems extremely limited, especially in the Mediterranean neighbourhood or for that matter anywhere outside the European continent, in the absence of sufficiently strong local actors and given Europe's limited appeal to local public opinion in the current international climate.

In view of the fact that the objectives of democratisation and stability seem to be difficult to reconcile, at least under the current circumstances, a debate seems in order on the desired end-state of the ENP. Perhaps the EU could be satisfied with incremental progress while maintaining the existing regimes, in the interest of stability. Yet, from the perspective of the provision of GPG, is it not evident that the enormous gap between haves and have-nots in many neighbouring countries means that stability is actually very fragile? In the longer term, this gap will certainly lead to unrest and crises of different types, which first of all threaten the security of people in the neighbouring countries. But, if this appears to indicate that in the long-term the objective must be full democratisation, then the methodology of promoting democracy is in urgent need of reassessment. This dilemma between democracy and stability is at the heart of the hesitant, even reluctant, attitude of the EU toward speaking up for 'human security' in its neighbourhood.

A very important related question is specific to the EU's southern neighbourhood: what is the Union's attitude towards political Islam, which often makes up an important part of opposition and reformist actors – and is often the winner of elections? Here the case of Palestine can serve as an illustration. By breaking off official relations with the Palestinian government after the Hamas election victory of January 2006, apparently under US pressure, possibly in return for the US subscribing to the negotiated approach towards Iran, the EU has missed an opportunity. The Hamas government did play into the hands of those favouring breaking off relations by refusing to condemn suicide attacks. Yet the decision contrasts sharply with established EU policy, which has always been that a lot more influence can be had by dialogue rather than by designating rogue states with whom one does not talk, even if like in the case of Hamas part of their programme is not acceptable. Although Hamas is on the EU list of terrorist organisations, pragmatism should have prevailed. Why after all refuse to speak with Hamas on the grounds that it does not recognise Israel, while simultaneously negotiating with Iran, the President of which has declared he would like to see Israel destroyed?

By condemning the results of what probably are the fairest elections in any Arab country, the EU has severely undermined the legitimacy of its democratisation project. Furthermore, by immediately breaking off relations and demanding changes in policy, the EU has left the initiative to resume the relationship with the other party and has thus made itself dependent on the most radical elements within Hamas. If, alternatively, the EU had continued to work with the Palestinian government, it could potentially have strengthened the more moderate wing of Hamas, which is focusing on the domestic governance of Palestine rather than on the confrontation with Israel and is therefore very interested in continued EU support.[3] It can safely be argued that Hamas won the elections not because it was more anti-Israeli than its competitors, but because of its socio-economic programme, which had gained credibility thanks to the network of social services that Hamas and affiliated organisations had built in the territories, and, simply, because Fatah, with its record of corruption and ineffectiveness, lost the elections. If the EU is now unforgiving vis-à-vis Hamas, in the past it has perhaps been too soft on conditionality.

Those who have welcomed the establishment of a Fatah-only government on the West Bank, after Hamas assumed power in Gaza, because a partner for dialogue has again been found, are mistaken. The existence of Gaza cannot be ignored, not only because of the humanitarian plight of its 1.3 million inhabitants, but also because no settlement is possible without Hamas. As much is demonstrated by the failure of the Annapolis Summit, following President George W Bush's call (16 July 2007) for an international meeting 'of representatives from nations that support a two-state solution',[4] to produce any results, and the ensuing stalemate. The EU must therefore open a channel for dialogue with Hamas. One cannot simply pretend they are not there. In Palestine, and indeed in the region at large, the EU cannot afford not to have a dialogue with political Islam – a critical dialogue, based on conditionality, just as with the regimes. Given its prominence in politics and in civil society, political Islam must be recognised, perhaps not as a partner but at least as an indispensable actor.

A security guarantee?

The politico-military dimension constitutes an integral part of the holistic approach of the ENP. Military instruments have a role to play in the permanent policy of conflict prevention and stabilisation, notably in the field of security sector reform (SSR) and disarmament, demobilisation and reintegration (DDR) as well as in the field of traditional confidence- and security-building measures (CSBMs). Clearly, though, in countries that are involved in armed conflict or in disputes carrying the risk of conflict, more forceful intervention may be necessary, from the deployment of observers and classic peacekeeping missions to preventive diplomacy and, in extreme cases, crisis management and the use of force. Just like an exclusively military solution that ignores the political, social and economic root causes of conflict will not produce durable results, a root causes approach will come to nothing if it ignores existing 'hard security' issues. The Middle East Peace Process (MEPP), or rather the lack of one, is a case in point, as the ESS itself emphasises: 'Resolution of the Arab/Israeli conflict is a strategic priority for Europe. Without this, there will be little chance of dealing with other problems in the Middle East.'

The question is whether this commitment to a resolution of the Arab-Israeli conflict can be considered part of a wider security commitment toward the 'neighbourhood' as a whole. Can the 'neighbourhood' as defined by the ENP be seen as a region in which the EU has committed itself to guarantee peace and security, up to the use of military means if necessary – and feasible? Does the EU have the capacity to live up to such a commitment and, if so, are the member states willing to engage that capacity? Or does the Union's commitment to its neighbourhood end at the moment military measures are required? An assessment of the EU's security engagement in the region since the coming into existence of the ENP produces a mixed picture.

Security in the Mediterranean neighbourhood

Within the EU's neighbourhood, the Middle East is obviously the most important flashpoint. Perennial tensions and regular violence and conflict overshadow relations with the whole of the region. Europe has a long history of diplomatic engagement with the MEPP, to the extent even that it can be said that the need to define a position on the issue was one of the driving forces behind the creation of European Political Cooperation (EPC), the predecessor of the Common Foreign and Security Policy (CFSP).[5] Through increasingly more specific and outspoken positions, the EEC and later the EU played a major role in the recognition of the demands of the Palestinians and of the PLO as negotiating party. Yet, in spite of this record and in spite of the priority accorded to the issue in the ESS, today Europe is still all too often seen as a 'payer' rather than a 'player': indispensable for its economic aid, without which notably the Palestinian Authority would long have collapsed, but sidelined when it comes to 'high politics'. The invasion of Iraq, against the advice of those adhering to the long-standing European view that 'the road to the Middle East goes through Jerusalem' rather than through Baghdad, was a sad low point of EU influence – also of course because the EU itself was deeply divided.

Progress has been limited. The acceptance by Israel of the deployment of an unarmed border assistance mission, EU Border Assistance Mission in Rafah (EU BAM Rafah), the European Security and Defence Policy (ESDP) operation at the crossing point between Gaza and Egypt that was launched in 2005, can be seen as a positive sign. By 2008 however violence caused the crossing point to be closed most of the time. As a result of the failure of Annapolis, the Quartet – of which the EU is a member with the US, Russia and the UN – remains lethargic as well. The EU remains committed to the two-state solution and still sees that as the key to the wider security problems in the region, but no EU initiative has any chance of success without parallel US engagement. That will also require a more active EU, for until now the member states have showed little willingness to try to stimulate peace initiatives. Furthermore, as mentioned above, since the intra-Palestinian conflict between Fatah and Hamas and the separation of the Palestinian Authority into two competing halves, the situation is even more difficult than before. Interestingly, though, at the same there seems to be a widespread consensus that if a settlement would emerge that would include a peacekeeping force, the EU and its member states would evidently make a substantial contribution.

The EU has shown more activity with regard to Lebanon, but with mixed results. Following the 2006 war in Lebanon, the UN clearly looked to the EU to provide the forces for an enhanced peacekeeping mission. If during the war the EU did not always act in a united manner, as notably the UK conformed with the US and delayed the call for a ceasefire, now the EU was quick to take up the call from the UN, shocked into action perhaps by the unexpected scale and intensity of the war and driven by its strong declarations of support for the UN in recent years. In the Political and Security Committee (PSC) the option was sincerely considered of launching an ESDP operation, that is with a UN mandate but under EU command. Why, indeed, not assume command and run the operation under the EU label if EU member states contribute the bulk of the forces anyway? In the end however – and perhaps not completely to the disappointment of all EU member states – only the UN framework turned out to be acceptable to all conflict parties, hence the reinforcement of the existing UN Interim Force in Lebanon (UNIFIL) rather than a new force. Interestingly, NATO was never an option, because of the connotations it carries in the Middle East – a sound argument for the maintenance of an alternative mechanism to launch operations, i.e. ESDP.

For the EU member states the decision to contribute to 'UNIFIL-plus' was clearly taken in an EU context. Deliberations on force composition and the force commander took place in the EU institutions, in close coordination with the UN – although EU member states rejected a Council Secretariat proposal for the EU to act as 'clearing house' managing the national contributions to UNIFIL.[6] On 25 August 2006 UN Secretary-General Kofi Annan participated in an extraordinary meeting of the EU Council, which 'welcome[d] Member States' intentions to commit a substantial number of troops to be deployed in Lebanon'.[7] Afterwards the Secretary-General declared his satisfaction with this outcome, stating that 'Europe has lived up to its responsibility'.[8] In spite of the troops wearing the blue helmet of the UN, UNIFIL-plus is thus clearly seen as an EU presence, by all relevant parties, and with all the implications that carries for the EU. The Council conclusions themselves state this clearly: 'The significant overall contribution of the Member States to UNIFIL demonstrates that the *European Union* is living up to its responsibilities. [...] This gives a leadership role for the *Union* in UNIFIL' [emphasis added].

It certainly is a success that the border with Israel is now being controlled by Lebanese armed forces rather than the Hezbollah militias. For the EU, its large presence in UNIFIL seems to imply increasing acceptance of a politico-military, rather than just an economic role, notably by Israel. Yet, UNIFIL will not disarm Hezbollah – it will demilitarise the border region below the Litani river, above which Hezbollah is likely to regroup. UNIFIL thus basically buys time for a political process that should integrate all actors in a democratic Lebanese polity. Only in such a wider political framework can SSR/DDR schemes result in the integration of the armed Hezbollah in a united Lebanese army, which seems the only peaceful way of consolidating Lebanese democracy. Secretary-General Annan explicitly confirmed this after his participation in the EU Council: 'I think it is also generally accepted that the disarmament of Hezbollah cannot be done by force. It has to be a political agreement between the Lebanese; there has to be a Lebanese consensus and an agreement among them to disarm.'[9] Commissioner for External Relations, Benita Ferrero-Waldner, confirmed the same: 'The disarming of Hezbollah [...] realistically can only be achieved as part of a process of political integration.'[10] As the assassination of several Lebanese leading figures since the deployment of UNIFIL-plus and the ensuing general political turmoil have shown, the situation remains fragile. Without consolidation of the political situation, the positive light in which UNIFIL is seen today could quickly fade away. As in Afghanistan, if insufficient benefits are seen to be forthcoming, the peacekeepers might easily come to be seen as occupiers, and as proxies for Israel. Deploying troops is of no use if not accompanied by diplomatic and political engagement.

As a security actor in its Mediterranean neighbourhood, the EU thus appears strangely active and hesitant at the same time, simultaneously playing a leading and a subservient role. The deployment of nearly 8000 blue helmets from EU member states is undoubtedly a very significant step toward an enhanced diplomatic and military presence in the region. Yet, the political follow-up to this deployment seems to be lacking, as if the member states are shying away from the expectations and responsibilities which it has brought. In a similar vein, the EU remains very reluctant to translate its long-standing position on the Arab-Israeli conflict in diplomatic initiatives. Important in this regard is the EU's difficult relationship with the US, the other crucial external actor in the region. While it can be argued that only a mutually supported strategy has any chance of success, Brussels and Washington continue to hold very different opinions about how to pursue their largely shared objectives for the region.[11] Furthermore, the US still seems to seek to avoid an important politico-military role for the EU, while a number of EU member states give priority to the alliance with the US over the pursuit of a joint European policy. Hopefully, the election of Barack Obama as US President will create the impetus for a joint reconsideration of policy.

Security in the eastern neighbourhood

In Europe's continental neighbourhood, the 'frozen conflicts' dominate the security agenda. Here until recently the EU as such has played a lesser role, because traditionally the forum to address these issues has been the Organization for Security and Co-operation in Europe (OSCE), while the focus of the Union is on the Western Balkans. Nevertheless, the eastern neighbourhood has been gaining prominence in recent years, as is witnessed by the statement in the ESS that 'We should now take a stronger and more active interest in the problems of the Southern Caucasus'. This commitment has been translated in the appointment of a Special Representative for the region, whose staff includes a Border Support Team offering strategic level advice to the Georgian government on matters of SSR. The EU also deployed an ESDP rule of law mission in Georgia, EUJust Themis (July 2004–July 2005), supporting Georgia in reforming the criminal justice system. There is also a Special Representative for Moldova, and an EU BAM to Moldova and Ukraine has been deployed since December 2005, advising the border and customs services.

Unlike in the Mediterranean neighbourhood, the EU is confronted with Russia, a regional actor – rather than an external actor like the US in the Mediterranean – that is a power in its own right and seeks to maintain and extend its influence in the region. In the face of not-too-hidden Russian involvement and support for breakaway regions in Georgia and Moldova, the EU has adopted a very careful policy, emphasising monitoring and capacity-building rather than grand initiatives aimed at conflict resolution. That proved insufficient to prevent the crisis of August 2008, when ongoing Russian provocations led to a rash Georgian offensive, ending with the inevitable defeat of its forces and recognition of the independence of South Ossetia and Abkhazia by Russia. Because the US sided rather too openly with Georgia and NATO was seen as part of the problem by Moscow, the EU was the only available mediator after the clash, a role which it fulfilled relatively effectively, be it to a large extent because France happened to hold the Presidency. If President Nicolas Sarkozy was able to broker the 'Six-Point Agreement' (12 August), that was thanks to his weight as French Head of State, with Russia apparently – but thanks to Sarkozy, vainly – attempting to avoid all EU involvement. On 1 October 2008 a 200-strong EU Monitoring Mission (EUMM) was deployed in Georgia to observe the implementation of the agreement.

For the EU, the crisis confirmed its long-standing view that only engagement with Russia can create a mutually beneficial relationship. The EU is best placed to negotiate a package deal with Moscow, precisely because, unlike NATO, EU-Russia relations cover much more than security. The EU is thus forced to improve its strategy toward Russia, and will hopefully be able to manage the internal divide between its Western and Eastern European members on this issue. Just like in the Middle East, one lesson seems clear, though: the EU must develop strategies and policies based on its own priorities – simply following or even just observing all-too-confrontational US policies has proved counter-productive for European interests. Brussels should not fear Moscow, but neither should it be in favour of an issue only because Moscow is against or vice versa: interests must dictate policy, not Alliance politics.

Multilateral frameworks and the broader region

The ENP puts the emphasis on bilateral relations, through the APs. Yet, in the southern and in the eastern neighbourhoods, existing multilateral frameworks might help the EU to attain its objectives, notably in the field of security.

In the south, the ENP de facto takes over the bilateral dimension of the Euro-Mediterranean Partnership (EMP) or Barcelona Process as APs are agreed with successive partner countries. On paper the EMP continues to function as a multilateral complement to the ENP, but in reality it has been moribund ever since 1996, when Arab-Israeli relations deterio-rated again after the initial success of the Madrid Process. With a few exceptions, partner countries have always continued to meet, which is a merit in its own right, but little of substance has been achieved. Yet, a multilateral framework is indispensable when addressing 'hard secu-rity' issues in the region, which requires 'south-to-south' confidence-building, between the neighbouring countries. However, the EMP, with its 37 participants, is at the same time too unwieldy as a forum, and too limited, because it does not include a number of countries that are crucial to security notably in the Middle East, such as Iran and Iraq. A more flexible approach is in order, bringing together relevant actors on a sub-regional basis, including non-EMP countries if necessary, but in the broad framework of the EMP. On the EU side as well, a flexible approach could be imagined, delegating authority to negotiate on the issue at hand on behalf of the EU to a limited number of member states. Together with High Representative Catherine Ashton, or perhaps her envoy, the member states with the most interests and expertise could thus take the lead in preparing and, after receiving a mandate from the Council, implementing policy. Such a more flexible format seems better suited to deal with the 'high politics' of conflict resolution and crisis management, while the overall EMP framework could continue to address some of the 'softer' security issues, such as cooperation on training, civil protection, etc. The transformation of the EMP into a 'Union for the Mediterranean' as announced at the Paris Summit for the Mediterranean (13 July 2008) envisages an institutionalisation of the Barcelona Process, for example the creation of a co-presidency and joint secretariat. Although undoubtedly useful, such institutional measures alone will not suffice to revitalise the EMP, if the EU does not address the fundamental political questions that are at the heart of the current stalemate.

In the east, following the Georgian crisis, Russia, fearing further expansion of NATO, is now calling for a new pan-European security organisation. The obvious answer is that the OSCE, as a forum convening all neighbouring countries plus Russia and the US, could already play that role today – the precondition is of course that Russia refrains from blocking the organisation, as it has done in the recent past. In the ESS, the OSCE is mentioned only very briefly, on a par with the Council of Europe: 'For the European Union, the strength and effectiveness of the OSCE and the Council of Europe has a particular significance.' The EU and its member states could probably make much better use of their prominent position in the OSCE, if there were more effective coordination between the two organisations, not only in the field of 'hard security', but also with regard to the APs.

Not only are the strategic objectives and approaches of the OSCE strikingly similar, but the OSCE can bring a wealth of experience and expertise to the table. In many of the neighbouring countries, the OSCE has a long-established and large-scale presence; with its norm-setting experience, it could help the EU in designing realistic objectives and benchmarks and in negotiating the APs. Even more importantly, through its missions and delegations, it could then collaborate in a very constructive way with the neighbours in helping them to meet those objectives. The OSCE could thus also profit from the increased leverage resulting from an EU-provided carrot to stimulate cooperation and reform, to the benefit of both organisations' objectives. Such constructive cooperation could meet the criticism by some Commonwealth of Independent States (CIS) countries that the OSCE focuses too exclusively on monitoring human rights and democratic institutions to the detriment of supporting the governments of the target states,[12] although of course political participation, respect for human rights and the rule of law constitute an important dimension of the ENP APs.

In both the eastern and the southern neighbourhoods, there are obvious links with countries that are not covered by the ENP and where the *problématique* is very similar, for example in the Gulf region and Central Asia. The question could therefore be asked whether the ENP should be extended to these regions, or whether perhaps separate but similar and linked frameworks can be imagined to deepen relations with them. The EU has established relations with the Gulf Cooperation Council (GCC), including annual ministerial meetings, but except for the economic dimension cooperation is limited. In June 2004 The European Council adopted the *EU Strategic Partnership with the Mediterranean and the Middle East*, which sought to apply the holistic approach of the ENP/EMP, without enlarging the frameworks themselves, to relations with the GCC countries of Yemen, Iran and Iraq. The latter have proved to have a very limited interest in this initiative however; thus not a lot has been heard about it since its adoption. The June 2007 European Council adopted *The EU and Central Asia: Strategy for a New Partnership*, a new framework for relations with the five Central Asian countries, focusing on political dialogue, education, rule of law, human rights and energy. Both in Central Asia and the Gulf region the dilemma between democracy and stability presents itself in even starker terms than in the ENP countries. Many of the regimes are even more intransigent and moreover possess important energy assets, which makes the balancing act, which a 'critical dialogue' always is, even more difficult for the EU, while the desired end-state is even vaguer. Thus, although on the one hand the linkages with the ENP region are evident, on the other hand if the EU earnestly wants to pursue a similar partnership with Central Asia and the Gulf, a thorough assessment of the holistic approach becomes even more pressing, given the additional difficulties which these regions entail. Otherwise the addition of ineffectual policies will further erode the Union's soft power.

Conclusion

From one perspective, the field of policies toward the neighbourhood is one in which the translation of the overall orientations of the ESS into sub-strategies, policies and actions has advanced the furthest. The ENP can really be seen as the implementation of one part of the ESS. In the policy cycle, implementation should be followed by evaluation, the results of which should be fed back into the policy design. In the case of the ENP, implementation has clearly revealed the practical difficulties of translating even a sound concept into practice. As the evaluation above has shown, this is not just a matter of the modalities of implementation – the assessment also reveals a number of remaining questions at the strategic level. The EU must address these in order to maintain the dynamic of the ENP and guarantee its effectiveness. The December 2008 report on the implementation of the ESS reconfirmed the importance of the ENP – hopefully on that basis a real strategic review of the Union's engagement with its neighbourhood will be launched.

As a first priority, the EU should find a renewed and more resolute commitment to react firmly to human rights abuses and apply conditionality effectively. Respect for human rights is at the very heart of the EU project and should be seen to be a core element of its foreign policy as well – without that, the EU can have no soft power. While more attention to human rights is a conditio sine qua non, at a more fundamental level the EU must assess the long-term objectives of the ENP, their feasibility and the effectiveness of the instruments at its disposal. This includes the question of how to interact usefully with authoritarian regimes as well as with religiously inspired political actors without renouncing the Union's values; conditionality should apply to relations with both. Without a more thought-through policy, the democracy versus stability dilemma risks paralysing the Union.

In the field of 'hard security', drawing up a specific sub-strategy for the ENP region would be counter-productive, by creating the perception that the EU sees its neighbours mostly as potential sources of insecurity. At a more general level, the ESS as a whole has to be translated into an overall military strategy, one level of abstraction below the ESS, outlining when, where and which use of the military instrument the EU aims to make, including the threshold for the use of force, for example in a Responsibility to Protect scenario. That will then also make clear how far the EU's security commitment toward its neighbours goes. Multilateralism is one of the core elements of the ESS and the EU's approach to security, but the multilateral fora in the ENP region have been paralysed by conflicts among the neighbours and by the intransigence of major participants. The EU should assess how they can be revitalised, for example by introducing a more flexible and sub-regional approach, and how, in the case of the OSCE, it can better coordinate its action with and within that organisation. All of these issues should probably have been addressed first, before creating new frameworks for relations with the Gulf and Central Asia, where the same difficulties are present to an even greater extent. Without an effective ENP, policies towards these regions cannot be effective either.

Neighbours just accidentally live next to each other – a neighbourhood does not automatically constitute a community. The first experiences of the ENP demonstrate that creating a community is a very slow and difficult process. But if the EU finds the will to assess its strategies and policies sincerely, and adapt them where necessary, it will at least be an ongoing process.

Notes

1. On this issue, see Hartmut Mayer and Henri Vogt (eds) (2006), *A Responsible Europe? Ethical Foundations of EU External Affairs*. Basingstoke, Palgrave Macmillan.
2. Sven Biscop (2005), *The European Security Strategy – A Global Agenda for Positive Power*. Aldershot, Ashgate Publishing. See also Sven Biscop and Jan Joel Andersson (eds) (2008), *The EU and the European Security Strategy – Forging a Global Europe*. Abingdon, Routledge.
3. The author thanks Dr Claire Spencer of Chatham House for pointing out this argument.
4. 'President Bush discusses the Middle East'. White House, Office of the Press Secretary, 16 July 2007.
5. Costanza Musu (2007), 'The EU and the Middle East Peace Process: A Balance'. In: *Studia Diplomatica*, 60(1), pp. 11–28.
6. Nicoletta Pirozzi (2006), 'UN Peacekeeping in Lebanon: Europe's Contribution'. In: *European Security Review*, 30, pp. 1–3.
7. Extraordinary EU Council Meeting: Conclusions on Lebanon. 25 August 2006.
8. Brussels, Belgium, 25 August 2006 – Secretary-General's Press Conference.
9. Brussels, Belgium, 25 August 2006 – Secretary-General's Press Conference.
10. Benita Ferrero-Waldner (2006), 'For a Sovereign and Independent Lebanon'. In: *The Wall Street Journal Europe*, 31 August.
11. Sven Biscop, 'For a "More Active" EU in the Middle East: Transatlantic Relations and the Strategic Implications of Europe's Engagements in Iran, Lebanon and Israel-Palestine'. In: Roby Nathanson and Stephan Stetter (eds) (2007), *The Middle East under Fire? EU-Israel Relations in a Region between War and Conflict Resolution*. Berlin, Friedrich Ebert Stiftung, pp. 65–87.
12. Monika Wohlfeld and Oleksandr Pavlyuk (2004), 'The European Neighbourhood Policy and the OSCE', *Challenge Europe Online Journal*, 12.

5
The ENP's Strategic Conception and Design Overstretching the Enlargement Template?

Carmen Gebhard

Introduction

Until very recently, the EU's relationship with its immediate neighbourhood was mainly framed by its enlargement and pre-accession policies. So far, enlargement has not only helped the EU to expand its sphere of strategic influence incrementally, it has also proved to be a strong policy tool for enhancing overall stability and security on the European continent. However, as the enlargement process lately moved toward an EU of 25 and 27 respectively, the European project entered a crucial geopolitical stage. While bringing the EU into direct contact with new areas of strategic interest, the enlargements in 2004 and 2007 also shifted the EU borders to the very eastern – and therefore probably ultimate – limits of Europe, leaving outside a number of states that are unlikely to ever become candidates for formal membership. When introduced in 2003, the European Neighbourhood Policy (ENP) with its underlying concept of a 'Wider Europe' was intended to counter the emergence of new dividing lines, which were likely to result from this post-enlargement setting. It addressed all neighbouring countries of the EU that did not have a mid-term perspective for accession.[1] The vision behind the policy initiative was to stabilize the so-called 'near abroad' to the service of the Union's security and prosperity, in essence by establishing a 'ring of friends' in the European neighbourhood without effectively enlarging the Union any further.

This chapter looks at the strategic foundations of the ENP and seeks to locate it accordingly in the broader context of previous EU policies directed toward the Union's neighbourhood. It investigates the policy solutions developed in the ENP framework, assesses their structural design and relates them to institutional models and policy instruments that the EU has employed in the past to achieve governance impact and compliance in its neighbouring regions, most importantly in the context of enlargement and in the course of the pre-accession processes. This is intended to help to answer the question of whether the ENP's overall strategic conception actually constitutes a policy departure that suitably accounts for the unprecedented challenges posed in the post-enlargement context, and thus, whether and to what extent the policy indeed has the potential of being effective and successful in the long run. In order to contextualise the ENP along these lines, this chapter employs a historical institutionalist perspective, mainly building on the theoretical argument of path-dependency and structural 'stickiness' in institutional development. The chapter is divided into three sections: the outline of the analytical framework, an empirical and a concluding section. It ends on a critical note, pointing at the inherent ambivalence of a policy conception that is intended to achieve 'integration without accession' while relying on the conditionality formula of enlargement.

The ENP as a case for path-dependent stickiness

Many studies analysing the ENP's strategic rationale and institutional set-up avail themselves of the argumentative framework of historical institutionalism, which in fact provides a useful explanatory model for the way institutions and policies emerge, develop and persist over time.[2] The basic assumption of this approach is that the general orientation and structural nature of policies is formed by the course of past developments and thus by strategic and structural choices made earlier in related policy-making processes.[3] Policies are assumed to be 'path-dependent', meaning in the first place that their generation and functioning can only be understood if embedded in the specific historical context.[4] Adding a more substantial claim, historical institutionalists mainly argue that this path-dependency causes constrained or 'sticky' change. It is thought to produce tracks of structural continuity over time, which to a certain extent lock the flow of institutional change.[5] In a next step, this is expected to reduce the overall potential for innovative shifts and factual departures within the policy system concerned.[6] The historical institutionalist approach thus regards policies as institutional instances bounded by political choices taken in

preceding policy-making contexts rather than, as rational institutionalists would suggest, as political tools deliberately established to serve a
specific political objective or tackle a certain strategic challenge.[7]

Applying this theoretical argument to the case assessed here, the
assumption is that concepts and practices established in other EU
'neighbourhood' contexts have had substantive impact on the overall
strategic conception and the structural design eventually adopted for
the 'new' ENP. This sort of 'policy transfer' is expected to become clear
from a comparative assessment of the ENP with the most relevant EU
policy introduced in another context of 'integration beyond borders',
which is – enlargement. In fact, looking back into the recent history of
European integration, one can see that the idea and aim of 'building
security in the European neighbourhood' as it has recently been
voiced in the ENP framework is not totally new to EU foreign policy.
Throughout the last two decades, the internal process of integration
has been accompanied by the progressive extension of the Union as an
established zone of prosperity, stability and security and as a normative centre of gravity to capture many adjacent regions and major parts
of the European continent. In the course of this development, the EU
has managed repeatedly to project its rules, norms and values extra-
territorially, most notably democracy, rule of law, human rights and the
market economy, and to shape its neighbourhood accordingly and in
its own interest.

In principle, the contention that the ENP shows strong path-
dependent traits in respect to the enlargement and pre-accession model,
and that it builds extensively on the enlargement template, is without
controversy among policy analysts and external observers. Scholars
have in fact found numerous different ways of describing the ENP's
alleged path-dependent 'stickiness', asserting for instance that the
European Commission as the main institutional player involved in the
development of the policy had shown a 'strongly mimetic behaviour',
that the ENP had suffered 'from almost reflexive reliance on prior
models',[8] that its overall design had featured 'significant mechanical
borrowing from the enlargement strategies' or that there was immediate
and 'strong evidence for a policy transfer from enlargement'.[9] Apart from
these general assessments, it could even be maintained that one of the
specificities of the ENP was that the very policy-making process behind
it has been *overtly* path- dependent from the beginning. An important
source in this context came in a seminal speech Romano Prodi, then
President of the European Commission, gave in late 2002, sharing his

thoughts on the plans for the establishment of a new 'Proximity Policy' for the EU: 'Let me try to explain what model we should follow. I admit that many of the elements which come to my mind are taken from the enlargement process.'[10]

Also in the key policy documents outlining the rationale and structural methodology of the ENP,[11] there are recurrent references to the 'successful foreign policy instrument' of enlargement, and most significantly, to the strategic objective of 'expanding the benefits of enlargement' to other neighbouring countries.[12] Even though in the first place the 'response to the practical issues posed by proximity and neighbourhood' should be seen 'as separate from the question of EU accession',[13] there was a strong if not striking similarity with the enlargement model inherent to the entire policy argument as well as to the instruments suggested for the operationalisation of the 'new' neighbourhood concept. Kelley has collected a series of very critical anonymous assessments made by Commission officials who were directly involved in the preparation and policy formulation processes: according to one official's point of view 'there [was] nothing new in the ENP except packaging.'[14] Another one claimed 'the ENP [was] nothing more than a diluted version of the enlargement policy' and provided impressive evidence on how obvious the inherent institutional 'stickiness' of the ENP got, reporting that in very early in-house drafts on the policy, 'the name of a recent candidate would sometimes accidentally appear'.[15] While the policy instruments developed in the ENP framework cannot simply be dismissed as cheap or copy-pasted remakes, the imitation of the enlargement template nevertheless remains conspicuously evident.

Wrapping up, from an historical institutionalist perspective, the formative power of the past is relevant to *any* process of policy-making, with only the degree and pattern of path-dependent 'stickiness' varying from case to case. Hence, the major analytical puzzle does not exactly emerge from the question *whether* the ENP has been and is subject to this sort of mechanism or not. Having asserted that there actually *is* significant evidence for this sort of structural linkedness and boundedness through time, the aim is rather to identify the specific traits and the pattern this line of imitation has followed in the case of the ENP. This can help to get an idea of the extent to which the ENP has been shaped by the legacy of past policy strategies and practices, a legacy that has not least been enforced by the enduring success the enlargement model has achieved in reforming and shaping the European neighbourhood.

The ENP and the enlargement template

The EU way of encountering the 'near abroad'?

Looking back into the recent history of European integration, it can be maintained that in recent years, the EU has continuously followed a certain strategic approach when encountering its neighbours and adjacent regions. In fact, when looking at the type and orientation of policy solutions adopted so far in the broader 'neighbourhood' context, it becomes evident that the EU has developed a specific strategy when it comes to addressing its 'near abroad' – be it prospective fellow member states or less engagingly, associates and neighbouring partners. Generally, the aspiration of shaping and transforming the adjacent regions has entered EU foreign policy only since the end of the Cold War, whereas before, the Union's external relations had been known for their apolitical content and distinct reluctance to interfere with the domestic systems of other countries. Since the early 1990s, however, EU rules, norms and values have become 'essential elements' in any institutionalised relationship with third parties, employed as both objectives and conditions for future cooperation, association and integration.[16] The pre-accession procedures in Central and Eastern Europe have vividly illustrated the EU's unique capability of influencing and shaping governance systems beyond its external borders according to its restrictive normative principles, namely through the strategic tool of positive conditionality, which Wallace circumscribed as 'the promise of integration linked to the fulfilment of political, economic and administrative conditions'.[17]

Apart from dominating the accession processes in post-communist Europe, this strategy of 'external governance projection through conditional integration' has not only made its way into the EU Stabilisation and Association Process (SAP) addressing the Balkans but has eventually also intruded the strategic conception of what has been promoted as the 'New Neighbourhood Policy': the ENP. The ENP can in fact be seen as the most recent instance on a continuum of domain-expanding EU policies that all share the strategic logic of conditionality and thus build on the power of carrots and incentives.[18] The adoption of the conditionality principle in the ENP framework in fact also constitutes one of the strongest and most decisive elements of path-dependent 'policy transfer' from the strategic template of enlargement. Analogous to the pre-accession relationships but also to the EU's international association policies, the ENP ties any re-evaluation of the bilateral relationship with a neighbouring partner country to progress in certain priority areas. Political, economic and social change in the countries addressed is sought to be achieved by way of incentives set out in return for reforms and achievements that comply with the basic values of the European project as well as with the structural and economic requirements of full membership.

Another instance of mimetic policy formulation on this strategic level is the ENP's reliance on the principle of socialisation, which again, has also been an essential tool during recent enlargement rounds. As much as in the pre-accession context, socialisation is now intended to effect change in the new European neighbourhood through the creation of reputational pressure, including tactical measures like shaming, persuasion or the support of reform-minded forces to trigger systemic change from within. Last but not least, the ENP has also taken over the principle of differentiated treatment as established during the pre-accession preparations in Central and Eastern Europe. Much like before in the case of enlargement, flexible standards taking into account the basic diversity and uniqueness of each of the partners are again expected to favour the overall success of governance transformation and reform in the respective ENP partner countries. This is done by way of specific Actions Plans for each individual ENP partner country that provide an extensive list of priorities as well as a detailed road map for reform and transformation.

Structural borrowing from enlargement

These structural elements of the ENP strongly evoke the operational and instrumental arrangements that have also been employed in the context of enlargement. On the level of methodology and policy instruments, the ENP's design could in fact hardly be more similar to what had before been established and applied successfully in the relationship with the Central and Eastern European candidate countries. Early issues of the ENP Action Plans were modelled most directly on the Association Agreements used in the pre-accession context, including some explicit references to the Copenhagen criteria.[19] The same holds true for the monitoring and evaluation tools suggested in respect to the 'new' neighbourhood policy: the unilateral reports – termed 'regular country reports' – produced in the ENP context are more than just akin to the 'progress reports' used during the accession negotiations. Just as in the enlargement context, these annual reports are also employed for the purpose of socialisation, for example to praise progress or to shame ENP partners for lacking reform or violation of human rights.

An important source of path-dependency can be found on the administrative level and the level of human resources, which in fact constitutes the most direct instance of 'policy transfer' from enlargement. As a matter of fact, several key officials now working on the ENP also have a distinct enlargement related background, and most teams working together on the preparation of one specific candidate have been retained and assigned together to deal with one of the ENP countries. 'Major parts of the Commission's personnel resources were simply shifted from the enlargement to the ENP corner'.[20] Employing the historical institutionalist terminology, this enormous transfer of know-how and people could be seen as 'sticky potential' likely to enhance a path-dependent and self-reinforcing process of institutional continuity over time. From a practical point of view, this obvious lack of major regroupment on the lowest level of single individuals involved in the process of implementation might have reinforced the above-outlined strategic reliance of the ENP on past models and solutions. By suggesting established tools and instruments for the realisation of an allegedly 'new' policy approach, and by appointing a body of staff that has been consigned to do very similar technical work over years but in a completely different geopolitical context, the makers of the ENP have most likely determined the extent to which the new policy conception could actually depart from the ethos of enlargement, and thereby, account for the essential difference of 'integrating *without* enlarging'.

The conditionality formula reloaded – what is 'new' about the 'new offer'?

In its 'Wider Europe Communication of 2003, the European Commission promoted a 'New Vision and a New Offer' for the post-enlargement neighbourhood.[21] As pointed out above, the ENP's strategic conception is – just as the enlargement policy used to be – fundamentally based on the principle of conditionality, and thus, on the conditional use of incentives. Conditionality may be seen as the quid pro quo principle of any policy of the EU aiming at the outside projection of values, policy standards and beliefs, since it is key to the compliance strategy lying behind these policy models. The 'New Offer' presented in the ENP framework thus contains the core substance that the conditionality method builds upon in this case: the incentives for compliance with EU values and those parts of the *acquis* that ought to be shared in the ENP framework.[22]

The incentives offered 'in return for concrete progress demonstrating shared values and effective implementation of political, economic and institutional reforms' are numerous.[23] They include the offer of a stake into the internal market and the expansion of regulatory structures, with the mid-term perspective of moving beyond cooperation to a significant degree of integration, and toward preferential trading relations, market opening and the reduction of trade barriers. Moreover, the catalogue of carrots counts in the perspective for lawful migration and movement of persons, ensuring that the new external border would not become or remain a barrier to trade, social and cultural exchange or regional cooperation, for example through the wider application of visa-free regimes. Another ENP incentive is the intensified cooperation to prevent and combat common security threats, prioritising issues like terrorism, trans-national organised crime, customs and taxation fraud, nuclear and environmental hazards as well as communicable diseases. This also includes cooperation on judicial and police cooperation, and the development of mutual legal assistance. The ENP furthermore offers the prospect for greater political engagement in conflict prevention and crisis management in the neighbouring countries concerned, including post-conflict security arrangements as well as additional funding for reconstruction and development. Another incentive set out in this context is concerned with the promotion of human rights, intensified cultural cooperation and measures for the enhancement of mutual understanding, such as dialogue, free exchange of ideas, contribution to the development of a flourishing civil society, establishment of student and professional exchange programmes, governance and human right trainings, twinning opportunities, etc. The catalogue also contains incentives in the area of transport, energy and telecommunication together with the prospect of integration into the European research area, including new regional dimensions for existing programmes like Galileo or Trans-European Networks. New instruments for investment promotion and protection aiming at the enhancement of a more stable and stronger climate for domestic and foreign investment are listed as much as the promise for a continued fight against corruption, the strengthening of the rule of law and the independence of the judiciary. Additional carrots are offered in relation to the inclusion in the global trading system, with WTO membership building the integral part of a positive economic agenda.

When trying to interpret this set of incentives essentially contained in the ENP's 'New Offer' from a historical institutionalist point of view, two main characteristics become evident. Firstly, most of the points suggest a mere continuation of already existing systems of bilateral cooperation, which as such would not require the specific framework of a policy as comprehensive and ambitious as the ENP. Others in turn again evoke elements of the conditionality system employed in the context of enlargement. What is then actually 'new' about the offer? Despite a few minor elements of adaptation, the most significant, and at the same time, the most obvious novelty about the ENP's 'offer' appears to be that the possibility of accession is clearly ruled out 'at this stage of the game'.[24] What is genuinely new is in fact the missing membership perspective. A country that is willing and able to comply with the common values may – no more and no less – 'come as close to the Union as it can without being a member'.[25] Lavenex and Schimmelfennig found a particularly mild description for the political significance of this limitation stating that 'The ENP does indeed promote enlargement – albeit only at the level of selected policy areas and without access to the core decision-making bodies of the EU'.[26]

There has been an extensive debate both within the European Commission and in academia, whether in the context of this 'New Offer', the carrot for the new neighbours was only smaller than in the pre-accession context, or whether the carrot was in fact missing altogether. Meloni, for instance, rightly pointed at the ambivalent nature of the conditionality deal at stake.[27] As a matter of fact, the ENP is asking the partner countries to engage in a particularly expensive and troublesome process of normative and legislative approximation, while the reward set out to them in return is all but clear, and absolutely non-committal. Accession conditionality used to be extremely successful in 'locking in democratic transformation and in ensuring the adoption of the *acquis communautaire* in the New Member States'.[28] However, the criteria employed in the context of enlargement conditionality were strictly linked to accession, and as such, were equal to reaching the 'capacity to assume the obligations of membership'.[29] The question remains whether the 'new' ENP offer of 'more than partnership and less than membership' is really able to compensate the power of attraction that the membership perspective once used to provide?[30] Prodi himself posed a similar albeit rhetorical question at an early stage of the ENP policy-making process, obviously trying to avoid calling the membership prospect an 'incentive' per se, and terming it a 'goal' instead: 'The goal of accession is certainly the most powerful stimulus for reform we can think of. But why should a less ambitious goal not have *some* effect? A substantive and workable concept of proximity *would* have a positive effect [original emphases].'[31]

Prodi did not offer a convincing answer to support the viability of his ambition to 'extend the area of stability without immediate enlargement of the Union'. Interestingly, the substantial power of the membership incentive was also emphasised in the 'Wider Europe' Communication, which in fact was to defend and legitimise the introduction of a diluted version of the old catalogue of incentives: 'The incentive for reform created by the membership prospect has proved to be strong. Enlargement has unarguably been the EU's most successful foreign policy instrument.'[32]

It could be observed that, at a later stage, this sort of clear statement gradually disappeared from the ENP documents and the political declarations by the Commission; yet the evidence of an inherently ambivalent compliance strategy remained as much as the unconvincing structural reliance on what used to build the basis for the more promising model of 'integration through prospective membership'.

Elements of change and adaptation

Given this strong evidence of structural borrowing from previous policy models, it should hardly be surprising that the rate of factual changes in the overall policy structure and set-up has to remain poor. Indeed, there are not many instances of modification or even innovation identifiable in the concept and making of the ENP. Recalling the idea of the policy continuum and the analytical argument that from a historical institutionalist and procedural point of view, the ENP should not be regarded as a new, entirely detached and stand-alone policy construct, we might expect two types of change: on the one hand, some elements of change might become evident from a direct comparison of the ENP to previous policy concepts and unveil instances of change and adaptation introduced in the course of the making of the new policy. Another type of change in turn might involve adaptations made ex post or on an ad hoc basis, and become manifest when assessing the implementation practice of the policy as well as analysing the respective follow-up documents. Interestingly, the ENP provides one, and no more, no less, example for each of these two types of change.

While there is no relevant strategic or formal departure from the enlargement template, the introduction of a new financial instrument for the ENP has to be regarded as a genuine innovation. It fundamentally revolutionised the old established funding procedures for regional cooperation programmes. In July 2003, the Commission formally launched the concept of a New Neighbourhood Instrument intending to enhance coordination and transparency in the field and seeking to solve the problems caused by the variety of financial programmes at hand.[33] It suggested a two-stage approach for the gradual reorganisation of EU external assistance within the catchment area of the ENP. After a transitional phase (2004–6) involving the launch of combined 'Neighbourhood Programmes', in January 2007, the European Neighbourhood and Partnership Instrument (ENPI) was put into place in order to bring convergence to the set of existing cross-border funding schemes.[34] The advantages resulting from the ENPI were in fact already evident during the first phase of implementation, and they are expected to become even more salient once all programmes have been consistently merged under the ENPI umbrella.[35]

Kelley in turn identified a particularly catchy example for the second type of change, that is of instances of modification introduced post hoc in the course of the implementation process.[36] She marked that since the early working drafts of the neighbourhood initiative, the language of conditionality has been significantly toned down. Initially, the Commission appeared to opt for a strict form of conditionality, using words like 'benchmarks' or 'targets' that were to be met as 'necessary preconditions' for specific rewards and efforts.[37] The 'Wider Europe' Communication still contained the clear statement that 'engagement should be conditional [...], setting clear and public objectives and benchmarks'. The following communication in turn clearly tried to avoid the hard elements of conditionality and rather employed terms like 'incentives', 'ambitions' or the 'degree of commitment.' The official policy of conditionality was then that 'the level of ambition of the EU's relationships with its neighbours will take into account the extent to which these values are effectively shared'.[38] Accordingly, also the rhetoric applied in the ENP Action Plans became remarkably 'softer' over time, as for instance evident in the case of Ukraine, where the Commission emphasised that 'the pace of progress of the relationship will acknowledge fully Ukraine's efforts and concrete achievements in meeting commitments to common values'.[39] Generally, however, this does not constitute any major innovation, which would, in a next step, alter or strengthen the basic strategic conception behind the ENP. This way of downplaying the importance of the factual decision of the ENP countries to align with the *acquis* rather adds another flaw to the overall picture.[40]

Overstretching the enlargement template?

Despite the apparent continuities between the ENP and enlargement as well as other established policies of the EU directed toward the Union's neighbourhood, there are important factors that turn the ENP into a special case. The catchment area it addresses is larger than the EU territory itself, and the range of countries that the policy seeks to lump together in one single superordinate policy framework is more diverse and structurally disparate than any other group of states or region addressed in other comparable EU policies.[41] Looking at the normative aspirations and the overall strategic objective behind the policy of 'integrating without enlarging', the ENP can be seen as the most ambitious plan of external governance projection the Union has envisaged so far. Apart from the grand vision behind the policy, there is a unique challenge the EU has to face at this point of its strategic, territorial and geopolitical development. In fact, the circumstances that the ENP is confronted with differ greatly from previous settings of 'governance export through integration'. Today, the EU faces the unprecedented challenge of having to institute and govern friendly neighbourhood relations across ultimate borders whereas before, every instance of expansion into the adjacent regions had merely brought new *preliminary* neighbours – and in a sense, future fellow members.[42]

While in the enlargement context, the notion of 'neighbourhood' used to denote some kind of intermediate status for prospective member states in the ENP framework, it has become much of a fatal label with unpromising implications for the 'neighbours' concerned. The question arises of why structurally the ENP has been designed on the existing enlargement model while today's strategic circumstances of having to deal with an 'ultimate neighbourhood' are clearly not comparable to the pre-accession setting in Central and Eastern Europe. Established policy solutions are in fact being translated into an entirely different geostrategic and political context, but are nevertheless expected to generate equally positive effects. How can the extent of structural conservatism behind the ENP be explained against the background of the *unprecedented* strategic challenges it is meant to tackle?

The classic model of enlargement has clearly passed the test in its original context, where, in fact, it has proved to be a strong tool for the sustainable enhancement of prosperity, stability and security on the European continent. When looking at the continuation of the policy model in the form of the ENP, it becomes clear that this success must have influenced remarkably the way policy-makers have decided to frame the new neighbourhood setting politically. Assessment of the strategic conception and the policy instruments developed in the framework of the ENP has shown that there is a strong reliance on the well-established model of enlargement. In many different respects, the ENP has been modelled directly on the pre-accession procedures employed in the Central and Eastern European context. It may be seen as the direct result of an institutional path continued over time. It constitutes much of the material outcome of the attempt to replicate the prominent policy formula of 'eliciting compliant transformation in adjacent areas by way of conditionality and socialization' and continuing the success story of the model through stages of decisive political change, or rather, notwithstanding this change. In many different respects, the ENP may thus be said to constitute a sort of diluted policy variation, or what Vahl called an overstretched and wannabe 'ersatz enlargement'.[43]

The ENP: structural conservatism and sensitivity to change

Wrapping up, in what way does the historical institutionalist strategy of tracing policy developments over time offer a helpful analytical toolkit for the assessment of whether the ENP has the potential to live up to outside expectations and strategic challenges in the long run? The link between the path-dependency argument and the potential inadequacy of a policy strategy lies in the various potential ways the alleged 'stickiness' or 'boundedness through time' described earlier in the chapter is thought to impact on the overall development of a policy model. On the one hand, path-dependent continuation directly influences current policy choices; on the other, this 'stickiness' also changes the costs and benefits associated with alternative political strategies.[44] Therefore, path-dependency has to be seen as a mechanism or 'way to narrow conceptually the choice set and link decision-making through time'.[45] Accordingly, Kay defines policy-making as a 'process all about sequenced choices' – choices about action or inaction, and between different policy instruments, procedural methodologies and strategic conceptions.[46] As North put it – 'at every step along the way, there are choices that provide [...] real alternatives'.[47] Path-dependent sequences can thus be said to constrain the strategic view on these alternatives by impacting on and potentially constraining future choice sets, and thus, the power and ability of a policy-making system to produce innovative policy solutions.

'Each step along a particular path produces consequences which make that path more attractive for the next round. As such effects begin to accumulate, they generate a powerful virtuous (or vicious) cycle of self-reinforcing activity'.[48] The potential 'viciousness' that Pierson is alluding to lies in the increasing probability of 'suboptimal policy outcomes'.[49] Accordingly, the ENP could be seen as the outcome of a sequence of institutional choices locked in a certain and, in view of the new strategic challenges currently faced, potentially unfavourable path. However, it is not the specific path that is to be perceived as 'wrong' or 'unfavourable'; it is rather the structural conservatism itself that risks reducing the effectiveness and success of the policy in the long run. Geopolitical reality presents a continuous challenge to the performative power of any policy. From this point of view, sensitivity to change has to be regarded as a key quality with major significance for the political and strategic adequacy of any respective policy. Evidence for this sort of sensitivity is likely to be found in the timeliness of policy choices and in the general flexibility of a policy system to adapt to changes in the overall strategic environment. Looking at the specific case of the ENP, it becomes clear that the mechanisms by which it has repeatedly been tried before to 'project rules beyond borders' have largely been preserved even though the circumstances for action have changed considerably.

The nature of the 'neighbourhood' relationship has changed in respect to enlargement: in contrast to the candidate countries, the ENP partners and the EU share a very different history of cooperation. Before launching the ENP, the EU has already had a decade-long active economic relationship with most of the countries. However, instead of proving an asset, the experiences had in these contexts rather constitute a bad legacy, since until now, most bilateral efforts have largely remained ineffective. Moreover, the recipients of 'external action directed towards the neighbourhood' have also changed in both quantitative and qualitative terms. The bilateral relationships have a lower starting point as a result of the stage of maturity of the ENP partners in respect to the values promoted by the policy. They partly face entirely new challenges and combinations of problems where the experience with post-communist transformation processes that the Union has gathered during the recent enlargement rounds is of little help. Not least, there is also a clear lack of positive competition between the ENP countries. While in the enlargement context the inherent competitive dynamism between the Central and Eastern European candidate countries used to constitute an important favourable factor, this effect is almost entirely missing within the ENP framework. The group of states that has been lumped together in the ENP is simply too diverse to allow this sort of dynamic. What generally appears inherent to the strategic conception of the ENP is a strong reliance on the belief that despite these very different circumstances the 'enlargement formula' may be replicated to the largest possible extent. When designing the ENP, the policy-makers in fact failed to innovate the strategic conception of enlargement to the extent of making the 'appropriate adaptations', and thus, to give evidence of their general sensitivity to change.[50]

Compliance and credibility

The logic of exclusion which 'integration without enlargement' and the idea of an 'ultimate neighbourhood' inevitably entail must be expected to have major repercussions on the way the Union will by seen by the very ones left 'outside', and consequently, on their readiness to comply with a set of rules that – at best – may lead them to 'everything but institutions'. The creation of the ENP as an umbrella policy to address both the EU's newly gained neighbourhood in the East and the entire group of Mediterranean partners has considerably raised the overall visibility of EU external action and, as a result, made its performative power in this respect subject to increased critical examination by external observers, not least all the third parties involved. Third-party perception is likely to have a decisive impact on the EU's overall power of attraction, which in turn, will determine the ENP's long-term success.

What does the specific ENP case tell us about the general ability of the EU to produce up-to-date policy solutions for the most crucial geostrategic challenges it is facing? Moreover, what implications may the apparent strategic inadequacy of the ENP be expected to have for the EU's role on the international scene and its credibility as a partner and global actor? The credibility issue evokes earlier discussions about the capability-expectations gap in the context of the EU's, or then rather the EC's, foreign political actorness.[51] While in the early 1990s, this 'gap' largely resulted from the outside load (often irrationally) imposed onto the Community 'following the Single Market and the Intergovernmental Conferences of 1991', the Union now appears to be in a situation where external expectations *and* self-proclaimed ambitions to an equal extent produce pressure on the EU to perform credibly and effectively in the global arena.

The European project is not expected only by others to generate appropriate outputs that 'expand the benefits of integration to the world' and, thereby, to live up politically to its given normative and economic power. To a very large extent, the EU has also 'talked itself up' into this exposed situation. The ENP has been harshly, and in most cases rightly, criticised for its lack of performative power in conflict resolution, most significantly, in the context of border conflicts in the European neighbourhood;[52] its weak performance in respect to the exertion of influence on autocratic regimes;[53] its oscillation between normative priorities and obvious strategic interests;[54] budgetary constraints and competing regional priorities within the policy framework[55] and, most importantly, for the structural weakness of its system of conditionality, given the absence of the membership carrot'.[56] In fact, looking at the policy tools produced in the ENP context, and taking stock of their potential effectiveness in view of the challenges faced, one could say that the European project has again – and probably more than ever – reached a 'point where it is not capable of fulfilling the expectations held of it'[57] and, most significantly, where the expectations it has recently encouraged by way of florid declarations and self-affirmative statements largely exceed its current performance capability.

What one could hold against this criticism is the aspect of timing. In fact, the ENP could certainly be regarded as – just what it is – a policy with a distinct long-term orientation, implying that the material gains are not yet conceivable but are to be expected in the long run. However, what should be discussed more openly is the overall suitability of the approach itself. Has the immediate and intuitive post-enlargement reflex actually led to a viable and useful set of policy solutions? Have the policy-makers taken appropriate account of the new geopolitical circumstances while constructing the new policy? Are the available policy tools capable of balancing the ENP's inherent logic of exclusion? What arguments support the distinct optimism that the 'enlargement formula' is expansible to any other strategic context and, most significantly, to a context where a very different political outcome is intended? Can conditionality be expected to work if the membership incentive is absent? The ENP partners might not be motivated to undertake domestic reforms if the prospect of accession is ruled out from the very beginning. The obvious reliance on the persistence and continuation of previous strategic trajectories has indeed no consistent or rational foundation. The ENP offers a set of weak tools, a softened and diluted version of the enlargement model, while the nature and level of challenges to be tackled in the European neighbourhood have reached an all-time high in terms of complexity and geopolitical disruption.

In 2007, the European Commission defined the very challenge the EU has to face: 'what is at stake, is the EU's ability to develop an external policy complementary to enlargement that is effective in promoting transformation and reform.'[58] It appears noteworthy that the necessity of *developing* such a policy was being asserted four years after the ENP's launch and, essentially, at a point where the outcomes of implementation should have been presented. However, apart from this very general awareness, there is no serious evidence for any efforts within the European Commission to revise the global approach of the policy, let alone to recalibrate it altogether. The ENP implementation process is about to enter its sixth year; in its first years, the institutional construct has been adapted and improved in some respects. However, the general inexpedience of the strategic conception behind it has remained.

While the Commission machinery is conducting implementation business as usual, the whole undertaking risks sliding into a failure on a grand scale. A failing neighbourhood policy would have decisive impact on the credibility of the EU as a global strategic actor and would significantly compromise its international standing and acceptance. The Union has no sort of depository of international legitimacy, nor does the course of global developments – in the European neighbourhood and elsewhere – appear to be moving into a clearly favourable direction to provide a window of opportunity for the Union to catch up with the challenges.

Notes

1. The ENP was initially also directed toward Russia. However, in May 2003, the EU and Russia agreed on the creation of the so-called 'Four Common Spaces' (common economic space; common space of freedom, security and justice; common space of cooperation in the field of external security and a common space of research and education, including cultural aspects, in the framework of the bilateral Partnership and Cooperation Agreement. For a critical discussion, see M. Emerson (2005), 'EU-Russia. Four Common Spaces and the Profliferation of the Fuzzy', *CEPS Policy Brief*, 71, May 2005.
2. J. Kelley (2006), 'New Wine in Old Wineskins. Promoting Political Reforms Through the New European Neighbourhood Policy', *Journal of Common Market Studies*, 44 (1), pp. 29–55. A. Magen (2006), 'The Shadow of Enlargement. Can the European Neighbourhood Policy Achieve Compliance?' *Columbia Journal of European Law*, 12 (2), pp. 383–427.
3. P. Pierson (1993), 'When Effect Becomes Cause: Policy Feedback and Political Change', *World Politics*, 45, pp. 595–628.
4. A. Kay (2005), 'A Critique of the Use of Path Dependency in Policy Studies', *Public Administration*, 83 (3), pp. 553–71.
5. P. Pierson (2000), 'Increasing Returns, Path Dependence, and the Study of Politics', *American Political Science Review*, 94 (2), pp. 51–74.
6. The notion of 'policy system' refers to the superordinate framework of a specific policy. A policy system is thought to embrace a set of interrelated policy subsystems (Baumgartner and Jones (2002), *Policy Dynamics*. London: Chicago University Press, p. 14). In line with this definition, the ENP is embedded in the wider system of EU foreign policy, including all external dimensions of Union and Community action, and most importantly, including all policies of the EU that in the widest sense address its geographical neighbourhood.

7. P. Pierson (1998), 'The Path of European Integration. A Historical Institutionalist Analysis' in W. Sandholtz and A. Stone Sweet (eds), *European Integration and Supranational Governance*. Oxford: Oxford University Press. M. Blyth (2002), 'Institutions and Ideas' in D. Marsh and G. Stoker (eds), *Theory and Methods in Political Science*, 2nd edn. Basingstoke and New York: Palgrave Macmillan.

8. A. Magen (2006), 'The Shadow of Enlargement. Can the European Neighbourhood Policy Achieve Compliance?' *Columbia Journal of European Law*, 12 (2), pp. 383–427.

9. J. Kelley (2006) 'New Wine in Old Wineskins. Promoting Political Reforms Through the New European Neighbourhood Policy', *Journal of Common Market Studies*, 44 (1), p. 32.

10. R. Prodi (2002), 'A Wider Europe – A Proximity Policy as the Key to Stability', Speech at the 6th ECSA World Conference (Brussels).

11. Commission of the European Communities (2003a), Communication from the Commission, *Wider Europe – Neighbourhood: A New Framework for Relations with our Eastern and Southern Neighbours* COM(2003) 104 final, Brussels, 11 March 2003. Commission of the European Communities (2004), Communication from the Commission, *European Neighbourhood Policy, Strategy Paper*, COM(2004) 373 final, p. 3, Brussels, 12 May 2004.

12. In the 'Wider Europe' Communication (COM(2004) 104) as well as in the ENP 'Strategy Paper' (COM(2004) 373).

13. Commission of the European Communities (2003a), Communication from the Commission, *Wider Europe – Neighbourhood: A New Framework for Relations with our Eastern and Southern Neighbours* COM(2003) 104 final, Brussels, 11 March 2003.

14. J. Kelley (2006), 'New Wine in Old Wineskins. Promoting Political Reforms Through the New European Neighbourhood Policy', *Journal of Common Market Studies*, 44 (1), pp. 29–55.

15. Ibid. p. 33.

16. F. Schimmelfennig (2007), 'Europeanization Beyond Europe', *Living Reviews in European Governance*, II (1).

17. W. Wallace (2003), 'Looking After the European Neighbourhood. Responsibilities for the EU-25', LSE European Foreign Policy Unit Working Paper, 3.

18. A. Magen (2006), 'The Shadow of Enlargement. Can the European Neighbourhood Policy Achieve Compliance?', *Columbia Journal of European Law*, 12 (2), pp. 383–427. Recent policy developments in the context of the Eastern Partnership of the EU and the Union for the Mediterranean have also started to point into a similar strategic direction. While in neither of the two cases conditionality has been mentioned overtly, the idea of 'stabilizing through attraction' has been present at all times.

19. M. Vahl (2005), 'Models for the European Neighbourhood Policy. The European Economic Area and the Northern Dimension', CEPS Working Document, 218.

20. J. Kelley (2006) 'New Wine in Old Wineskins. Promoting Political Reforms Through the New European Neighbourhood Policy', *Journal of Common Market Studies*, 44 (1), p. 32.

21. Commission of the European Communities (2003a), Communication from the Commission, *Wider Europe – Neighbourhood: A New Framework for Relations with our Eastern and Southern Neighbours* COM(2003) 104 final, Brussels, 11 March 2003.
22. G. Bonvicini (2006), 'The European Neighbourhood Policy and its Linkage with European Security', in F. Tassinari, P. Joenniemi and U. Jacobsen (eds), *Wider Europe. Nordic and Baltic Lessons to Post-Enlargement Europe.* Copenhagen: Danish Institute for International Studies.
23. Commission of the European Communities (2003a), Communication from the Commission, *Wider Europe – Neighbourhood: A New Framework for Relations with our Eastern and Southern Neighbours* COM(2003) 104 final, Brussels, 11March 2003.
24. R. Prodi (2002), 'A Wider Europe – A Proximity Policy as the Key to Stability', Speech at the 6th ECSA World Conference (Brussels).
25. Commission of the European Communities (2003a), Communication from the Commission, *Wider Europe – Neighbourhood: A New Framework for Relations with our Eastern and Southern Neighbours* COM(2003) 104 final, Brussels, 11 March 2003.
26. S. Lavenex and F. Schimmelfennig (2006), 'Relations with the Wider Europe', *Journal of Common Market Studies*, Annual Review, 45 (1), pp. 143.
27. G. Meloni (2007), 'Who's My Neighbour?' *European Political Economy Review*, 7, pp. 24–37.
28. S. Lavenex and F. Schimmelfennig (2006), 'Relations with the Wider Europe', *Journal of Common Market Studies*, Annual Review, 45 (1), p. 138.
29. G. Meloni (2007), 'Who's My Neighbour?' *European Political Economy Review*, 7, p. 31.
30. R. Prodi (2002), 'A Wider Europe – A Proximity Policy as the Key to Stability', Speech at the 6th ECSA World Conference (Brussels).
31. Ibid.
32. Commission of the European Communities (2003a), Communication from the Commission, *Wider Europe – Neighbourhood: A New Framework for Relations with our Eastern and Southern Neighbours* COM(2003) 104 final, Brussels, 11 March 2003.
33. Commission of the European Communities (2003b), Communication from the Commission, *Paving the Way for a New Neighbourhood Instrument*, COM(2003) 393.final, Brussels 1 July 2003.
34. Since 1 January 2007, the ENPI replaces all existing programmes, including INTERREG, PHARE and CARDS as well as TACIS and MEDA. The official name of the new financial instrument has been changed from 'New Neighbourhood Instrument' (NNI) into 'European Neighbourhood and Partnership Instrument' (ENPI) in order to mark the inclusion of Russia. Even though Russia decided not to be part of the overall ENP, and instead to opt for the formally different, but practically similar strategic partnership with the EU, the ENPI has been extended to Russian partners as well. See also note 1.
35. N. Copsey and A. Mayhew (2005), *Neighbourhood Policy and Ukraine*. Brighton: Sussex European Institute.

36. J. Kelley (2006), 'New Wine in Old Wineskins. Promoting Political Reforms Through the New European Neighbourhood Policy', *Journal of Common Market Studies*, 44 (1), pp. 29–55.
37. Commission of the European Communities (2003a), Communication from the Commission, *Wider Europe – Neighbourhood: A New Framework for Relations with our Eastern and Southern Neighbours* COM(2003) 104 final, Brussels, 11 March 2003.
38. Ibid.
39. Commission of the European Communities (2004), 'EU/Ukraine Action Plan', available at http://ec.europa.eu/world/enp/pdf/action_plans/ukraine_enp_ap_final_en.pdf
40. G. Meloni (2007), 'Who's My Neighbour?' *European Political Economy Review*, 7, pp. 24–37.
41. The ENP catchment area amounts to approx. 7.1 million m^2 excluding Russia (EU territory: 4.4 million m^2) and involves a population of 280 million. Today, the ENP covers 16 countries including Algeria, Armenia, Azerbaijan, Belarus, Egypt, Georgia, Israel, Jordan, Lebanon, Libya, Moldova, Morocco, the Palestinian Authority, Syria, Tunisia and Ukraine.
42. S. Lavenex (2004), 'EU External Governance in Wider Europe', *Journal of European Public Policy*, pp. 680–700.
43. M. Vahl (2005), 'Models for the European Neighbourhood Policy. The European Economic Area and the Northern Dimension', *CEPS Working Document*, 218, p. 9.
44. P. Pierson (1993), 'When Effect Becomes Cause: Policy Feedback and Political Change', *World Politics*, 45, pp. 595–628.
45. D.C. North (1990), *Institutions, Institutional Change and Economic Performance*. Cambridge: Cambridge University Press, p. 99.
46. A. Kay (2005), 'A Critique of the Use of Path Dependency in Policy Studies', *Public Administration*, 83 (3), p. 556.
47. D.C. North (1990), *Institutions, Institutional Change and Economic Performance*. Cambridge: Cambridge University Press, p. 98.
48. Ibid., p. 253.
49. A. Kay (2005), 'A Critique of the Use of Path Dependency in Policy Studies', *Public Administration*, 83 (3), p. 554.
50. C. Knill and A. Lenschow (1998), 'Change as "Appropriate Adaptation". Administrative Adjustment to European Environmental Policy in Britain and Germany', European Integration Online Papers, 2 (1).
51. C. Hill (1993), 'The Capability-Expectations Gap, or Conceptualizing Europe's International Role', *Journal of Common Market Studies*, 31 (3), p. 315.
52. N. Tocci (2004), 'Conflict Resolution in the European Neighbourhood. The Role of the EU as a Framework and Actor', EUI Working Papers, 2004/29. F. Cameron (2006), 'The European Neighbourhood Policy as a Conflict Prevention Tool', EPC Issue Paper, 47. R. Gillespie (2006), 'This Stupid Little Island. A Neighbourhood Confrontation in the Western Mediterranean', *International Politics*, 43 (1), pp. 110–32.
53. V. Poselsky (2004), The Frontiers of Europe in the Light of the Wider Europe's Strategy', *European Political Economy Review*, 2 (1), pp. 251–267. M. Cremona

and C. Hillion (2006), 'L'Union fait la Force? Potential and Limitations of the European Neighbourhood Policy as an Integrated EU Foreign and Security Policy', Sussex European Institute Seminar Paper Series, I.

54. S. Lavenex and F. Schimmelfennig (2006), 'Relations with the Wider Europe', *Journal of Common Market Studies*, Annual Review, 45 (1), pp. 137–54.

55. A. Missiroli (2007), 'The ENP Three Years On: Where From – And Where Next?', EPC Policy Brief.

56. J. Kelley (2006), 'New Wine in Old Wineskins. Promoting Political Reforms Through the New European Neighbourhood Policy', *Journal of Common Market Studies*, 44 (1), pp. 29–55.

57. C. Hill (1993), 'The Capability-Expectations Gap, or Conceptualizing Europe's International Role', *Journal of Common Market Studies*, 31 (3), pp. 305–28.

58. Commission of the European Communities (2007), Communication from the Commission, *A Strong European Neighbourhood Policy*, COM(2007) 183 final, Brussels, 18 April 2007.

Part II

Making Sense of the European Neighbourhood Policy – Contextualising a Policy Departure

6
Lessons from the Balkans: The ENP as a Possible Conflict Management Tool?

Stefan Wolff and Annemarie Peen Rodt

Introduction

The 2004 and 2007 enlargements moved the European Union (EU) closer – geographically, politically and security-wise – to a number of frozen and violent ethnic conflicts in its so-called 'new neighbourhood'. These conflicts include ongoing disputes in Israel/Palestine, Lebanon, Algeria, Moldova (Transnistria), Armenia/Azerbaijan (Nagorno-Karabakh), Georgia (Abkhazia and South Ossetia), Morocco/Western Sahara, Egypt, Ukraine, Jordan and Syria. EU foreign policy-makers have in recent developments of the Common Foreign and Security Policy (CFSP) and Common European Security and Defence Policy (CESDP)[1] stressed the importance of managing these conflicts. With the 2003 European Security Strategy and the launch of the 2004 European Neighbourhood Policy (ENP) the Union explicitly articulated its intention to take a more active stance in the management of violent ethnic conflicts in the ENP area (and beyond).

The failed European attempts to handle the violent disintegration of Yugoslavia in the 1990s, were, according to the large majority of CFSP scholars, the first real push for European foreign policy-makers more actively to seek to develop a common EU approach to dealing with violent ethnic conflicts in the Union's near abroad. The atrocities in the Western Balkans had illustrated the inadequacy of the tools available to the Union at the time and left the EU embarrassed. After NATO came to the rescue of the EU over Kosovo for the second time in 1999, the EU was eager to develop its own crisis management capabilities, and consequently did so with the Yugoslav experience in mind and reflecting past and present failures, as well as a few successes, in the Western Balkans. The EU's approach to violent ethnic conflicts thus arguably being born and bred in the Balkans, and the Union's experience in this region is therefore an important aspect of any debate on the EU's potential future global role as a conflict manager. This chapter therefore examines the EU's capabilities and recent track record in dealing with the ethnic conflicts in the Western Balkans in order to assess what, if any, lessons can be learnt from the Balkan experience and to consider whether the ENP could potentially serve as a tool for the management of violent ethnic conflict in the rest of Union's 'new neighbourhood' and beyond.

The EU's early experiences of ethnic conflict management

The European Union as a collective of its member states has been concerned with ethnic conflicts since its very beginning. On the one hand, the EU, and its predecessor organisations, has always prided itself in being, among other things, a community of values in which democracy, human rights and the rule of law take on concrete meaning for the benefit of all its citizens, regardless of ethnic, linguistic or religious background. This normative perspective has informed the EU's non-discrimination directives and policies, and has thus been one instrument of the management of minority-majority relations within EU member states. Yet its success in addressing ethnic conflicts effectively within the Union itself, and even more so beyond its boundaries, has been limited. Conflicts in Northern Ireland, the Basque Country and Corsica have persisted at different levels of violence and intensity, causing loss of human life and material damage. The states directly affected by these conflicts, and other countries outside the present boundaries of the EU, share a second area of concern in relation to ethnic conflicts – security. This relates to the physical security of both individual citizens and the state, but also involves a wide range of other dimensions of security, for example ethnic conflict has immediate and longer-term consequences for socio-economic security, to name but one.

The conflicts within the EU as it existed before the 2004 enlargement were relatively well contained and did not pose major threats to the security and stability of the EU as a whole, but were rather perceived as internal matters not to be dealt with at the EU level. The perception of far graver threats in post-communist Europe, large parts of which had aspired to EU membership since the early 1990s, prompted the EU to adopt a much more proactive policy of managing ethnic conflicts outside its boundaries than within them. This approach was deemed necessary because of the greater risk posed by such actual and potential conflicts in likely new member states and the EU's 'new neighbourhood'. It was made possible as a consequence of the collapse of communism, the end of the Cold War division of Europe and the greater political and economic leverage that the EU gained over these respective countries. EU-internal conflicts had remained relatively contained for decades and member states facing such threats generally resented and actively blocked EU involvement in their management,[2] but conflicts outside the Union were perceived as potentially far more dangerous in the short-term as well as in the potential longer-term of their becoming EU-internal conflicts by way of enlargement. This resulted in the EU beginning to create a framework of policies and institutions for the management of ethnic conflict that was primarily aimed at non-member states. It became most closely associated with the CFSP and increasingly also with the EU's enlargement policy, through the Stabilisation and Association Process for the Western Balkans, which effectively allowed the EU to impose conditions on candidate states that it did not implement on its own territories, and more recently through the ENP, which explicitly states the Union's ambition to 'reinforce stability and security and contribute to efforts of conflict resolution [in the ENP area].[3]

Institutional reform and capability-building: the EU after its Balkan failures

Based on its respect for state sovereignty and its own experience of ethnic conflict, the initial response of the EC (later EU) to the Yugoslav crisis in the early 1990s was to attempt to contain the problem by seeking to keep Yugoslavia intact. European countries faced with ethnic conflicts of their own feared that if they supported the dissolution of Yugoslavia, this might encourage ethnic minorities elsewhere to push for independence. The Union therefore sought a neutral role as negotiator between the belligerent parties and was reluctant to recognise any one side as the aggressor. These negotiation efforts failed repeatedly, as violence broke out first in Slovenia and later in Croatia, Bosnia and Kosovo.[4] The EU's further failures to respect its self-set criteria for the recognition of Slovenian and Croatian independence and its inability (along with that of the rest of the international community) to prevent the increase in, and extent of, the violence and large-scale disasters such as the 1995 atrocities in the 'UN protectorate' of Srebrenica,[5] illustrate the continued failures of EU conflict management efforts in the former Yugoslavia throughout the 1990s.[6] These failures were largely the result of the EU's internal struggle with its own inexperience in providing 'soft' as well as 'hard' security; it lacked the institutional structure and the military strategy and strength to back up its infant CFSP, which was simply not ready to deal with a challenge as complex as Yugoslavia.[7] What the EU as a conflict manager lacked more than anything in the 1990s; however, was the political will to act – and to act in unison.[8]

Lessons from the failures of the EU and the broader international community during the ethnic conflicts in the Western Balkans throughout the 1990s were gradually learnt and a new European security architecture started emerging in which different international organisations play their part and contribute to a cooperative, rather than merely collective security order.[9] Characterised by principles of task- and burden-sharing, this new cooperative security structure emerging at the beginning of the twenty-first century, involves the same principal security institutions – the UN, the Organization for Security and Co-operation in Europe (OSCE), NATO and the EU – but with a new set of mandates, instruments and policies that (in principle) enable them to face existing and emerging security challenges. Within this new European security architecture the EU occupies a central role: strengthened in its political weight through the enlargements and the accession and association processes, and diplomatically and militarily more capable as a result of the development of its security and defence identity and policy.

For the EU, lesson-learning happened within an existing institutional framework: begun by the Treaty on European Union (TEU) (1992) and revised by the Treaty of Amsterdam (1997), crisis management is a policy area within the CFSP Pillar and the CESDP, but owing to the complexity of the tasks, it also requires input from policy areas in Pillars 1 and 3 (see Figure 6.1). Specifically, the Treaty of Amsterdam expanded the range of tasks of the Union to 'humanitarian and rescue tasks, peacekeeping tasks and tasks of combat forces in crisis management, including peacemaking' (Article 17). These so-called Petersberg Tasks have their origin in the June 1992 Ministerial Council of the Western European Union (WEU) at which the WEU member states agreed to make available military units for tasks conducted under WEU authority.[10]

For the military component of crisis management, the European Council in Helsinki (1999) followed up on the decisions made at the Cologne Council meeting earlier the same year.[11] Comparing existing

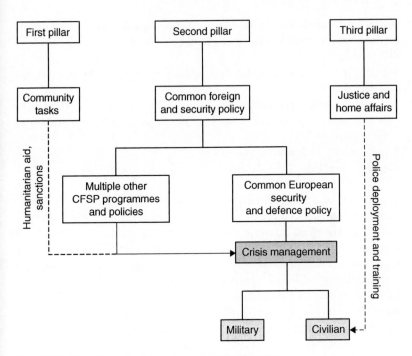

Figure 6.1   The place of crisis management in EU policy

capabilities with the ambitious Petersberg Tasks, the heads of state and government agreed on the Helsinki Headline Catalogue, which determined 144 areas in which capabilities and assets needed to be developed in order to enable the Union to fulfil the Petersberg Tasks:

- commitment by the member states to make available 50,000–60,000 military personnel deployable within 60 days and sustainable for up to 12 months;
- establishment of coordinating political and military structures within the Union's single institutional framework; and
- development of a framework for cooperation with NATO and third states.

Subsequent meetings of the European Council contributed to the further development of EU crisis management policy, particularly in relation to the improvement of its civilian component. The 2000 Feira

European Council determined four priority areas for the improvement of the Union's civilian crisis management capabilities:

- police (commitment to the deployment of up to 5000 officers and training of local forces);
- strengthening of the rule of law (identification of 200 experts readily available for deployment, development of common training modules for human rights monitors);
- civilian administration; and
- civil protection.

The Treaty of Lisbon, which was signed by EU leaders in December 2007 (but has yet to be ratified in a number of member states) reiterates the EU's continued commitment to 'assist populations, countries and regions confronting natural or man-made disaster' and 'promote an international system based on stronger multilateral cooperation and good global governance'. In particular, it confirms the EU intention to 'develop a special relationship with neighbouring countries, aiming to establish an area of prosperity and good neighbourliness, founded on the values of the Union and characterised by close and peaceful relations based on cooperation'.[12]

Four key innovations in the Treaty of Lisbon seek institutionally to improve CFSP capabilities and may thus have an effect of the EU's future role as a conflict manager in the ENP area and beyond:

- a new High Representative of the Union in Foreign Affairs and Security Policy, also the Vice-President of the Commission, is to increase the impact, coherence and visibility of EU external action;
- a new European External Action Service, is to provide support to the High Representative and work in cooperation with the member states' diplomatic services. The External Action Service shall comprise officials from the relevant departments of the General Secretariat of the Council and of the Commission as well as staff seconded from the national diplomatic services of the member states;
- a single EU legal personality is intended to strengthen the Union's negotiating power by making it a more visible partner for third countries and international organisations; and
- special decision-making arrangements are to pave the way to reinforced cooperation amongst a smaller group of member states in the CESDP.[13]

As far as the decision-making process is concerned, the Commission will no longer be able to make proposals in the area of the CFSP, but should support specific initiatives of the High Representative, who because s/he is also Vice-President of the Commission will ensure consistency of the Union's external action. At the same time, the principle of unanimity is largely confirmed for the CFSP, thus preserving member states' ability to cast a veto on specific policy proposals. The Lisbon Treaty limits the available CFSP instruments to European decisions (on actions, positions and arrangements for implementation). The so-called Common Strategies under the TEU are preserved in the Lisbon Treaty as strategic guidelines set by the European Council and further elaborated by the Foreign Affairs Council.[14]

Developing European crisis management: civilian and military capabilities

Lord Robertson, the Secretary-General of NATO (until the end of 2003) shortly after taking office in October 1999 emphasised that the three most important elements for securing the future of the Alliance were 'capabilities, capabilities, capabilities'. What is true for NATO, the most powerful military alliance (albeit largely dependent on the US in this context) is equally valid for the EU's crisis management capabilities, be they military or civilian in nature. In the EU context, the 'capabilities, capabilities, capabilities' dogma can be broken down into three main areas: capabilities to act, to fund and capabilities to cooperate and coordinate (see Figure 6.2).[15]

In terms of capabilities to act, issues of personnel and hardware were addressed by several European Council meetings following the inauguration of crisis management as a distinct policy under CESDP in Cologne in 1999. Specifically, the Helsinki European Council in 1999 agreed on the Helsinki Headline Goal, which was to set up the rapid-response capabilities needed to fulfil the Petersberg Tasks (see above). By the time the heads of state and government of EU members met again

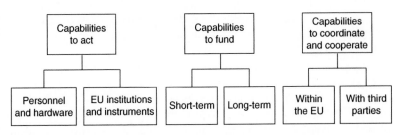

Figure 6.2 The EU's 'capabilities, capabilities, capabilities' problem

in Laeken in 2001, the Headline Goal had, in their view, been partially met, and they found that:

> through the continuing development of the ESDP, the strengthening of its capabilities, both civil and military, and the creation of appropriate structures within it and following the military and police Capability Improvement Conferences held in Brussels on 19 November 2001, the Union is now capable of conducting some crisis management operations.[16]

However, the Council also recognised that there was a large number of deficiencies in areas crucial for the EU's ability to take on more demanding operations and emphasised that the Union had to improve coordination between the resources and instruments of military and civilian crisis management, strengthen its military capabilities, finalise agreements with NATO to gain access to resources (planning, military assets and command options) and implement already existing arrangements with other non-NATO partners.[17] NATO-EU cooperation has subsequently made significant progress in the form of the Berlin Plus Agreement, a Framework Agreement on the EU-NATO partnership and an Agreement on Security of Information.

The development of appropriate institutions and policy instruments also progressed significantly. The creation of the post of Secretary-General of the European Council and High Representative for CFSP (and the appointment of former NATO Secretary-General Javier Solana to the post) was a significant step forward and indicated that the Union was prepared to follow up on its intentions with substantive commitments.[18] The new institutional structure, made permanent under the Treaty of Nice (see Figure 6.2) has to date proved reasonably efficient and effective. As for EU policy instruments, and emphasising the multifaceted nature of CFSP, Hill has aptly summarised the situation, '[t]he arrival of Joint Actions, Common Positions and now Common Strategies in the CFSP has spawned new initiatives such as the Stability Process in South-East Europe'.[19] In addition to these three policy instruments, 'statements' also form part of the range of options available to the Council for the conduct of its CFSP.

Capabilities to fund various crisis management operations in the short and the long-term do exist within the EU. The provision of long-term funds for CFSP activities is normally not a problem – it certainly was not a shortage of financial means that impeded EU policy in the Western Balkans. However, the complicated system within the Union for making the use of its funds transparent and accountable, for the first two years of the existence of crisis management as a distinct Union policy, often hindered their rapid disbursement. An important contribution to the improvement of the EU's short-term funding capabilities, therefore, was the creation of the Rapid Reaction Mechanism (RRM) in February 2001. Its main aim is to 'allow the Community to respond in a rapid, efficient and flexible manner, to situations of urgency or crisis or to emergence of crisis'.[20] The RRM covers six dimensions of EU crisis management: 'assessment of possible Community responses to a crisis, conflict prevention in countries and regions showing significant signs of instability, acute crisis management, post-conflict reconciliation, post-crisis reconstruction and the fight against terrorism'.[21] Actions financed with funds from the RRM may be carried out by 'authorities of Member States or of beneficiary countries and their agencies, regional and international organisations and their agencies, NGOs and public and private operators with appropriate specialised expertise and experience' (Article 6) and must be implemented within six months. The RRM has a fixed amount of funds at its disposal each year, determined annually by the budgetary authority (Article 8). This was €20 million in 2001, €25 million in 2002 and €30 million in 2005. Of the 2001 funds, 64 per cent were spent on Macedonia alone, while in 2002 all new activities financed by the RRM took place outside the Western Balkans, since by then only one programme was taking place in Macedonia. This clearly underlines the importance of the Balkans experience to other areas in which the EU is engaged in conflict management: institutions created in direct response to EU conflict management needs in the Balkans now form an integral part of the Union's broader approach to conflict management beyond this region, including in the ENP area.

Coordination and cooperation capabilities here relate to EU-internal processes as well as to the EU's relations with third parties. Within the EU, these have two dimensions: a horizontal one (coordination among the three pillars) and a vertical one (between the EU as a supranational organisation with its own institutional structures and the EU member states). At the external level, coordination and cooperation is essential in particular with NATO (see above) and, while potentially increasing EU dependency on NATO resources, has so far worked well. In the Western Balkans, especially, there has been a longer tradition of cooperation anyway (Bosnia and Herzegovina, Macedonia and Kosovo), and the Union took over from NATO's Stabilization Force (SFOR) as EUFOR in 2004 after having already assumed responsibility from an earlier NATO force in Macedonia. Cooperation with third countries (i.e. non-EU and non-NATO members) and international organisations (the UN, OSCE, UNHCR and non-governmental organisations (NGOs)) is accorded high priority by the Union. This is the case for two reasons: the EU is strongly committed to a multilateral approach and it recognises the mutual benefits of cooperation with organisations that 'specialise' in different crisis management tasks. In the case of cooperation with NATO, permanent consultation structures have been created in the wake of the Berlin Plus Agreement; in the case of cooperation with third parties the EU has clear procedures for coordination, including the establishment of so-called committees of contributing countries meant to give third parties an adequate role in the day-to-day running of a particular crisis management operation while leaving responsibility for overall strategic direction with the relevant institutions inside the Union. In addition, as recent experience in the Western Balkans indicates, the EU also uses its ability to conclude bilateral agreements with third parties to put any crisis management cooperation on solid legal foundations.

The changes proposed in the Treaty of Lisbon, if it is ratified, are intended to improve further the Union's institutional capability to cooperate and coordinate better both internally and externally and to act in a more coherent and efficient manner with regard to the CFSP. Furthermore, the amended Article 28 of the Lisbon Treaty states that the Council shall adopt a decision establishing the specific procedures for guaranteeing rapid access to appropriations in the Union budget for urgent financing of initiatives in the CFSP framework and, in particular, for preparatory activities referred to in Article 28 A(1) and Article 28 B, namely, joint disarmament operations, humanitarian and rescue tasks, military advice and assistance tasks, conflict prevention and peacekeeping tasks and tasks for combat forces in crisis management, including peacemaking and post-conflict stabilisation. The Treaty also states that preparatory activities for such tasks, which are not charged to the Union's budget, shall be financed by a start-up fund made up of member state contributions. In this way the Lisbon Treaty also increases the Union's short-term capability to fund its conflict management efforts.[22]

Testing capabilities in the Western Balkans

The EU police mission in Bosnia and Herzegovina

The 2003 EU Police Mission (EUPM) in Bosnia and Herzegovina (B-H) was the first ever CESDP mission. It is part of a comprehensive programme of measures aimed at establishing rule of law in B-H and is envisaged to accomplish its tasks by the end of 2008. It succeeds the UN's International Police Task Force. EUPM's annual budget is €38 million budget (50 per cent provided directly by Brussels), its personnel consists of 207 staff from 34 EU and non-EU countries. EUPM derives its legitimacy from Security Council Resolution (SCR) 1396 and a decision by the Peace Implementation Council (PIC) to accept EUPM to follow the UN Mission in B-H. EUPM is a crisis management operation and as such has a unified command structure within the single EU institutional framework, comprising the European Council and its Secretary-General and High Representative (SG/HR), the Political and Security Committee (PSC) and the EU Special Representative (EUSR) for B-H. The Head of Mission/Police Commissioner, who leads EUPM and is in charge of day-to-day operations, communicates with the SG/HR through the EUSR. The EUPM has two key priorities – fighting organised crime and ensuring the security of returnees. Apart from technical and professional assistance and training, EUPM is therefore also involved in the creation and consolidation of new institutional structures. Following an invitation by B-H authorities the EUPM refocused its mission in 2004 to support the B-H police reform process to develop and consolidate local capacity and regional cooperation in the fight against organised crime.[23]

Operation CONCORDIA in Macedonia

2003 Operation CONCORDIA also followed on from a previous international mission, in this case NATO's operation Allied Harmony. The background of this mission was to ensure sufficient levels of security and stability in Macedonia to enable the implementation of the 2001 Ohrid Agreement. CONCORDIA derived its legitimacy from a request by Macedonian President Trajkowski and UN SCR 1371. The operation fell within the remit of EU military crisis management operations and was the first ever CESDP deployment of military forces. It comprised 400 soldiers from 26 countries, again including non-EU contributor states. Operation CONCORDIA was the first case for EU-NATO cooperation under the Berlin Plus Agreement, that is the EU made use of NATO capabilities. Initially only assumed to last for six months, Operation CONCORDIA was extended at the request of the Macedonian government until December 2003. Command of the operation rested with EUFOR headquarters.[24] Contributions to Operation CONCORDIA were made by EU member and non-member states, the budget of €6.2 million was contributed by the EU with non-common costs borne by the participating states. As part of the day-to-day management structures, a Committee of Contributors had a consultative role its decision-making procedures.

Operation PROXIMA in Macedonia

In 2003 Operation PROXIMA became the second EU police mission in the Balkans. The establishment of the mission followed an invitation by Macedonia's Prime Minister. Its implementation was closely linked to the implementation of the Ohrid Agreement. The mission was extended beyond its initial 12 months following another request by the Macedonian Prime Minister and was completed in December 2005. The mission personnel comprised staff from EU member and non-member states. Operation PROXIMA was deployed to five locations across Macedonia to monitor, mentor and advise Macedonia's police force and promote European policing standards. The budget was €7.3 million for start-up costs and €7 million for 2004 running costs to be financed from the Community budget. For the 12-month extension a budget of €15.95 million was agreed.

Operation ALTHEA in Bosnia and Herzegovina

In 2004, the European Council decided to take over responsibility from NATO for securing the conditions for the implementation of the Dayton Peace Agreement.[25] The initial budget for common costs was €71.7 million to be administered by the ATHENA mechanism,[26] which relies on financial contributions by EU member states determined on a GDP basis. EU member and non-member states participate in this operation. Perhaps more than any other ESDP operation to date, Operation ALTHEA exemplifies the importance of cooperation among the international organisations making up Europe's security architecture. The EU takeover from NATO was only possible following the work of NATO's SFOR and the resulting improvements in the security environment on the ground.[27] The EU was able to rely on NATO assets and capabilities. NATO's Deputy Supreme Allied Commander Europe was appointed as the Operation Commander for the military component of Operation ALTHEA, and SHAPE simultaneously became the EU Operation Headquarters.[28] The command structure of Operation ALTHEA again underlines the close cooperation between NATO and the EU under the political control and strategic direction of the EU's PSC, the EU Operation Headquarters at SHAPE in Mons, the EU Command Element at the Allied Joint Forces Command in Naples and the Headquarters of EUFOR at Camp Butmir in Sarajevo. The EU Command Element at the Allied Joint Forces Command is a particularly crucial element in the coordination process with NATO as it ensures the EU's operations in the Balkans conform to the EU's regional approach, on the one hand, and cooperate closely with NATO operations in the Balkans, on the other.

In addition, the EU closely coordinates its military mission with its police mission. As both are meant to contribute to the implementation of the Dayton Agreement, cooperation is also essential with the PIC, the Office of the High Representative (OHR) and other international actors engaged in the region: primarily, the UN and OSCE.

Lessons learnt for future challenges of ethnic conflict management

In 1993, Christopher Hill predicted six future functions of then European Community (EC) as an international actor, including that of 'regional pacifier' and 'mediator of conflicts'.[29] In each case, he made explicit reference to former Yugoslavia and pointed out that it fell to the EU 'to act as mediator/coercive arbiter when the peace of the whole region seems under threat' and that there had been 'considerable diplomatic effort and creativity in the early stages of the Yugoslav imbroglio'.[30] Judging the EU's performance in the 1990s, however, only since the NATO intervention in Kosovo in 1999 has the EU played an increasingly important role as a regional pacifier and mediator of conflicts in the Western Balkans, albeit with varying success over time. No matter which perspective one takes on the Union's conflict management policy in the Western Balkans, it remains the largest donor and the organisation with the biggest presence throughout this region, having contributed significantly (partly in cooperation with third parties) to the stabilisation of the countries in the region and their reconstruction to date. This general view, at least partly, testifies to the existence of EU conflict management capabilities in the Western Balkans. However, only a closer look at the operations conducted there allows making better informed statements about the status of capability-development in general.

Current EU capabilities appear to be sufficient to take on tasks of the kind required in the Western Balkans at present. The EU was able to mobilise sufficient personnel, hardware and the funds to sustain them. It had the institutional framework and instruments available to make the necessary decisions and proved itself capable of a certain level of cooperation and coordination within its own structures as well as with third parties. This relatively positive assessment of EU crisis management capabilities in the Western Balkans since 1999, however, cannot necessarily be taken as a general indication of the readiness of the Union to manage conflict elsewhere and with a similar degree of success. While it is undoubtedly true that the 'CFSP, through the position of the HR for CFSP, has experienced in a very short time a substantial improvement in its coherence and visibility',[31] improved coherence and visibility do not necessarily translate into effectiveness. With respect to the Western Balkans one could question whether the Union has indeed been successful. In Macedonia, for example, it could be argued that early stage of conflict management, despite the mobilisation of significant resources, failed, and that it was only once the violent conflict had erupted that the EU (through conflict management measures) succeeded in brokering a deal between the fighting factions.[32]

Taking into account the complexity of the situation the EU had and has to deal with in the Western Balkans and the intensity of the conflicts it had to manage (in post-Dayton Bosnia and Herzegovina and in Macedonia) the Union has demonstrated that it has developed an institutional framework and a set of policies that enable it to make decisions quickly, provide adequate funds and personnel and cooperate and coordinate activities with third parties in ways that enhance its own capabilities and maximise the chances of successful crisis management. It is equally important in this context to bear in mind that since the failure of conflict management in the early and mid-1990s, the Union's capabilities have been improved significantly, enabling it now to undertake both civilian and military operations, that is being able to back up its diplomatic efforts with credible threats of force where necessary. This evolution of expertise at both the HQ and ground level demonstrates a significant process of lesson-learning at the institutional and operational levels of EU conflict management capabilities.

However, the EU's relative success of late in the Western Balkans has its sources not only in improved capabilities. In our view, the Union's experience in the Western Balkans cannot be generalised or exported easily. The distinct advantage that the EU has in this region is that its policy of conditionality is much more effective vis-à-vis countries where the promise of closer association with, and potentially accession to, the EU is credible and where both political elites and the general public are ready to make significant compromises in order to attain what many believe to be the only option for a viable future, even though there is now growing Euroscepticism in Croatia, Serbia and B-H, because the imagined solutions are not forthcoming as quickly as envisaged. In other words, the success of EU conflict management in the Western Balkans must be seen in a larger context, in which conflict management is only one element in a comprehensive EU approach to a region. As Javier Solana pointed out as early as 2000, '[t]he European

Union is uniquely placed for comprehensive action in the Western Balkans' and is 'the only institution capable of comprehensive action, ranging from trade, economic reform, and infrastructure, humanitarian assistance, human rights and democratisation, justice and police to crisis management and military security'.[33] Without the clear long-term commitment of the EU to the Western Balkans' prospect of EU membership, the incentives for political elites and the various ethnic groups they represent would be less powerful and thus the Union's ability to elicit short- and long-term compliance, which has been a major factor in the success of its conflict management operations so far, diminished.

We must sound a second note of caution regarding the EU's readiness to engage successfully in conflict management operations elsewhere concerns the availability of personnel and especially military assets. The commitments made by EU member states have not yet been tested to the full – the two police missions in B-H and Macedonia have required only about 10 per cent of the total number of police officers committed by EU member states, and the two military operations CONCORDIA and ALTHEA have similarly required only around 12 per cent of total committed troops. At the same time, the EU is now, for better or worse, locked into a framework of cooperation with NATO which will perpetuate its dependency on NATO resources.[34] This may significantly decrease the Union's capability for autonomous action in situations where NATO resources are stretched or where disagreement within NATO prevents the use of certain resources by the EU.

A final factor limiting the generalisability or indeed the transferability of the relative success of recent EU conflict management operations in the Western Balkans is at the same time one of the very reasons for this success – increasing familiarity with, and sensitivity toward, the situation in the region and the countries concerned, a long-standing network of information sources (EUMM) and previous experience in dealing with the political elites and populations in the area. One of the main shortcomings of EU capabilities, identified by the Director General of the European Union Military Staff,[35] namely 'shortfalls in all areas of intelligence gathering' and a lack of a 'common system for intelligence fusion' could thus be at least partially neutralised.

Nevertheless, even the limited conflict management operations that the EU is currently conducting in the Western Balkans are very valuable for its future role as a serious international actor. While it might be too early to proclaim the overall success of EU conflict management in the region, there are some indicators that a certain degree of success might not elude the Union on this occasion.[36] First of all, they have proven the success of institutional reforms within the Union and of the development of credible policies and instruments for conflict management. Second, they underscore that the overall approach of the EU to the conduct of international affairs is fruitful: commitment to multilateralism (within the EU and with its partners elsewhere),[37] constructive and long-term engagement with conflict regions, combining short-term crisis management with long-term structural conflict prevention and a fair balance between civilian and military strategies to maximise the short- and long-term impact of its policies. Third, by highlighting remaining deficiencies in EU conflict management capabilities, the Union now has an opportunity to draw lessons for the future before engaging in more ambitious and demanding operations elsewhere in its 'new neighbourhood'.

The ENP as a possible conflict management tool?

In order to draw an accurate parallel from the lessons learned in the Western Balkans to an assessment of the prospect of the ENP as a potential policy instrument for conflict management in the EU's 'new neighbourhood', it is important to stress that the countries in the ENP area have an all together different relationship with the EU than the countries in the Western Balkans. Although, the EU is a key aid and trade partner to these countries, the ENP explicitly excludes them from the promise of future EU membership. In effect, the EU has significantly less leverage in terms of conditionality compliance in these countries than it does in the Western Balkans, where the accession prospect is the key to the Union's success. Consequently, the EU is not seen as an equally important partner in these countries, and it often suffers a lack of credibility in terms of its capability to deliver on its threats as well as its promises. It is important here to stress that the relationship with the EU also varies significantly between the different ENP countries.[38]

The international context with regard to the ENP partner countries is also different from that of the Western Balkans, where the key international security actors (for the most part) respect the EU's current leading role. In the ENP area, other international actors, such as Russia, China, a number of Middle Eastern countries and the US, have vested interests and are already engaged in a number of the conflicts in question (albeit in different ways, to different degrees and at different levels in the different countries).[39] The ENP's prospect as a conflict management tool therefore depends on whether the EU is both able and willing to implement a conflict management policy despite other international actors being engaged and potentially having conflicting interests in the country in question. Although the Union may have learned valuable lessons with regard to what means are necessary for successful EU conflict management, this does not by any means guarantee that the Union is able or indeed willing to undertake such missions throughout the ENP area, especially where such efforts would conflict with the interests of the other actors engaged or indeed those of the EU itself. As argued above conflict management in the Western Balkans is comparatively much more important for the EU. Finally, the EU has relatively few capabilities in terms of intelligence and understanding of the conflicts in these countries and it lacks the institutional memory and know-how, which have gradually been built up over time in the Western Balkan context, which means that if the EU was indeed willing to commit to the extent necessary for EU conflict management to be successful in the ENP area, it may not necessarily be able to do it with the same relative success as it has had in the Western Balkans since 1999.

What then are the tangible prospects of ENP conflict management in the EU's 'new neighbourhood'? As far as the Southern dimension is concerned, the Israeli-Palestinian conflict, Lebanon, Algeria and Morocco/ Western Sahara, we argue, are far beyond the individual conflict management capacity the EU (and within it the ENP) at present. Nevertheless, the EU has an important role to play here alongside the US, Russia and the Arab world in bringing about conditions under which international, multilateral conflict management would be possible. Here, the EU has significant long-term potential in facilitating conflict management through aid, trade, mediation and long-term governance reform assistance, to mention but a few areas, all of which could well be facilitated through multifaceted ENP country strategies, and it is in the formulation of such strategies that the EU could make the best use of the lessons it learned in the Western Balkans.

In the Eastern dimension, its geographical proximity and political leverage arguably presents the Union with a relatively positive prospect in playing a more significant role in the conflict in Transnistria. A positive outcome of any ENP initiative to manage (resolve and prevent) further conflict in Moldova, however, depends on the cooperation of the respective governments in these countries and the role of Russia.[40] The conflict between Armenia and Azerbaijan over Nagorno-Karabakh presents the EU with an even more complex regional situation involving Russia, Iran and Turkey. In particular, the nature of the incumbent regimes in relation to this particular conflict presents the ENP with a significantly greater challenge than the conflict in Moldova.

Much more concretely than in most other cases in the EU's neighbour-hood, the recent confrontation between Russia and Georgia (August 2008) has tested the EU's emerging conflict management capabilities in the Southern Caucasus. Taking into account the complexity of the situation the EU has had, and continues to have, to deal with in Georgia and the complexity of the underlying conflicts it has to help manage (resolve and prevent) in the region, the Union demonstrated that it has indeed developed an institutional framework and a set of policies that enable it to make decisions quickly, provide adequate funds and personnel and cooperate and coordinate activities with third parties in ways that enhance its own capabilities and maximise the chances of successful crisis management in this context, too. Shortly after the outbreak of the war between Georgia and Russia in August 2008, on 1 September 2008 the Council of the EU expressed 'grave concern at the open conflict which had broken out in Georgia, and expressed the readiness of the European Union to commit itself to supporting every effort to secure a peaceful and lasting solution to the conflict'.[41] To this end the Council appointed Pierre Morrel as European Union Special Representative for the Crisis in Georgia to 'enhance the effectiveness and visibility of the European Union in helping to resolve the con-flict in Georgia'[42] and on 15 September the Council adopted a Joint Action to launch a European Union Monitoring Mission in Georgia (EUMM Georgia). Two days later Hansjorg Haber was appointed Head of the EUMM and within two weeks of the Council decision, the Union had successfully launched the mission and deployed more than 200 monitors from 22 member states on the ground.

Although the EUMM has already encountered a number of problems in the field[43] and it is still far too early to proclaim the overall success of EU's reaction to the crisis in Georgia, the quick reaction in terms of condemning the conflict, appointing the EUSR and launching the EUMM, there are some indicators that a certain degree of success might not elude the Union on this occasion. First, as already men-tioned, the EU underscored the success of its internal institutional reforms and of the development of credible policies and instruments for conflict management. Second, the rapid EU response to the recent developments in Georgia highlighted once again the Union's emerg-ing approach to conflict management through commitment to multilateralism (within the EU and with its partners) and constructive and long-term engagement with conflict regions, combining short-term crisis management with long-term structural conflict prevention. The Union now has an opportunity in Georgia to draw on the lessons from the Balkans before engaging in more ambitious and demanding operations elsewhere in its 'new neighbourhood'. The track record so far suggests that the EU might after all be on the right track to establish itself as a credible international security actor.

Notes

1. Initially it was simply referred to as ESDP in the Presidency Conclusions of the Cologne European Council in June 1999; the Helsinki Council of December 1999 introduced the acronym of CESDP 'to signify the determination, on the part of the EU member states, to develop a distinct European politico-military project, with its own institutional infrastructure and a significant military capacity'. Howorth, J. (2000), 'Britain, NATO and CESDP: Fixed Strategy, Changing Tactics', *European Foreign Affairs Review*, 5 (3), pp. 377–396.
2. This is not to deny that the EU has had two successive programmes in support of the Northern Ireland peace process since the mid-1990s (PEACE I from 1995 to 1999, and PEACE II from 2000 to 2006) and that European integration has provided institutional structures and incentives for cross-border cooperation both in Northern Ireland and in South Tyrol that have had a generally positive, albeit hardly quantifiable impact on conflict resolution in both of these cases.
3. Commission of the European Communities (2004), Communication from the Commission, *European Neighbourhood Policy, Strategy Paper*, COM(2004) 373 final, p. 3, Brussels, 12 May 2004.
4. A.G. Kintis (1997), 'The EU's foreign policy and the war in former Yugoslavia' in M. Holland, *Common Foreign and Security Policy.* London: Pinter. L. Silber and A. Little (1996), *The death of Yugoslavia.* London: Penguin Books.
5. It is estimated that between 7000 and 8000 Muslim men and boys were killed by Serb nationalists in Srebrenica in 1995. L. Silber and A. Little (1996), *The death of Yugoslavia.* London: Penguin Books.
6. A.G. Kintis (1997), 'The EU's foreign policy and the war in former Yugoslavia' in M. Holland, *Common Foreign and Security Policy.* London: Pinter. N. Morris (2004), 'Humanitarian intervention in the Balkans', in J. Welsh, *Humanitarian intervention and international relations.* Oxford: Oxford University Press. P.C. Pentland (2003), 'The EU and Southeastern Europe after Dayton' *Europe-Russia Working Chapters.* Ottawa: Carleton University.
7. The EU did, however, go through a learning process in the Balkans. After the Dayton Agreement ended the war, the EU gradually began a more coherent and effective response to political stabilisation and economic recovery in the region. The EU assumed a modest role in the first three years of the international protectorate in Bosnia-Herzegovina and contributed significantly in terms of humanitarian aid and assistance in the post-conflict reconstruction in the wider region, but it was not until after the Kosovo campaign that the EU re-emerged with a comprehensive vision for the Western Balkans and a renewed claim to leadership. Today the EU, heavily engaged in crisis management is widely recognised as one of if not the most important international actor in the region. F. Cameron (2006), 'The European Union's

role in the Balkans' in B. Blitz (ed.) *War and change in the Balkans*. Cambridge: Cambridge University Press; E. Faucompret (2001), *The dismemberment of Yugoslavia and the European Union*. Antwerp: University of Antwerp. L. Silber and A. Little (1996), *The death of Yugoslavia*. London: Penguin Books.

8. E. Faucompret (2001), *The dismemberment of Yugoslavia and the European Union*. Antwerp: University of Antwerp.

9. Wolff, Stefan and Rodt, Annemarie Peen, (2008), 'The EU and the Management of Ethnic Conflict', In: Weller, Marc, Blacklock, Denika and Nobbs, Katherine, eds. *The Protection of Minorities in the Wider Europe*. Basingstoke: Palgrave.

10. The Petersberg Declaration was the WEU's response to calls for greater burden-sharing within NATO through the elaboration of a coherent European Security and Defence Identity (ESDI) built around the WEU. In the context of the European Convention, important amendments and revisions to the Petersberg Declaration were proposed by the so-called Barnier Report. European Convention (2002), Final Report of Working Group VIII on Defense, Chaired by Michael Barnier (Barnier Report). Brussels, 16 D http://register.consilium.europa.eu/pdf/en/02/cv00/cv00461.en02.pdfecember 2002, accessed on 7 January 2010.

11. The Cologne Summit, importantly, happened just at the end of NATO's intervention in the Kosovo crisis, which in turn visibly influenced the decision-making by Heads of State and Government in Cologne.

12. European Union (2007), Treaty of Lisbon amending the Treaty on European Union and the Treaty establishing the European Community (2007/C 306/01), *Official Journal of the European Union*, English Edition, C 306, Volume 50, 17 December 2007, available online at http://eur-lex.europa.eu/JOHtml.do?uri=OJ:C:2007:306:SOM:en:HTML, accessed on 7 January 2010.

13. Ibid.

14. Ibid.

15. For a somewhat different take on the capabilities problem, see U. Schneckener (2002), *Developing and Applying EU Crisis Management: Test Case Macedonia*. ECMI Working Paper No. 14. Flensburg: European Centre for Minority Issues, pp. 37–39. Available at http://www.ecmi.de/doc/download/working_paper_14.pdf.

16. Presidency Conclusions, European Council Meeting in Laeken, 14 and 15 December 2001. SN 300/1/101 REV 1.: paragraph 6.

17. Presidency Conclusions, European Council Meeting in Laeken, 14 and 15 December 2001. SN 300/1/101 REV 1. Annex II.

18. This has also been emphasised by Piana, C. (2002), 'The EU's Decision-Making Process in the Common Foreign and Security Policy: The Case of the Former Yugoslav Republic of Macedonia', *European Foreign Affairs Review*, 7 (2), pp. 209–226; in relation to the crisis in Macedonia: 'The creation of the post of High Representative definitely brought the visibility/continuity element that was lacking in the CFSP.'

19. C. Hill (2001), 'The EU's Capacity for Conflict Prevention', *European Foreign Affairs Review*, 6 (3), p. 328.

20. European Council (2001), Council regulation (EC) No 381/2001 of February 26 2001 creating a rapid reaction mechanism.

21. Commission of the European Communities (2002). Information Note, 'The Rapid Reaction Mechanism Supporting the European Union's Policy Objectives in Conflict Prevention and Crisis Management', Council

Regulation (EC) No 381/2001 of 26 February 2001 creating a rapid-reaction mechanism http://eur-lex.europa.eu/smartapi/cgi/sga_doc?smartapi!celex plus!prod!DocNumber&lg=en&type_doc=Regulation&an_doc=2001&nu_ doc=381, accessed on 7 January 2010.

22. European Union (2007) Treaty of Lisbon amending the Treaty on European Union and the Treaty establishing the European Community (2007/C 306/01), *Official Journal of the European Union*, English Edition, C 306, Volume 50, 17 December 2007, (available online at http://bookshop.europa.eu/ eubookshop/FileCache/PUBPDF/FXAC07306ENC/FXAC07306ENC_002. pdf; accessed on 3 April 2008).

23. European Council (2008), 'European Union Police Mission in Bosnia and Herzegovina', available at http://www.consilium.europa.eu/cms3_fo/ showPage.asp?id=585&lang=EN&mode=g; accessed on 9 March 2008).

24. EUFOR was established in 1995 in Lisbon as a military force under the Petersberg Tasks. Contributing nations are France, Italy, Portugal and Spain. Operational since 1998 and listed in the force catalogues of the EU, NATO, the OSCE and UN, it has been part of NATO operation Allied Guardian in Albania in 2000.

25. Council Joint Action of 12 July 2004 on the European Union military operation in Bosnia and Herzegovina. 2004/570/CFSP.

26. The ATHENA mechanism was established by the Council of the European Union on 23 February 2004 to administer the common costs of EU operations having military or defence implications. It provided a funding mechanism for the common costs of military operations, ready in advance, which could cover both the preparatory phase and the involvement of third states.

27. The Operations Field Commander was EUFOR military staff, but also part of the command structure of this particular operation. He reported to the EU Operation Commander, in this case NATO's Deputy Supreme Allied Commander for Europe. The EU Military Committee monitored the conduct of the operation and received reports from the Operation Commander as well as providing the first point of call for him in relation to the Council. Even though the Operation Commander simultaneously had a position within the NATO command structure, he only reported to EU bodies and the chain of command remained under the EU's political control and strategic direction. In contrast to the EUPM, the EUSR to Macedonia, Alexis Brouhns, was not part of the command chain, but acted, together with the SG/HR, as primary point of contact for Macedonian authorities and as key liaison for EU commanders in the field. This was in many ways similar to what had happened one year earlier in relation to the EU's Operation CONCORDIA taking over from NATO's Operation Allied Harmony in Macedonia.

28. NATO, 'SHAPE-EU Cooperation: Background Information. Available at http:// www.nato.int/shape/issues/shape_eu/background.htm; NATO, 'Operation Althea', available online at http://www.nato.int/shape/issues/shape_eu/althea.htm.

29. C. Hill (1993), 'The Capability–Expectations Gap, or Conceptualising Europe's International Role', *Journal of Common Market Studies*, 31 (3), p. 312.

30. C. Hill (1993), 'The Capability–Expectations Gap, or Conceptualising Europe's International Role', *Journal of Common Market Studies*, 31 (3), p. 311f.

31. Müller-Brandeck-Bocquet, G. (2002), 'The New CFSP and ESDP Decision-Making System of the European Union', *European Foreign Affairs Review*, 7 (3), pp. 257–282.

32. This is the problem of CFSP as a 'moving target'. See F. Cameron (2002), 'The European Union's Growing International Role: Closing the Capability – Expectations Gap?'. Paper presented at the conference on The European Union in International Affairs, National Europe Centre, Australian National University, July 2002, available at http://www.anu.edu.au/NEC/fraser_cameron.pdf.

33. Solana, J. (2000), Report on the Western Balkans Presented to the Lisbon European Council by the Secretary-General/High Representative together with the Commission. Brussels, 21 March 2000. SN 2032/2/00/REV2.

34. For example, the decision of extending Operation CONCORDIA in Macedonia was contingent upon a decision of the North Atlantic Council to extend the availability of NATO assets to the EU.

35. Schuwirth, R. (2002), 'Hitting the Helsinki Headline Goal', *NATO Review*, Autumn 2002. http://www.nato.int/docu/review/2002/issue3/english/art4.html, accessed on 7 January 2010.

36. The two big (known) unknowns in this respect are the closure of the OHR in Bosnia and Herzegovina and the outcome, and impact, of the Kosovo final status negotiations.

37. The preference of a multilateral approach to crisis management can also be deduced from the fact that in both current crisis management operations in the Western Balkans and in the brief military operation in the Democratic Republic of Congo, the European Council either did not move before the UN (DRC) or explicitly inferred the legitimacy of its operation, at least in part, from a *preceding* UN resolution. M.E. Smith (2001) 'Diplomacy by Degree: The Legalisation of EU Foreign Policy', *Journal of Common Market Studies*, 39 (1), p. 99.

38. For a more in-depth investigation of the role of the EU and the ENP in different geographical contexts, see the chapters by Echeverria, Bicchi, Ghazarian and Sasse in this volume.

39. For some examples, please see Rynning and Jensen and Haukkala in this volume.

40. For a more in-depth discussion, Haukkala in this volume.

41. European Council (2008), Council Joint Action of 25 September 2008 on appointing the European Union Special Representative for the crisis in Georgia. 2008/760/CFSP http://eur-lex.europa.eu/LexUriServ/LexUriServ.do?uri=OJ:L:2008:259:0016:0018:EN:PDF, accessed on 7 January 2010.

42. European Council (2008), Council Joint Action of 25 September 2008 on appointing the European Union Special Representative for the crisis in Georgia. 2008/760/CFSP http://eur-lex.europa.eu/LexUriServ/LexUriServ.do?uri=OJ:L:2008:259:0016:0018:EN:PDF, accessed on 7 January 2010.

43. The successful implementation of the EUMM mandate in Georgia has so far been hampered by the blockage of access for EU monitors to South Ossetia and Abkhazia and, according to the EU itself, limited cooperation with the Russians. Some observers, such as the International Crisis Group, Radio Free Europe and reportedly Human Rights Watch, have also raised concerns about the limited mandate of the mission and the inability of the EU observers to intervene directly when faced with violence. (Crisis Group Europe Briefing No. 51, 26 November 2008; EUMM Press conference with Hansjorg Haber, 24 October, 2008; Radio Free Europe interview with Hansjorg Haber, 4 November 2008).

7
The ENP and Transatlantic Relations

Sten Rynning and Christine Pihlkjær Jensen

Introduction

It is common to portray the European Neighbourhood Policy (ENP) as a reasonable and indeed functional response to a gap in the European Union's (EU) panoply of external relations tools. The standard practice of influencing neighbours via the promise of EU membership had run its course with the December 2003 decision to enlarge in a big bang – with ten new countries – and a new partnership policy was in demand. The ENP promised close partnership, that is 'everything but institutions,' which is to say growth and modernisation in the partner countries and relief in an EU struck by enlargement fatigue.

The ENP should also be seen as a geopolitical event, however, which illuminates the EU's growing presence in its near abroad and its inevitable involvement in conflicts on its periphery. As such, the ENP highlights both strengths and weaknesses in the EU's external presence, and this is where transatlantic relations are important. It is no scoop that the EU's foreign and security policies – the Common Foreign and Security Policy (CFSP) and the European Security and Defence Policy (ESDP) – are marked by member states' disagreements and therefore vary in strength and impact. Less noted is the need for strategic policy given the advent of the ENP. This is so for at least three reasons. First, the ENP lumps together disparate countries and regions – Eastern Europe, the Caucasus, the Levant and North Africa – and the challenge is not to tailor ENP policies to individual countries but to address the regional level falling between the individual (country) and collective (ENP) levels. Second, the ENP has moved into the Russian sphere of influence and challenges Russian policy notably with respect to liberal values, and the EU can hope to cope with Russia only if it

135

is clear on its priorities on such issues as democracy promotion and energy imports. Finally, and most fundamentally, the ENP overlaps with American interests in Europe and its peripheries. Geopolitically speaking, the US has an interest in influencing events in the Eurasian rim areas – particularly Europe and South-East Asia – and organising relationships with local partners that enable this influence. The ENP may signal that the EU is more ready and able to engage in this type of partnership, but it will depend on the development of an ENP strategy that builds explicitly on the transatlantic geopolitical link and seeks the alignment of Atlantic positions.

This, then, is a geopolitical fact: it is within an American sphere of interest and influence that the EU engages in embedded regional conflicts and Russia's near abroad. Transatlantic alignment will be of benefit to both the EU and the US: to the EU because it lacks the inner unity and strength to circumvent US policy and take on these conflicts and Russia; to the US because a reasonable burden-sharing agreement will advance the management of its Eurasian presence. Transatlantic relations are thus the bedrock of the ENP. The question is whether the EU is in the process of gaining a strategic perception of geopolitics, and whether the ENP is indicative thereof, and also whether the US perceive the ENP as a constructive contribution to transatlantic relations. To the extent we can answer in the affirmative, the ENP will rest on solid ground and have significant potential for development.

This is far from certain, however, although there are positive indicators. First, the US did not see the ENP at its time of inception as a threat or nuisance to transatlantic relations. Moreover, the ENP has in a number of instances been instrumental in advancing an EU policy agenda that is better tailored to individual cases and more in tune with American policy. However, and inversely, the ENP is so large that it is almost useless as a foreign policy guide, which reflects negatively on the EU's ability to deal strategically with its environment. American policy-makers have consistently ignored its potential, perhaps because they deem it too limited. Moreover, the ENP cannot in any instance be credited as a cause of improved transatlantic relations, although the ENP can be, and in fact has been, an instrument in the improvement of relations that are already on track. The future of the ENP will not depend on the tinkering with details of ENP Action Plans but on the EU developing a strategic view of Europe, the inevitable US engagement here and finally the EU's role parallel to that of the US.

In the following section we assess transatlantic relations up to and around the publication of the ENP in 2003–2004. We then turn to two key regions – the post-Soviet space and the Middle East – and in each assess major challenges, European and American approaches to them and the potential contribution of the ENP to an alignment of approaches. The conclusion reflects on the future of the ENP.

The beginning

The months of March and April 2003 reveal the extent to which European and American security agendas are interrelated. On 11 March, the European Commission issued its 'Wider Europe' report outlining the ENP and the ambition to create a 'ring of friends.'[1] On 1 April the EU Nice Treaty entered into force and thus gave life to the new organisation intended to strengthen the CFSP. Meanwhile, a coalition led by the US invaded Iraq on 20 March, an event preceded by extraordinary diplomatic rift within Europe. Both the ENP and the Iraq War sought to enhance security in Europe's peripheries, and both had much to do with the American presence in Europe.

The remarkable feature of European security since the end of the Cold War is not really the emerging foreign and security policy of the EU but the continuing American willingness to play a leading role in an overseas region absent the communist threat. Continuity, not change, is what we must bring to bear in our understanding of the ENP and transatlantic relations.

William Wohlforth finds the source of continuity in the unrivalled power of the US (i.e. unipolarity) and the incentive for other states not to balance but to cooperate with the US (i.e. 'hedging, free-riding and bandwagoning'). The EU is subject to this same dynamic, although EU-US relations are rendered complex by the fact that the EU is an economic peer to the US and that their contrasting 'power portfolios' feed 'status rivalry.'[2] Some scholars contend that 'status rivalry' is in fact a type of balancing.[3] That is, they challenge the view of continuity, arguing that change is in the making, albeit modestly so. Still, the concept of 'soft' balancing is both elastic and controversial and there is scant evidence that the EU is motivated by balancing.[4] There is instead the argument to be made that much of the agony of transatlantic security relations for the past 15 years evolves around the organisation of America's presence in 'the democratic bridgehead' – Europe – as part of a larger American strategy to influence Eurasian politics.[5] More than 60 years ago Nicholas Spykman assessed US access to 'the Old World' and argued that 'In the transatlantic zone, it will not be sufficient for her to accept obligations to aid Britain against a threat from the continent or to aid the continent against a threat from outside if she is not physically in a position to carry out such an obligation.'[6]

Continuity has resulted notably in NATO's geographic and functional enlargement: NATO now comprises 28 allies, and NATO has operationally gone out-of-area. This deepening engagement has not come about smoothly but has, significantly, encapsulated EU processes. Consider enlargement:[7] it was only in 2002 that the EU's big eastern bang happened, bringing EU membership to 27; NATO had at this point twice decided to expand eastward and so the EU stepped into new but also transatlantic territory.[8] Moreover, NATO is more likely than the EU to enlarge again in the near future.

A similar dynamic has taken place in virtually every security domain. From 1993 to 1995 the EU developed programmes to handle the new neighbourhood, beginning with the so-called Balladur Stability Pact directed toward Central Europe, moving on to Partnership and Cooperation Agreements (PCAs) entered with Eastern European countries, including Russia, and a stability pact directed toward South-Eastern Europe and a Euro-Mediterranean policy (the Barcelona Process) toward the Southern neighbours.[9] NATO had prior to this, in 1991, established a North Atlantic Cooperation Council (NACC) that included nine Eastern European countries, all members of the Commonwealth of Independent States, and also Georgia and Albania, and in 1994 extended the NACC with individual (bilateral) Partnership for Peace Agreements (PfP). The EU took the lead in the Yugoslav conflict but did not pass the test. NATO's operational lead was subsequently written into Atlantic Agreements – the Berlin Agreement of 1996 and the Berlin Plus Agreement of 1999.[10]

As noted, smooth transatlantic relations have not always prevailed. The US and its European allies diverged significantly on the Bosnian crisis in 1992–93; later, the US had to convince reluctant allies of NATO enlargement's importance;[11] and transatlantic disagreement marked the Kosovo intervention in 1999 and the potential scope of the ESDP that also came to life in that year. The perhaps most dramatic disagreement took place in the context of the Iraq War, in 2002–2003, and resulted in France's aborted attempt – along with Germany, Belgium and Luxembourg – to establish an independent EU operational planning headquarters in the Brussels suburb of Tervuren.[12]

This brings us back to the analytical starting point, the durability of the US presence in Europe. When initiatives, such as the ENP, surface we can probe their impact on and contribution to this presence. We should ask whether such an initiative will strengthen EU coherence and

Table 7.1 Ideal-typical views of Europe

	Military autonomy	Military dependence
Complementary	A strong EU partner enabling common action	A limited EU working within an Atlantic division of labour
Competitive	A strong and autonomous EU undermining US influence and NATO's survival	US entrapment in European conflicts by revisionist but weak EU

whether EU policy-makers are motivated by Atlantic cooperation. We should also ask whether American policy-makers see in the initiative a potential contribution or threat to the transatlantic relationship. In this context it is intriguing how little attention the ENP attracted in Washington – or in the American delegation to Brussels.

To situate the reaction of official America we refer to Table 7.1. It asks whether American policy-makers see in European initiatives first of all a desire to compete with the US (vertical axis) and second a capacity to undertake autonomous military action (horizontal axis). Four ideal-typical views of Europe emerge.

The official American position is located in the upper left square, which is a conclusion reached by induction. A systematic review of official American statements from 2000 onward, including inquiries to the U.S. Mission to the European Union in the matter, reveal no explicit American ENP statements. Put differently, the US did not comment on the birth of the ENP. We detect the first mention of the ENP in official documents in 2005 but merely as an item on a long list of existing European and American initiatives aimed at spreading and consolidating democracy and development.[13] In short, officially the US had preciously little to say about the ENP in 2003–04.

We do know something about the overall US view of EU foreign policy, however. The Bush administration chose from the outset, January 2001, to continue the Clinton period's support of the ESDP, hoping that it could bring about *'a more effective and balanced partnership'*[14] – an often-repeated phrase. American support of a strengthened European defence dimension was conditional in so far as primacy had to be accorded to NATO, a historical condition turned into three D's by Madeleine Albright in 1998[15] and one confirmed by the George W. Bush administration.[16]

Thus, the official position was generally positive but with explicit reservations, and it seems obvious that at least some members of the American strategic community must have harboured doubts about the ESDP's potential and political impact. Naturally, the ESDP is not the ENP. Still, had the ENP evoked similar worries, we feel certain that US policy-makers would have articulated them.

Table 7.1 tells us what to look for in the subsequent analytical sections: indications that US policy-makers see in the ENP a movement either in the direction of greater political competition (because a strong EU now defines and pursues its own goals in the neighbourhood) or greater military dependence (because the EU builds on traditions of 'soft' power – also sometimes labelled 'civil' or 'normative' power).

We know that American commentators and observers fall into the different categories of Table 7.1, and we thus know that potential fertile ground for a shift of perception exists. Most observers seem to fall into the lower left box where the EU becomes a kind of revamped Gaullist bloc motivated by multipolarity.[17] However, EU limits are apparent and the question may not be whether the EU will do too much but too little, and whether competition or cooperation ensues.

In looking for signs of greater concern with either political competition or military dependence we will not examine all the twists and turns of Washington policy-making and debate. Tracing policy statements would easily miss the target because the ENP is a minor subject matter in transatlantic relations. Instead we will work our way through two distinct regions that have their own geopolitical logic: the post-Soviet space and the Middle East. The research strategy is then straightforward: we must assess transatlantic relations prior to the launch of the ENP and the way in which the ENP subsequently impacted on these relations.

In this section we have established the geopolitical significance of the continued US presence in Europe. We have outlined the American interest behind the view that Europe is now 'whole and free.'[18] We have examined the official American reaction to the ENP and found little of significance. By implication we have embedded the ENP in the larger debate on transatlantic relations. The US officially encouraged Europe's participation in the defence of democracy and the effort to combat radicalism, terrorism and the proliferation of weapons of mass destruction.[19] The US thus spearheaded NATO's transformation, which began with the Prague Summit of 20–21 November 2002. Would the allies follow suit? Would the members of both NATO and the EU see a similar security situation in Europe's peripheries and seek to align the new ENP with the other arrows in the transatlantic quiver? Conversely, did the ENP signal that the EU was set on a course of confrontation related either to greater self-confidence or a legacy of normative power?

The ENP and the post-Soviet space

The post-Soviet space between Russia and the EU is indeed a unique setting for the politics of transatlantic relations The presence of a former great power, eagerly attempting to sustain its diminishing influence in the region, invariably conditions policy in the area by forcing both the EU and the US to factor in Russian interests and sensibilities when promoting their own strategic interests.

To what extent has the ENP contributed to the harmonisation of transatlantic positions in this geopolitically crucial space? The case of Georgia suggests that a certain alignment of interests has taken place over time. Since the breakup of the Soviet bloc Georgia has attracted particular US attention because of its status as a key energy transit country. American interest has manifested itself in terms of heavy investments in the construction of a pipeline connecting Azerbaijani oilfields with Western markets via Georgia, in the form of intensive pressure applied on President Eduard Shevardnadze to resign in the period leading up to the Georgian 'Rose Revolution' in November 2003 and through extensive diplomatic and economic support to the reform and development policies of the new pro-Western leadership.[20] The US has in addition become a forceful advocate of Georgia's inclusion in NATO, to the extent that the US in late 2008 sought to have NATO grant Georgia (and the Ukraine) a special and unprecedented path of Alliance entry.[21]

The EU has been cooperating with Georgia since 1992, supporting the state through a range of assistance instruments. A PCA with the objective of fostering respect of democratic principles, rule of law and human rights, as well as consolidation of the market economy, entered into force on 1 July 1999.[22] This relationship has gained new momentum since the Rose Revolution; after having initially been left out,[23] Georgia and the two other South Caucasian states were included in the ENP in June 2004. The EU-Georgia Action Plan adopted on 14 November 2006 elaborates on Georgia's PCA by envisaging the establishment of a free trade area between Georgia and the EU, calling for additional efforts in settling the conflicts in South Ossetia and Abkhazia and offering a perspective of deeper integration with the EU.[24]

Russia has reacted negatively to the Rose Revolution and Georgia's association with NATO.[25] While it remains unclear who initiated the hostilities that erupted in outright war in August 2008 – it lasted for five days – the effects of the war are clear: Russia has recognised the independence of two parts of Georgia, South Ossetia and Abkhazia, and is deliberately blocking Georgia's smooth path to Alliance membership.[26] The policy of the George W. Bush administration remains the same, although relations to Russia have deteriorated, namely to push for NATO membership and take on the sphere of influence contest.[27] We thus observe great continuity in American policy, beginning with the 2002 'Train and Equip Program' that in 2006 grew into the Intensified Dialogue on its NATO membership aspirations and more generally America's embrace of Georgian democracy. Continuity is hardly a quality of EU policy. The August 2008 ceasefire was negotiated by the rotating EU Presidency, France, which was a laudable achievement, but it left the EU split on subsequent policy and unable to bolster the ENP as a means to help solve the conflict.[28] To what extent should the EU confront Russia and support Georgia's democracy, in effect aligning with the ENP's promise to create a neighbourhood governed by the rule of law and also with US policy, or instead criticise both parties (partly considering Georgia's likely proactive role in provoking the August 2008 war) and thus placate Russian sensibilities in the hope of promoting a new European security architecture and securing European energy supplies? Having frozen strategic partnership talks with Russia on 1 September, the EU decided in mid-November to unfreeze them – while countries such as the UK, Sweden and Lithuania voiced their marked concern.[29] Russian President Medvedev in the meantime seeks to woo the Europeans, outlining a new security architecture that emphasises the vices of US leadership or dominance as well as the virtues of multipolarity.[30] Russia has effectively clarified the choice with which the EU is faced: in the Russian-American game of Eurasian influence, the EU must choose which side to support. Georgia has thus come to embody a strategic choice for the EU. At the time of writing the EU is likely to postpone choosing and await the policies of the American president-elect Barack Obama. The EU will find no guidance in the ENP; but its sense of strategic priorities in the Georgian context will significantly guide the ENP in the years ahead.

Ukraine is a similar strategic pivot in East-West relations. Its integration into the West has the potential to transform the geopolitical map of Europe by pulling other states in the area westward and thereby seriously curtailing the prospects of Russian reassertion.[31]

Thus Poland – who in fear of Russian imperialism desires to expand the Union's borders further eastward[32] – tries to link Ukraine to the case of Turkey, hoping to advance Ukrainian prospects of EU membership by representing it as a similarly complicated membership candidate.

The EU and the US engaged Ukraine at the same time and set up similar cooperation schemes. Although the EU Action Plan is more operational than the American one, neither of them is overly ambitious. In other words, the two approaches appear not only to be parallel in terms of the priority of issues but also synchronous – in alignment from the beginning.

The 'Orange Revolution' in November 2004 ushered in a new, more democratic era in Kiev with the Western-oriented Victor Yushchenko taking over the presidency, having defeated the Putin-backed Yanukovitch. The demonstrations and demands for a re-vote and democratic reform unleashed by election fraud and media discrimination made Ukraine a signpost for both the ENP and the US campaign promoting democracy – a clear setback for Russian hegemonic inclinations.[33] Nevertheless, the reform process has faltered with Ukraine going from one political crisis to another, involving most notably power struggles between President and parliament and opaque political marriages of convenience between the parliamentary majority and its opposition. The reform process is faltering, and the public appears unconvinced about the desirability of NATO membership.

American relations with Ukraine had not been a priority until Yushchenko came into power, but in April 2005 a broad agenda for cooperation on a range of issues was defined. President Bush at this occasion expressed his support for Ukraine's ambitions to pursue NATO membership.[34] The broad agenda was tantamount to ambiguity but the NATO issue has since gained steam. Ukraine, a NATO partner since 2004 and privilege to an Intensified Dialogue since April 2005, was singled out for NATO membership by the George W. Bush administration in 2008, as was the case for Georgia. Russia has issued dire warnings on the issue[35] but neither Russian warnings nor Ukrainian political turmoil have altered the US course.

The EU has only in recent years developed substantial relations with Ukraine and it lacks the strategic sense of priorities that characterise the US. The EU urges political and economic transition, which is in line with its European policy generally, and which led to Ukraine's inclusion in the ENP in May 2004. The EU adopted the Ukraine ENP Action Plan in February 2005.[36] Ukrainian political turmoil causes hesitation in the EU. While some EU members – Poland, the Baltic states, Scandinavia and Germany – support Ukrainian EU membership, southern European member states oppose it. This ambiguity resulted in the attachment of a somewhat vague letter of reform support to the Action Plan – a distinctively non-binding commitment.[37] It is not surprising, therefore, to witness Ukrainian dissatisfaction with the ENP and its demand for a special status – as in the Commission-sponsored ENP Conference in September 2007.[38]

Strategic ENP thinking appeared under the German EU Presidency in 2007, one should note. Introducing a *Neue Ostpolitik* and drawing on a legacy of historical German *Drang nach Osten* and Willy Brandt's *Ostpolitik*, the German Foreign Office envisioned, first, an 'ENP plus'[39] offering Moldova, Ukraine, Belarus, Georgia, Armenia and Azerbaijan a more attractive policy with a perspective of influence on decisions in areas with overlapping interests, a reallocation of funds benefiting the Eastern neighbourhood and the integration of regional initiatives in the programme; second, a realignment of European-Russian relations on the basis of a renegotiated PCA and, third, a strategy for Central Asia, where the EU had hitherto been strategically underrepresented compared to the US and Russia.[40]

The reorientation was not particularly successful. The Commission's adaptation of Berlin's proposal avoided shifting the priority of the ENP toward the East and precluded any institutional innovations. Thus, the proposal added little more to the policy than a thematic approach to cooperation in overlapping sectors, simplified travel restrictions, extended political dialogue, offered support for Black Sea cooperation and additional funding from individual EU member states and financial organisations[41] – all relatively uncontroversial issues. Russia was once again at the heart of EU challenges. The 2007 cessation of Russian oil deliveries to Belarus, Vladimir Putin's confrontational Munich Conference speech[42] and the issue of US missile defences had created deep rifts – and the May 2007 EU-Russia Summit in Samara ended in a dramatic verbal confrontation between Putin and Merkel. The Presidency's ambitions were also challenged from within the Union: Poland was consistently in opposition to the process. At the EU-Russia summit in Helsinki in November 2006 it had vetoed the renegotiation of the PCA in an attempt to compel the German Presidency to first deal with the Russian embargo against Polish meat exports and to acknowledge that a new agreement should to a greater extent reflect the interests of the countries in the post-Soviet space.[43] Hence, the only real success of the *Ostpolitik* was the adoption of a Central Asian strategy aiming at building bilateral and regional cooperation – and as such the impact of the German Presidency on the ENP was limited.

The German Presidency's priorities were strategic because they sought to prevent the establishment of a security gap between the EU and Russia in which Russia and the US could compete.[44] It was a step away from the Union's 'Russia-first-policy' and an attempt to pursue an anti-bloc-strategy – which could potentially set off unpredictable and unmanageable democratic developments with which Russia clearly felt uncomfortable. The US did not openly assess the priorities of the German Presidency, but the German policy could have been seen as unsolicited competition or a bid for equal partnership. As a strategy it was neither credible nor coherent enough to force the US to respond, however; Germany was pursuing its own ambition and its chances for success were limited. The Central Asian strategy was a step toward matching the US rather than setting an independent agenda – and in that sense the EU realigned with the US.

Both the EU and the US have strong interests in the wider Black Sea region. With the accession of Romania and Bulgaria to the EU, it has become the Union's new South-Eastern border. The region's geo-strategic importance is unquestionable as it provides a corridor for energy pipelines between the Caspian region and the EU – a corridor outside Russian territory, that is. For the US, the Black Sea region has gained in strategic significance since the 11 September terrorist attacks: it is now an important buffer zone between the West and the greater Middle East and an attractive platform for military operations in the fight against terrorism.[45]

Within the framework of the ENP plus, the German Presidency introduced the Black Sea Synergy initiative in April 2007, adding a regional dimension to the programme by inviting cooperation within the Black Sea region itself and between it and the EU on areas such as energy, environment, transport, internal security and democratic institutions.[46] EU and US policies in this context do not seem to differ significantly. Core US priorities in the region are the promotion of democracy, security and commerce – not least in the energy sector – but at the same time it *'want[s] to start kind of small'*, that is, work within existing frameworks and bilaterally on a voluntary basis.[47] This modesty probably reflects an overburdened US foreign policy agenda which does not allow spending significant efforts on this specific engagement.[48] In the Black Sea, the ENP thus reinforces transatlantic relations.

Russia, along with Turkey, is not involved in the ENP Black Sea initiative. Russia's reactions to the Black Sea Synergy initiative have been cautious, but both the prospective threat against its dominant position in the energy field and the European attempt to modernise the region are potentially able to undermine Russian influence. Russia's response to the Black Sea dimension of the ENP will once again reveal the extent of its support for regional pro-democratic and pro-market developments, although the debate at the regional level will be less pitched than in the controversial case of Georgia.

In the Black Sea region as elsewhere, the EU and the US will find it difficult to exclude Russia – if only because they need Russia to deal with countries such as North Korea, Iran and Afghanistan[49] – but they also find cooperation difficult given Russia's inclination to divide the EU by playing up bilateral relations with individual European countries and also split the Atlantic Alliance by driving wedges between the EU and the US.[50] Still, we observe a tentative alignment of EU and US positions in the post-Soviet space. The cases vary in terms of the sequence of involvement of the US and the EU: in the Black Sea region, the EU took the policy initiative; in the case of Ukraine the US and the EU act simultaneously and in the cases of Georgia and the Central Asian Strategy the EU tends to follow in the footsteps of the US. Alignment should not be exaggerated: the case of Georgia, particularly, reveals flaws in the transatlantic line-up. The US has combined geopolitics and democracy promotion in a policy of Georgian support; the EU is split between a policy of democracy promotion, which would imply support for Georgia, and a policy of geopolitics, which would imply partnership with Russia. US policy may be controversial but it is stringent; EU policy is not. Strategic ENP initiatives are either weak, like in the case of the Black Sea region, and therefore possible or they are strong and therefore controversial, and in the end they become impossible, like in the case of Germany's new *Ostpolitik*. The ENP contributes little to EU policy coherence and outlook. The best that can be said for it is its role as a vehicle for EU debate and coordination.

The ENP and the Middle East

In what ways has the ENP impacted on EU-US relations in the making of peace in the Middle East? These relations were never simple to account for, and the Iraq War – along with the collapsed peace process – complicates matters further. Still, we can see in the ENP a number of developments that on balance give reason to believe that the two sides of the Atlantic maintain a tenuous alignment. This is so because general threat perceptions, the specific positions on an Israeli-Palestinian peace agreement and the approaches to Iran converge. However, neither side of the Atlantic has a comprehensive approach to the region, which makes their positions vulnerable to almost inevitable bursts of conflict.

The contribution of the ENP in respect of these issues of cooperation and discord is mixed. The ENP has clarified EU interests in creating stability and steering processes in individual countries, and it has thus stimulated transatlantic cooperation. However, the ENP does not offer ENP countries reciprocity on issues such as market access, labour movement and multilateral trade – instead it offers various types of positive conditionality related to EU aid – with the implication that neighbouring adherence to the ENP is weak and in danger of weakening further. Moreover, the ENP is distinctively bilateral, which is to say that the EU has yet to develop strategic visions for specific neighbourhoods such as the Middle East: the EU is, for instance, silent on linkages between Israel-Palestine issues and Persian Gulf security.

The EU's approach to the flanking region of the Mediterranean was defined in 1995 as a distinctively multilateral and regional one with the Euro-Mediterranean Partnership (EMP) programme, also known as the Barcelona Process. The ambition was to create a 'multilateral and lasting framework' with the potential to transform 'the Mediterranean basin' into an area of prosperity and dialogue.[51] Results have not been impressive, however.[52] The ENP does not represent revolutionary change but it does introduce a reordering of priorities. First, the ENP is strong on bilateral relations, which we witness qua the ENP stress on tailored Action Plans and monitoring mechanisms. The ENP is a new instrument of positive inducement to produce national change. Moreover, the ENP is weak on multilateralism, which is a natural outgrowth of the ENP's geographical reach and also a consequence of the stalled EMP process.[53]

Greater bilateralism grew out of the frustrations of the Barcelona Process and also the way in which the ENP headed south: as the ENP originated in response to the 2002 *Eastern* enlargement, the Southern EU states feared a policy designed exclusively for Eastern Europe and pushed for the South's inclusion. Internal balancing rather than strategic vision lay behind the geographical scope of the ENP. The resulting lack of coherence naturally draws ENP officials to focus on country-by-country solutions – bilateral relations. Bilateralism is not merely a consequence of 'domestic' EU affairs, however. The complexity of the region is in itself an incentive for bilateralism, as it apparently offers the stronger part (the EU or the US) a fast-track to diplomatic efficacy.

Bilateralism is no substitute for overall coherence, however, which is why the US organised the Annapolis Middle East Peace Conference in November 2007 meant to revive the Israeli-Palestinian peace process, and which is why the EU not only supported this initiative but also, prior to the conference, outlined how 'themes' such as public health, energy and transport could be introduced into the ENP to strengthen its collective dimension.[54] Paradoxically considering its track record, the EU has even suggested drawing on the experiences of the Barcelona Process in shaping a new initiative for the Black Sea region.[55] The decisive question seems to be whether the diplomacy of the Atlantic partners is synchronised – whether the ENP and Middle East peace processes interact positively. This would be the best case for the ENP.

The Iraq War was anything but multilateral, but the gist of American policy for the region sought to be so, as it aimed to establish a framework programme for democratisation in the Middle East and North Africa. The US blueprint for the 'Broader Middle East and North Africa' (BMENA) thus resulted in the G8, June 2004, 'Partnership for Progress and a Common Future' and an ongoing and broadly inclusive Forum for the Future.

The trouble behind this initiative lay in its prior synchronisation, or rather lack hereof, with European policy. European policy – the Barcelona Process and also the involvement in the Israeli-Palestinian process – was seen as 'more inclusive' than American policy and 'the only game in town' for many countries.[56] The EU thus wanted to protect European multilateralism against American multilateralism, which led to an awkward compromise in June 2004: the G8 first launched the broad framework program; subsequently the EU and the US declared that 'We will build upon our respective policy frameworks and instruments.'[57] Adding to this plethora of instruments, the Atlantic allies decided two days later to strengthen NATO's Mediterranean Dialogue – never much of a policy instrument – and establish a new Istanbul Cooperation Initiative offering partnership notably to the countries of the Gulf Cooperation Council (GCC).[58]

The transatlantic challenge vis-à-vis the Middle East is therefore the synchronisation of multilateral policies and the definition of a common view of the balance between multilateral and bilateral instruments. In this context the EU has benefited from the ENP to articulate specific goals and interests that enhance transatlantic cooperation. However, this ENP effect should not be overestimated, nor should its shortcomings be overlooked.

We begin with the positive contribution visible in the Israel-Palestine peace process. The onset of the second Intifada in 2000 and the disintegration of the Oslo peace process shattered the investments made by the EU in creating peace bottom-up through economic reform, civil society and regional cooperation. At that time, the EU invested economically in the Palestinian areas and tended to criticise Israeli policy, which strained relations to the US. Today, the ENP Action Plans for Israel and the Palestinian Authority reflect a differentiated approach, with the Palestinian plan involving more demands on the part of the EU where the Israeli plan is more symmetric.[59] With the ENP the EU has thus improved its historically tense relations to Israel and it has flexed its muscle vis-à-vis the Palestinians.

The alignment of Atlantic positions began tentatively in June 2002 when the EU called for a two-state solution based on the 1967 borders and the US declared itself in favour of a Palestinian state granted it was democratic and desisted from terrorism.[60] A quartet of the US, the EU, the UN and Russia then defined a new 'road map' and revived the peace process in the early months of 2003. The alignment was not complete, however. Some European countries, France in particular, called for an international peace conference early in the process but this was rejected by the US with reference to the step-by-step logic of the road map. Moreover, in April 2004 the US endorsed Israel's plan for a unilateral Gaza withdrawal and held out the prospect that Israel could retain some settlements in the West Bank and refuse the Palestinian refugees' right of return. President Bush did seek to grant the Palestinians some favours – declaring that security barriers must be 'temporary' and a Palestinian state 'viable and contiguous' – but he plucked from the hands of the Palestinian negotiators 'formidable negotiating levers' and distanced the US from the European position.[61]

The stalemated road map process and Hamas' election victory in January 2006 caused the US to shift course, once again bringing transatlantic alignment into view. Secretary of State Condoleezza Rice began in late 2005 an engagement to establish the foundations for final status talks (partly in a failed attempt to prevent the Hamas victory), which brought about an agreement to have the EU monitor the Gaza border[62] and ultimately led to the common support for the Annapolis Middle East Peace Conference in November 2007. Europeans had eagerly pushed for this conference – President Chirac renewed the French call for it in September 2006, and Javier Solana urged in January 2007 'It's time to enter final status talks'[63] – and are committed to supporting the process politically as well as financially[64] while the US had changed tracks to make the conference possible. The conference achieved a short-term gain in so far as bilateral negotiations between Israel and the Palestinian Authority began anew; however, the two Palestinian camps, Hamas and Fatah, failed to agree on a platform prior to the conference and Annapolis did not seriously address the key outstanding issues. Momentum was therefore soon lost.[65]

In sum, alignment happens because the US has turned away from the stalemated 'flexibility' of the road map and now seeks to use the road map along with the Annapolis Summit to promote final status talks. The EU on its part is ready to work more even-handedly with the local parties. The EU and the US are thus for the moment synchronised in the desire to reinvent multilateralism in the search for regional peace. The EU has positively used the conditionality and specificity of the ENP to bolster its role.

We detect a similar positive contribution in the case of Lebanon where the 2005 assassination of Rafik Hariri led to the withdrawal of Syrian forces from the country and the formation of a new government more in tune with the policy of the EU as well as the US. The EU Action Plan for Lebanon, on which work began in 2005, was a prime occasion for the EU to align with the new government and bolster its commitment to reform.[66] The EU momentum continued in the wake of the 2006 war between Hezbollah and Israel where the EU managed to balance its criticism of the war, of American peace initiatives (or what was perceived as the lack thereof), and to contribute around 7000 troops to a reinforced UN border mission, the UN Interim Force in Lebanon (UNIFIL) that provided the warring parties with an exit strategy. Remarkably, the EU is now monitoring borders in both Israel's north and south. True, the EU must now show itself capable of dealing with intransigent players such as Hamas and Hezbollah, which is no small challenge.[67] Continued transatlantic cooperation is one way to meet it, and the Atlantic partners were off to a promising beginning in 2007 when they agreed on a first step toward engaging Syria in regional diplomacy.[68] The ENP can again be useful because it is the economic boon that awaits the conclusion of an association agreement between Syria and the EU, and because it is built into the EU's 2006 'ENP instrument' – the 'country Strategy Paper' for Syria.[69] This instrument has every type of conditionality built into it that the EU needs to align with US policy and sustain regional peace initiatives. Its contribution will depend on continued transatlantic alignment.

The contribution of the ENP should be put into perspective. The ENP is not a cause of these events: the ENP facilitates the EU's involvement and alignment with the US on some issues. Moreover, the ENP has limits that it is important not to overlook.

In the case of the Middle East, it is a fact that the peace process is more sensitive to events in Iraq and Iran than in the Ukraine or elsewhere within the ENP domain. The EU signed a cooperation agreement with the Gulf Cooperation Council (GCC) in 1989 and has since then not developed coherent policies toward the area. To be sure, the EU troika of France, the UK and Germany has since 2002–2003 negotiated with Iran to secure its commitment to non-proliferation, which was an important diplomatic initiative. Moreover, the United States finally backed EU diplomacy in the spring of 2005, which was the most explicit American recognition hitherto of the EU's worth as a diplomatic actor. However, and apart from the fact that the EU negotiations faltered and that the United Nations Security Council took charge, to no greater effect, the EU has yet to devise the general implications of its Iranian engagement. It is worth noting that this engagement is part of the EU's general foreign policy (i.e. the CFSP) run by governments whereas the ENP is a community instrument run by the Commission; thus we encounter the habitual problem of internal coordination and the resulting lack of strategic vision.

This is too bad, partly because Western economies are set to remain dependent on Persian Gulf stability,[70] partly because peace is a regional issue and because Iran's foreign policy increasingly impacts on Israel's security and thus Israel's willingness to enter peace agreements. Israel will not support regional peace if non-proliferation is used against Israel while countries such as Iran retain a free hand to become threshold nuclear weapons states. Moreover, existential threats to Israel will naturally undermine peace and inflame diplomatic relations of the entire region. It may be that Iran's 'Khatami compromise' ('we will honor what the Palestinian people accept' – which is another way of indirectly accepting the prospect of recognising Israel) remains alive despite President Ahmadinejad's pronouncements to the contrary, and it may thus be that the EU can focus predominantly on an Israel-Palestine peace as a lever to moderate Iran.[71] It would be more coherent to address all the issues in the Middle Eastern basket, however. Up to this point the EU has not done so. The ENP is of no help because it draws a line between EU neighbours and other states, privileging relations between states in the Levant and the Baltic at the expense of regional relations. Cross-cutting themes might strengthen the ENP's collective dimension but they will not help solve this problem. The EU must continue to think outside the box, outside the ENP, if it is to continue to clarify its strategic interests and its ability to promote an alignment of EU and US policy. If it can do so, the ENP will be of significant use and a contributor to, not a source of , improved transatlantic relations.

Conclusion

The ENP has not figured prominently on the radar screen in Washington and has in fact often fallen below it. The US occasionally recognises the ENP as one of several instruments that advance transatlantic coop-eration but only in the grand statements of summits. There is little or no evidence of the ENP entering into policy considerations and opera-tional thinking in Washington and thus little evidence that the ENP has made any significant contribution to transatlantic relations. Still, the ENP signals a change of EU outlook and it is reasonable to expect at least some effect of the ENP on transatlantic relations. From this article we draw four major conclusions.

First, the ENP represents a strategic challenge to the EU. The ENP is almost cosmic in scope and reach: it stretches from the Baltic to the western tip of North Africa and covers a vast range of political, economic, social and religious systems. Making sense of the ENP in this context is in itself a strategic challenge. Moreover, the EU will increas-ingly encounter external great powers and embedded conflicts, and the ENP should logically align with the EU's other foreign policy instru-ments, notably the CFSP and ESDP. This is the true stuff of strategy. Considering limits and constraints internal to the EU, transatlantic cooperation appears a necessity for the EU to succeed.

Second, the ENP has demonstrably made a difference in transatlantic relations because it has facilitated agreement. This was apparent in the cases of Israel, Lebanon, Georgia and the Black Sea Region. Specifically, the ENP enabled the EU to establish more symmetric relations with Israel and thus align with the US on important issues in the peace process, provided the EU with a chance to support the new Lebanese government at a time when both sides of the Atlantic were in opposition to Syria and in favour of political change in Lebanon and gave the EU the opportunity to define its relationship to Georgia and thus connect to the US policy agenda for the Caucasus, but in the Black Sea Region it serves as a complementary tool in the transatlantic tool box. This said, there is no hiding the fact that the ENP is an auxiliary instrument whose value varies with underlying transatlantic trends.

Third, the ENP has a perverse internal effect on the EU politi-cal system in so far as its wide focus and scope inhibit discipline and encourage controversial, nationally motivated proposals. The German

Presidency is a case in point in so far as its proposals for a new Eastern Dimension to the ENP dovetailed with German political tradition but not with the collective outlook. The Portuguese Presidency followed suit by replacing this dimension with a Southern Dimension, after which Slovenia re-focused attention, this time on the Western Balkans. Put differently, the ENP does not discipline the Council Presidency and instead invites conflicts over foreign policy resource allocation. New institutions built into the Treaty of Lisbon (a Council President and an EU High Representative for Foreign Affairs and Security Policy) may help but there is above all a need to rethink the multilateral dimension of the ENP and clarify its basic purpose.

Finally, the ENP is really hostage to EU coherence broadly conceived. The ENP is a reflection of political ambiguity within the EU and it would be naïve to expect the ENP to discipline EU politics. It is the inverse relation that matters, which is also to say that the EU ought to reflect strategically independently of the ENP. The EU is in the process of revising its 2003 Security Strategy, which is much needed considering this document's broadness. The new or updated strategy should notably define where and how transatlantic relations will be useful in the EU's near abroad. The EU's internal development is stalled, however, alongside the Reform Treaty that Ireland rejected in June 2008. It is not certain that the EU will emerge reinforced from this process of internal debate and reform. To wriggle out of it, the EU heads of state and government should *not* think about the ENP; they should instead ponder the turbulent security environment and common transatlantic interests in it. Clear-sightedness regarding these common interests can lead to a better ENP, not vice versa.

Notes

1. Commission of the European Communities (2003), Communication from the Commission *Wider Europe – Neighbourhood: A New Framework for Relations with our Eastern and Southern Neighbours*, COM(2003) 104 final, p. 4, Brussels, 11 March 2003. http://ec.europa.eu/world/enp/pdf/com03_104_en.pdf, date accessed 3 August 2007. This report became a strategy in May 2004.
2. W.C. Wohlforth (2004), 'The transatlantic dimension', in R. Dannreuther, (ed.), *European Union Foreign and Security Policy: Towards a Neighbourhood Strategy*. London: Routledge, pp. 192, 194.
3. R.A. Pape (2005), 'Soft Balancing Against the U.S.', *International Security*, 30 (1), pp. 7–45; T.V. Paul (2005), 'Soft Balancing in the Age of U.S. Primacy', *International Security*, 30 (1), pp. 46–71. Also B. Posen (2006), 'European Union Security and Defense Policy: Response to Unipolarity?' *Security Studies*, 15 (2), pp. 149–86; B. Posen (2004) 'ESDP and the Structure of World Power,' *The International Spectator*, 39 (1), pp. 5–17.

4. S.G. Brooks and W.C. Wohlforth (2005), 'Hard Times for Soft Balancing', *International Security,* 30 (1), pp. 72–108; K.A. Lieber and G. Alexander (2005), 'Waiting for Balancing: Why the World is not Pushing Back', *International Security,* 30 (1), pp. 109–39.

5. Z. Brzezinski (1998), *The Grand Chessboard.* New York: Basic Books; see also his (2004) *The Choice.* New York: Basic Books.

6. N.J. Spykman (1944), *The Geography of the Peace.* New York: Harcourt, Brace and Company, p. 57.

7. We should note that the Council of Europe was in fact the first organisation to expand its membership: the first Warsaw Pact country became a member of the Council in 1990.

8. The EU began its post-Cold War enlargement in 1995 but with three neutral Western countries (Sweden, Finland and Austria).

9. For an overview, A. Missiroli (2004), 'The EU and its changing neighbourhood', in R. Dannreuther (ed.), *European Union foreign and security policy: Towards a neighbourhood strategy.* London: Routledge, pp. 12–26.

10. The 1996 Berlin Agreement concerned the realisation of a European Security and Defence Identity (ESDI), and the Western European Union (WEU) – not the EU – was defined as NATO's European partner. The 1999 Berlin Plus Agreement changed the substance of the agreement in minor ways but more importantly replaced the WEU with the EU. Given diplomatic wrangling on the issue notably of Turkey and its relation to the EU, the Berlin Plus Agreement entered into effect only in March 2003. The Berlin Agreement can be found in the North Atlantic Council's *Final Communiqué* of 3 June 1996 (M-NAC-1 96(63)); the Berlin Plus agreement in the *Washington Summit Communiqué* of 24 April 1999 (NAC-S 99(64)).

11. See R. Asmus (2002), *Opening NATO's Door.* New York: Columbia University Press.

12. The Tervuren proposal did not fall entirely flat, though: it resulted in the establishment of an EU planning cell at NATO military headquarters, SHAPE, as well as a similar operational planning cell in the EU military staff.

13. U.S. Department of State (2005), 'U.S.-EU Cooperation in the Broader Middle East,' *Fact Sheet,* 17 February 2005, available online http://www.state.gov/p/eur/rls/fs/42531.htm, date accessed 10 March 2008.

14. The United States Mission to the European Union (2001), 'U.S, Representative to EU Morningstar on U.S.-EU Relations', 29 January. Available online http://useu.usmission.gov/Article.asp?ID=707BBDED-7486–474D-9832–5FADB350DE60, date accessed 10 March 2008; see also C.L. Powell (2004), 'A strategy of Partnerships', *Foreign Affairs,* 83 (1), The White House (2002), 'President Bush Thanks Germany for Support Against Terror', *Remarks by the President to a Special Session of the German Bundestag,* Office of the Press Secretary, 23 May, available online http://www.whitehouse.gov/news/releases/2002/05/20020523–2.html, date accessed 10 March 2008.

15. No decoupling, no duplication, no discrimination. See M. Albright (1998), 'The Right Balance Will Secure NATO's Future,' *Financial Times,* 7 December. The policy was not new: it represented a continuation of the traditional policy since the early 1980s, see I. Peters (2004), 'ESPD as a Transatlantic

Issue; Problems of Mutual Ambiguity', *International Studies Review,* 6, pp. 381–401.

16. This sentiment finds expression in official statements most openly at the beginning of the Bush presidency, for example The United States Mission to the European Union (2001), 'U.S. Representative to EU Morningstar on U.S.-EU Relations'; The White House (2001a), 'Joint Statement by President George W. Bush and Chancellor Gerhard Schroeder on a Transatlantic Vision for the twenty first century', 29 March, available online http://www.whitehouse.gov/news/releases/2001/03/20010329–5.html, date accessed 10 March 2008; The White House (2001b), 'Press Availability with President Bush and NATO Secretary General Lord Robertson,' NATO headquarters, 13 June 13, available online http://z22.whitehouse.gov/news/releases/2001/06/20010613–10.html, date accessed 10 March 2008; see also K. Archik and P. Gallis (2004), *NATO and the European Union,* CRS Report for Congress, Congressional Research Service, Library of Congress. Later statements focus more on the need for the EU to develop capabilities to share the burdens of meeting new challenges, but the three 'red lines' appear to be widely recognised by commentators, for example N. Gardiner and J. Hulsman (2004), 'A Historic Moment for NATO', *WebMemo # 465,* The Heritage Foundation; *Financial Times* (2000), 'Europe: US Diplomat Warns Europe over Defense,' 19 May, Friday USA 2nd Edition.

17. N. Gardiner, J. Spencer, J.J. Carafano and Will Schirano (2003), 'Secretary Powel's message to Europe: Measuring NATO's Future Performance', *WebMemo # 364,* The Heritage Foundation; N. Gardiner and J. Hulsman (2005),'The Bush Administration Should Not Back the European Constitution', *WebMemo # 668,* The Heritage Foundation; J.L. Cimabalo (2004), 'Saving NATO from Europe', *Foreign Affairs,* 83 (6), pp. 111–20; see also P.H. Gordon (2004) in: N. Gnesotto (ed.), *EU Security and Defense Policy: The First Five Years (1999–2004).* Paris: Institute for Security Studies; C. Grant (2003), 'Reviving European Defence Cooperation', *NATO Review,* Winter 2003.

18. An expression first used by President George Bush in an address to the citizens of Mainz, Germany, shortly before the fall of the Berlin wall in 1989 (G. Bush (1989), 'A Europe Whole and Free,' *Remarks to the Citizens in Mainz,* Rheindgoldhalle, Mainz, Federal Republic of Germany, 31 May) and later re-introduced by George W. Bush in Warsaw June 2001. The White House (2001c), 'Remarks by the President in Address to Faculty and Students of Warsaw University,' 15 June, . available online http://www.whitehouse.gov/news/releases/2001/06/20010615–1.html, date accessed 10 March 2008). The expression has been used extensively to designate the American accomplishment of transforming Europe since the Second World War.

19. The White House (2002), 'President Bush Thanks Germany for Support Against Terror,' *Remarks by the President to a Special Session of the German Bundestag,* Office of the Press Secretary, 23 May, available online http://www.whitehouse.gov/news/releases/2002/05/20020523–2.html, date accessed 10 March 2008; U.S. Department of State (2002), 'Charting a New Course in the Transatlantic Relationship,' *Remarks by Richard N. Haas to the Centre for European Reform,* available online http://www.state.gov/s/p/rem/10968.htm, date accessed 10 March 2008.

20. D. Anable (2006), 'The Role of Georgia's Media – and Western Aid – in the Rose Revolution', *The Harvard International Journal of Politics/Press*, 11 (3), pp. 7–43; G. Sanikidze (2004), 'The Georgian "Rose Revolution": Causes and Effects', *Caucasus and Central Asia Newsletter,* The Caucasus and Central Asia Program at the University of California, Berkeley, 5, Winter 2004, pp. 13–14.

21. Having failed at the April 2008 Bucharest Summit to secure access for Georgia and the Ukraine to NATO's Membership Action Plan (MAP), the outgoing Bush administration in November–December sought to prepare NATO membership for these countries outside the MAP. *New York Times* (2008c), 'U.S. Presses NATO on Georgia and Ukraine', (26 November).

22. Commission of the European Communities (1999), *Partnership and Cooperation Agreement between the EU and Georgia,* available online http://ec.europa.eu/external_relations/ceeca/pca/pca_georgia.pdf, date accessed 10 March 2008.

23. Commission of the European Communities (2003), Communication from the Commission, *Wider Europe – Neighbourhood: A New Framework for Relations with our Eastern and Southern Neighbours* COM(2003) 104 final, p. 4, Brussels, 11 March 2003, available online http://ec.europa.eu/world/enp/pdf/com03_104_en.pdf, date accessed 3 August 2007.

24. Commission of the European Communities (2006), *EU/Georgia Action Plan*, available online http://ec.europa.eu/world/enp/pdf/action_plans/georgia_enp_ap_final_en.pdf, date accessed 10 March 2008.

25. For example *The International Herald Tribune* (2006), 'U.S. Eager to Court Thorn in Russia's side; Georgia's Strategic Value Draws Attention,' 5 July.

26. Roy Allison (2008), 'Russia resurgent? Moscow's campaign to "coerce Georgia to peace"', *International Affairs* 84 (6) (November), pp. 1145–71.

27. Stephen Sestanovich (2008), 'What Has Moscow Done?' *Foreign Affairs* 87 (6) (November–December), pp. 12–28.

28. *The Economist* (2008), 'Too soon to kiss and make up' (18 October).

29. *New York Times* (2008b), 'European Union to Resume Russian Partnership Talks' (November 11); *BBC News* (2008), 'EU to end freeze on Russia talks' (10 November.), available online http://news.bbc.co.uk/2/hi/europe/7719666.stm, date accessed 1 December 2008.

30. President Medvedev's idea of a new security architecture predates the August 2008 war but got boosted in the diplomatic wake of the war, especially as a means to appeal to Europeans. See *The Daily Telegraph* (2008), 'Russian president Dmitry Medvedev calls for Europe to freeze out US', (8 October).

31. S.F. Larrabee (2006), 'Ukraine and the West', *Survival,* 48 (1); Z. Brzezinski (1998), *The Grand Chessboard*. New York: Basic Books, p. 46.

32. N. Copsey (2007), 'The Member States and the European Neighbourhood Policy', *European Research Working Paper Series,* No. 20, European Research Institute, University of Birmingham.

33. A. Karatnycky (2005), 'Ukraine's Orange Revolution', *Foreign Affairs* (March/April).

34. The White House (2005), *Joint Statement by President George W. Bush and President Viktor Yushchenko: A New Century Agenda for Ukrainian-American*

Partnership, Office of the Press Secretary, 4 April, available online http://www.whitehouse.gov/news/releases/2005/04/20050404–1.html, date accessed 10 March 2008.

35. *Washington Post* (2008), 'Putin Threatens Ukraine on NATO' (13 February).
36. Commission of the European Communities (2006), *EU/Georgia Action Plan,* available online http://ec.europa.eu/world/enp/pdf/action_plans/georgia_enp_ap_final_en.pdf, date accessed 10 March 2008.
37. For a discussion of the issue see G. Gromadski, O. Sushko, M. Vahl, K. Wolczuk and R. Wolczuk (2005), *Will the Orange Revolution bear fruit? EU–Ukraine relations in 2005 and the beginning of 2006.* Warzaw: Stefan Batory Foundation, pp. 18–20. Available online http://www.batory.org.pl/doc/orange.pdf, date accessed 10 March 2008.
38. *EU observer* (2007), 'EU neighbourhood policy divisions exposed' (4 September).
39. Although the term 'ENP plus' has been adopted by many commentators, it should be noted that it was invented by the German Presidency and does not appear in EU documents, which instead speak of an 'enhanced' or 'strengthened' ENP. Its current contents remain somewhat vaguely defined, as not all proposals have been implemented yet. For details on the process, see Commission of the European Communities (2008), 'European Neighbourhood Policy – Strengthening the ENP', available online http://ec.europa.eu/world/enp/strengthening_en.htm, date accessed 10 March 2008.
40. I. Kempe (2007), 'A New Ostpolitik? Priorities and Realities of the German EU Council Presidency.' *C.A.P. Policy Analysis,*4 (August), available online http://www.cap.lmu.de/download/2007/CAP-Policy-Analysis-2007–04.pdf, date accessed 10 March 2008.
41. Commission of the European Communities (2006), *Communication from the Commission to the Council and the European Parliament on Strengthening the European Neighbourhood Policy,* Brussels 4 December 2006, COM(2006)726 final, available online http://ec.europa.eu/world/enp/pdf/com06_726_en.pdf, date accessed 10 March 2008.
42. V.W. Putin (2007), Speech at the 43rd Munich Conference on Security Policy, 10 February, available online http://www.securityconference.de/konferenzen/rede.php?sprache=en&id=179, date accessed 10 March 2008.
43. M.A. Cichocki (2007), 'The German EU Presidency – The Polish Point of View', *Foreign Policy in Dialogue,* 8, (21), pp. 55–60.
44. For example *Frankfurter Allgemeine* (2006), 'Berlin entwickelt neue Nachbarschaftspolitik für die EU' (2 July).
45. A. Cohen and C. Irwin (2006), 'US Strategy in the Black Sea Region', *Executive Summary Backgrounder,* The Heritage Foundation, No. 1990; R.G. Nation (2007), *Russia, The United States and the Caucasus,* Strategic Studies Institute of the Army War College, available online http://www.strategicstudiesinstitute.army.mil/pdffiles/pub764.pdf, date accessed 10 March 2008.
46. Commission of the European Communities (2007), Communication from the Commission to the Council and the European Parliament, *Black Sea Synergy – A New Regional Cooperation strategy,* Brussels, 11 April 2007

COM(2007) 160 final. http://ec.europa.eu/world/enp/pdf/com07_160_en.pdf, date accessed 10 March 2008.

47. U.S. Department of State (2006), 'Economic Development and Security in the Black Sea Region', Remarks at the 'Economic Development and Security in the Black Sea Region', Center for Strategic and International Studies Conference, Washington, DC, 31 October, available online http://www.state.gov/p/eur/rls/rm/76035.htm, date accessed 10 March 2008.

48. B. Shaffer (2003) 'U.S. Policy in the South Caucasus,' in D. Lynch (ed.), *The South Caucasus: a challenge for the EU*, Chaillot Paper 65, EU ISS, pp. 54–61; R.G. Nation (2007), *Russia, The United States and the Caucasus*, Strategic Studies Institute of the Army War College, pp. 31–32, available online http://www.strategicstudiesinstitute.army.mil/pdffiles/pub764.pdf, date accessed 10 March 2008.; See U.S. Department of State (2006), 'Economic Development and Security in the Black Sea Region', Remarks at the 'Economic Development and Security in the Black Sea Region', Center for Strategic and International Studies Conference, Washington, DC, 31 October, available online http://www.state.gov/p/eur/rls/rm/76035.htm, date accessed 10 March 2008.

49. A. Cohen and C. Irwin (2006), 'US Strategy in the Black Sea Region', *Executive Summary Backgrounder,* The Heritage Foundation, No. 1990.

50. Z. Brzezinski (1998), *The Grand Chessboard*. New York: Basic Books, pp. 118–22; L. Spetschinsky (2007), 'Russia and the EU: The Challenge Ahead', *Studia Diplomatica* 60 (1), pp. 151–170 at pp. 162–63; see also L. Alieva (2006), 'EU and the South Caucasus,' CAP Discussion Paper, presented at the conference 'Looking Towards the East: Connecting the German and Finnish EU presidencies', Bertelsmann Group for Policy Research, pp. 5–6; A. Cohen and C. Irwin (2006), 'US Strategy in the Black Sea Region', *Executive Summary Backgrounder,* The Heritage Foundation, No. 1990, p. 5.

51. Europa (1995), *Barcelona Declaration* (27–28 November), available online http://ec.europa.eu/external_relations/euromed/bd.htm, date accessed 10 March 2008.

52. The multilateral, regional framework was conceptually 'flawed,' argues Mark Heller: a lack of results followed from the fact that the Euro-Mediterranean space does not 'in any meaningful sense' constitute a region. Heller (2001), 'Reassessing Barcelona', in F. Tanner (ed.), *The European Union as a Security Actor in the Mediterranean*. Zurich: Center for Security Studies, pp. 75–82. External events such as the faltering Middle East process thus impacted all the more directly on the process. See C. Spencer (2001), 'The Euro-Mediterranean Partnership: Changing Context in 2000', *Mediterranean Politics*, 6 (1), pp. 84–88.

53. For a comparison see R.A. Del Sarto and T. Schumacher (2005), 'From EMP to ENP: What's at Stake with the European Neighbourhood Policy towards the Southern Mediterranean,' *European Foreign Affairs Review*, 10 (1), pp. 17–38.

54. See Commission of the European Communities (2006), 'Non-paper: Expanding on the Proposals Contained in the Communication to the European Parliament and the Council on 'Strengthening the ENP' – COM (2006) 726 Final of 4 December 2006', available online http://ec.europa.eu/

world/enp/pdf/non-paper_thematic-dimension_en.pdf, date accessed 10 March 2008.

55. Council of the European Union (2007), *Outcome of Proceedings* (19 June), p. 3, available online http://register.consilium.europa.eu/pdf/en/07/st11/st11016.en07.pdf, date accessed 10 March 2008.

56. R. Dannreuther (2004), 'The Middle East Peace Process,' in R. Dannreuther (ed.), *European Union Foreign and Security Policy: Towards a Neighbourhood Strategy*. London: Routledge, p. 158.

57. U.S. Department of State (2004), *U.S.-EU Declaration Supporting Peace, Progress, and Reform in the Broader Middle East and in the Mediterranean* (26 June), available online http://usinfo.state.gov/xarchives/display.html?p=washfile-english&y=2004&m=June&x=20040627112537retnuh.ategdirb0.2226068, date accessed 10 March 2008.

58. NATO (2004), *Istanbul Summit Communiqué* (28 June), paragraphs 36–38, available online http://www.nato.int/docu/pr/2004/p04-096e.htm, date accessed 10 March 2008.

59. K. Smith (2005), 'The outsiders: The European neighbourhood policy,' *International Affairs*, 81 (5), pp. 757–73.The individual Action Plans are available online at http://ec.europa.eu/world/enp/documents_en.htm. The fact that the Action Plan with Israel was delayed because of the clash between the EU's policy of non-proliferation and Israel's implicit policy of nuclear deterrence is less important: this issue can only be resolved regionally, and for now the bilateral relationship has improved.

60. European Council (2002), *Declaration by the EU on the Middle East*, Sevilla European Council, 21–22 June 2002. For the US policy see The White House (2002), 'President Bush Calls for New Palestinian Leadership' (24 June), available online http://www.whitehouse.gov/news/releases/2002/06/20020624-3.html, date accessed 10 March 2008.

61. *New York Times* (2004a), 'Sharon coup: U.S. Go-Ahead' (April 15); *New York Times* (2004b), 'In Major Shift, Bush Endorses Sharon Plan and Backs Keeping Some Israeli Settlements' (April 15).

62. At the Rafah crossing. The EU mission is known as EU BAM Rafah.

63. J. Chirac (2006), speech before the United Nations General Assembly, New York, September 19; for Solana see *New York Times* (2007), 'U.S. Picks an Inauspicious Time to Restart Mideast Talks' (January 25).

64. J. Solana and B. Ferrero-Waldner (2007), 'Statebuilding for Peace in the Middle East: An EU Action Strategy,' *Joint Paper*, S378/07, available online http://www.consilium.europa.eu/ueDocs/cms_Data/docs/pressdata/EN/reports/97949.pdf, date accessed 10 March 2008.

65. K. Argyll (2008), 'Halfway Through Annapolis', *Washington Report on Middle East Affairs*, 27 (6) (August 2008), pp. 56–57; *New York Times* (2008a), 'Middle East Negotiators Press Pursuit of a 2-State Solution' (10 November 10).

66. The EU issued a country report on Lebanon in March 2005. In December 2005 the EU and Lebanon agreed to open negotiations on an ENP Action Plan which were successfully concluded in 2006.

67. *The Economist* (2006), 'Just a moment, or possibly more' (2 September).

68. *Middle East Economic Digest* (2007), 'Europe's shift on Damascus fails to draw economic ties' (16 March).

69. Commission of the European Communities (2008), *ENP Instrument: Syrian Arab Republic, Strategy Paper 2007–2013 & National Indicative Programme 2007–2010,* available online http://ec.europa.eu/world/enp/pdf/country/enpi_csp_nip_syria_en.pdf, date accessed 10 March 2008.
70. J. Barnes and A.M. Jaffe (2006), 'The Persian Gulf and the Geopolitics of Oil', *Survival,* 48 (1), pp. 143–62.
71. R. Takeyh (2006), 'Iran, Israel and the Politics of Terrorism,' *Survival,* 48 (4), pp. 83–96.

8

Explaining Russian Reactions to the European Neighbourhood Policy

Hiski Haukkala

Introduction

The post-Cold War era has largely been one of Western liberal hegemony.[1] Yet all is not well in the world of Western hegemony. Increasingly it seems that the appropriateness of liberal models is being challenged by other non-Western powers. To make a long story short – as it would deserve a book-length exposition of its own – the liberal agenda is being challenged both in its role as the only legitimate form of *internal* governance for the states (entailing a certain challenge to the role of democracy, human rights, etc. in the internal constitution of states) as well as eroding the consensus concerning the viability of certain neo-liberal principles (in short: the Washington Consensus as the organising principle for the global trading regime). Underlying these two trends is a broader undercurrent where the more traditional understandings of sovereignty as being based on essential non-interference in the affairs of states seems to be making a comeback at the expense of more recent attempts at qualifying the sovereignty of states by references to concepts such as 'the responsibility to protect', that have essentially been based on a liberal agenda concerning the primacy of individual rights and autonomy over those of states and other corporate actors.[2]

It seems, therefore, evident that the Western liberal hegemony is increasingly being challenged, even rejected. Yet it remains unclear what could come in its stead: the actors that have recently questioned the viability of these ideals – especially Russia and China – have thus far largely refrained from putting forward explicit normative agendas of their own. At the same time we should point out that from the vantage point of theory there is nothing particularly controversial about these processes: the constitution of international society and the role the question of sovereignty has played in the process has been redefined many times over the last four centuries.[3] What is more controversial, however, is the impact these changes have on the actual actors and their agendas. What is being argued here is that the future prospects may not be all bright and glowing for the West, the EU included.

This chapter seeks to give a rough sketch of the 'microfoundations' of the ongoing global normative recalibration. In this respect, it is argued that Russia's flat rejection of the European Neighbourhood Policy (ENP) is an instance where the Union's hopes of acting as a regional normative hegemon in the spirit to be discussed below has been seriously dented. It is in the context of 'battles' like this where ideas and agendas on the one hand are proposed, promoted or even imposed on others and either adopted, adapted, resisted or rejected on the other that the eventual constitution of international society will take its shape. In this respect, it is highly significant that Russia has successfully resisted Union's attempts at including Moscow in the process.

The chapter is divided into three parts. Drawing from my earlier work, the first part will make a brief case for conceptualising the ENP as the EU's attempts at regional normative hegemony based on the unidirectional imposition of its norms and values on its neighbourhood. The second part takes a look at Russian reactions to the initiative with particular reference being made to the role of normative convergence in the process. The chapter ends with some conclusions.

The ENP and the EU's regional normative hegemony[4]

In its foreign policy, especially in Europe, the Union seems to prefer bilateral relationships. This is reflected in a dense network of bilateral agreements that the EU has with countries in its neighbourhood both in the East and the South. The most obvious point where this process is manifested is of course the accession process where the Union in effect uses its economic and normative clout to create a set of highly asymmetrical bilateral relationships between itself and the candidates where the projection of norms and values is entirely one-sided.[5] The candidates are supposed to internalise not only the approximately 80,000 pages of *acquis communautaire* but also the value-basis of the Union, as exemplified by the Copenhagen criteria of 1993 which set out the other prerequisites for European belonging and full accession. It is this dual effect of cultivating normatively and materially asymmetrical relationships, together with the Union's insistence on the universal applicability of its own *internal* mode of governance for third parties, too, that resides at the heart of the Union's claim at regional normative hegemony, especially in Europe and its immediate neighbourhood.

Yet the application of the EU's normative hegemony in Europe is by no means confined to its future members alone. During the post-Cold War period the Union has built an extensive web of bilateral relationships in Eastern Europe that are based on the same set of norms and values as the accession process. For example, the EU has negotiated 11 Partnership and Cooperation Agreements (PCAs) with the so-called newly independent states of the former Soviet Union. Here as well the Union has sought the asymmetric bilateral approach but with a crucial difference, as accesssion has not been on the cards (but to be precise, not all of the post-Soviet states have aspired to membership, either). As a consequence, the key component of the Union's active leverage, political conditionality, has been weak and inefficient.[6] The Union's own half-hearted attempts at applying conditionality in practice seem to suggest that it, too, has been aware of this. The EU's discouraging track record in conditioning Russia's policy in Chechnya is a case in point, and Ukraine – especially during the reign of President Leonid Kuchma – is another. In both cases the EU has been content to let domestic events take their own course without seeking active change in the respective policies of the two of the most important Eastern neighbours of the Union.[7]

The ENP can be seen as having a dual function. On the one hand it is an attempt to devise an alternative to further enlargements of the Union. On the other it is an attempt at (re)injecting the Union's normative agenda and the application of conditionality more strongly to the relations with non-candidate countries as well.[8] As such, it is a conscious attempt at squaring the circle of relinquishing enlargement while retaining the Union's normative power in Europe. These aims were present already in the Commission's first blueprint concerning the policy, presented in March 2003.[9] The communication clearly stated that the new policy was meant for countries that did not enjoy the perspective of EU-membership. However, the document took great pains to make the case that the Eastern enlargement was not about exclusion and new dividing lines in Europe but that it would bring tangible benefits to new neighbours, too.

At the heart of the initiative was the EU's offer of enhanced relations and closer integration based on shared values between the Union and its neighbours. The mechanism is simple: in return for effective implementation of reforms (including aligning significant parts of national legislation with the EU *acquis*), the EU will grant closer economic integration with its partners. The approach is twofold, as the EU wanted first to tap the full potential of the already existing PCAs, namely the gradual harmonization of certain legal norms with the EU *acquis* and the creation of a free trade area, and only then move beyond with the prospect of realizing the so-called four freedoms (persons, goods, services and capital) within the 'Wider Europe' that would have included the Southern shores of the Mediterranean, Russia and everything in between.[10]

The concept was further developed in the Commission's strategy paper of May 2004.[11] The paper largely reiterated the points of departure of the earlier communication but it went further by identifying better the priorities and how to inscribe them into the neighbourhood action plans to be jointly adopted with the neighbours. The paper also envisaged a process based on clear differentiation between countries and regular monitoring of progress. It is, however, here that the Union's attempt at also creating a normative hegemony in its neighbourhood becomes clearly visible, as the process is built on a set of bilateral relationships between the individual neighbours and the EU. Scholars seem to be in agreement that this is a deliberate choice on the part of the Union to maximize its leverage over its neighbours.[12] Moreover, according to the strategy the Union does not give any meaningful say to the neighbours in setting the normative agenda: the objectives and the means are non-negotiable and the only place where the partners would be consulted is when the individual Action Plans with clear benchmarks and timetables, are being agreed upon. As such, the Union is offering (or withholding) economic benefits depending on the neighbours' ability and willingness to implement the Union's normative agenda and the EU is willing to give its neighbours influence only over *when* they want to implement the Union's demands and not *how* that is to be done.[13] In sum, it seems evident that the neighbours are not likely to have a large say in matters that will have a profound effect on their future development and place in Europe.

Although perhaps a slight caricature of the actual content and evolution of the ENP, this account nevertheless captures its essential gist. But even if the reading above should prove to be incorrect, the analysis below will show that Russian readings, at least, of the Union's initiative have largely corresponded to the model of the Union's regional normative hegemony outlined above. In essence, this is the background against which we must examine Russian reactions to the

Union's initial proposal also to include Russia in the policy template that we turn to next.

Russian reactions to the ENP and the Union's wider attempts at normative hegemony

In the recent years EU–Russia relations have become increasingly problematic, even conflictive. This has been reflected in Russia's growing insistence on a more equal role with the European Union that would be consummate with its regained sense of power. Increasingly, Russia has come to view the European Union and its policies, even if well-meaning, as overly intrusive and unwanted encroachments on Russia's own sovereignty. These modes of thinking have been gaining in prominence in Russia, especially during President Vladimir Putin's two terms as President that witnessed a certain consolidation of a more pragmatic nationalistic position promoted by Putin and his circle.[14]

It is against this background that Russian reactions to the ENP must be examined. On the one hand, there seems to have been certain appreciation of the rationale for the adoption of the policy. The bureaucratic and political necessities for bringing the various strands of the Union's proximity policies, especially, have received a nod of approval from the Russians.[15] Some voices have noted how the ENP is in fact a rather shrewd strategy from the supranational European Union to adapt itself to the processes of globalisation by pooling the resources of its neighbours, too, to the service of the centre in Brussels.[16] As such, the ENP has been seen as 'a graphic example' of how the internal methods of European integration are transferred into the realm of international relations outside the EU itself.[17] This has resulted in the abandonment of traditional geopolitics through the exploitation of 'gradual, sometimes latent, yet always effective, economic and legislative mechanisms to transform the states from inside.'[18]

But on the other hand, there has been an outright rejection of the applicability of the concept in the case of Russia. It has been seen as entailing a harmful intrusion into Russia's own sovereign prerogatives, including relations with its neighbours. As such, the ENP has been seen as essentially conceptually flawed. According to Deputy Foreign Minister Vladimir Chizhov: 'this [the ENP] is an attempt to reduce to the least common denominator groups of countries and individual states that are entirely different in their level of development and that, in addition to this, have different objectives with respect to the EU itself – objectives that are oftentimes incompatible with one another.'[19]

In essence, Russia felt insulted that it was grouped together with Moldova, Morocco and other countries in the Southern Mediterranean as a mere 'neighbour' of the Union.[20] Instead of becoming part of the Union's neighbourhood, Russia has insisted that its relations with the European Union must rest on the separate basis of an equal and mutually beneficial strategic partnership.[21] Chizhov's later words are worth quoting again in this context as they put the official Russian thinking on the issue in a nutshell: 'Russia is a large self-sufficient country with its own views on European and Euro-Atlantic integration. In contrast to some smaller Eastern European or South Caucasus countries striving for EU-membership Russia is neither a subject nor an object of the European Neighbourhood Policy.'[22] In any case, the Union's push for the ENP can be deemed a success, as it did inject the rather stale atmosphere between the Union and Russia with some new dynamism. It spurred Russia to react, first opting out from the ENP and then demanding a more privileged status as a 'strategic partner' based on equality.[23] The initiative for the development of a new and wider basis for relations in the form of Four Common Spaces at the St Petersburg EU-Russia Summit in May 2003 can be seen as a response to these Russian demands.

This is not the place to discuss the negotiations leading to the road maps for the Four Common Spaces that were adopted at the EU-Russia Summit in Moscow two years later.[24] Nor should scarce words in a short chapter like this be used to discuss the content of the documents as such, as works to that effect already exist.[25] Instead, attention will be drawn to the role that the question of Russia's normative convergence toward the rules, norms and standards of the European Union has played in the Russian debate. The question of normative convergence is, after all, at the heart of the Union's normative hegemony, the ENP and the Four Common Spaces included.

Since the beginning of the 1990s, the Union has sought to impose its norms and values onto Russia. This aim was originally codified in the Article 55 of the PCA between the EU and Russia which unambiguously stated that 'Russia shall endeavour to ensure that its legislation will be gradually made compatible with that of the Community.' Yet in actual fact the process of normative convergence has been slow in the coming with Russia dragging its feet at every possible instance. In fact, one way to read the Union's proposals for the Four Common Spaces and the Common European Economic Space (CEES) that predated them is to see them as attempts at 'operationalising' the rather monolithic and abstract obligation for Russia to harmonise its trade-related laws and rules with those of the EU *acquis*.[26] In essence, they can be seen as attempts at generating incremental forward momentum in a process that from the vantage point of the Union had so far been disappointing, to say the least.

It should be pointed out that the idea of normative convergence is highly challenging to sovereignty, akin to economic, even political integration. Such an extremely intrusive process in fact goes against the very grain of prevailing Russian understandings concerning what is feasible and desirable in international relations. By contrast, the idea of seeking equality and recognition for Russia's sovereignty runs like a red thread through most of the recent official Russian interventions in international politics in general and its relations with the European Union in particular. All of the major figures ranging from President Putin, both present and former ministers, parliamentarians, ordinary diplomats and even to judges in the Constitutional Court have conveyed basically the same message of Russia's equal rank and status in the contemporary world and the need to treat the indivisibility of state sovereignty as the main building block for the world order.[27] The expectation of equal treatment has started to filter also into official doctrines and documents in Russia. For example, the Russian Medium-Term EU Strategy takes equality between the partners as its starting point. More recently, material published from an ongoing review of Russian foreign policy has framed the same issue in the most explicit terms:

> A new important factor in European politics is the understanding that Russia is an independent player with global interests: This leaves no grounds for illusions about the possibility of co-opting this country into the loose Western alliance on terms dictated to us. This last circumstance highlights the non-viability of the unilateral policy pursued by the **European Union** in dealing with Russia. There is a pressing need to come to terms with Moscow on the basis of equality, which will require respect and consideration for the Russian position in the EU decision-making process – that is to say, a drastic revision of the modalities of our relations.[28]

Keeping this discussion in mind, it should not come as a surprise that Russia has started increasingly to question the very feasibility and legitimacy of normative convergence with the Union.[29] Perhaps the most scathing attack against Union's attempts at imposing its own norms and values on Russia has come from Oleg Ziborov, Senior Counsellor at the European Department of the Russian Foreign Ministry. According to him, only 'great powerism' corresponds with Russia's conditions, and any 'attempts, for example, to impose the dubious wisdom of the European Lilliputians on Russia should be seen as psychological aggression.'[30] Ziborov is by no means alone in these sentiments. An analysis of Russian stances on the issue, to be discussed in more detail below, produced a rather uniform picture of rejection of the Union's attempts at projecting its values and norms on Russia. This is also a finding that is supported by the existing research literature and scholarly commentary on the topic in Russia.[31] Russian public opinion also seems to concur. According to a public opinion poll conducted by the Levada Center in the summer of 2007, 74 per cent of respondents agreed with the sentence 'Russia is a Eurasian state that develops according to its own rules,' with only 10 per cent thinking that Russia should implement 'Western' rules at home.[32]

Behind this emphasis on equality and sovereignty seems to be an underlying understanding of world politics as 'an arena of uncompromising battle of interests and struggle for domination'.[33] The notion of ruthless global competition – economic, military and normative – seems to have strong resonance in the Russian elites. Perhaps the most famous occasion when such sentiments were voiced in public was in the aftermath of the tragic school siege in Beslan in September 2004 when President Putin argued how Russia had shown itself to be weak and that the weak get beaten. In addition, he warned that there exist actors who 'would like to tear from us a "juicy piece of pie". Others help them. They help, reasoning that Russia still remains one of the world's major nuclear powers, and as such still represents a threat to them. And so they reason that this threat should be removed.'[34]

Furthermore, especially in the aftermath of the Eastern enlargement to Central and Eastern European former Soviet satellites in 2004, there seems to be a growing understanding that in certain respects the European Union might prove to be a more serious challenger to the Russian position in the East than the traditional adversary, NATO.[35] Alternatively, leading Russian politicians also appear to bracket the EU and NATO together as organisations seeking to dictate policies, norms and values to Russia.[36]

A curious flip side to this stance seems to be the constant worry in Russia that European integration is progressing without Russia and that it might result in new dividing lines detrimental to Russia's economic and social development. Often this worry is framed in the way how the EU decisions, policies, norms and standards that affect Russia are prepared and taken without Russia's participation.[37] For example, the former Ambassador to Russia's Permanent Representation to the European Union, Vassily Likhachev, has noted how 'cooperation between Russia and the EU can be effective only when it is governed by international law rather than the whims or rules of one of the negotiating sides.'[38] More often than not, Russian reasoning seems to be that such developments are highly detrimental and that Russia remains committed to mutually beneficial cooperation 'on an equitable basis without dividing lines'.[39] This offer is, however, often made conditional on the Union's willingness to offer Russia the possibility of affecting its internal decision-making processes.

These understandings and demands seem to be entirely incompatible with the Union's views that emphasise the mutually beneficial win-win logic of its aims and actions (at the level of rhetoric) and the hegemonic projection, even imposition, of its norms and values (at the level of actual policies) while preserving its own decision-making autonomy. In the words of the Head of the European Commission Delegation in Russia, Richard Wright, the harmonisation of norms and standards is single-handedly beneficial for Russia:

> EU laws facilitate business effectiveness, and here unified approaches to standards would give Russia easy access to a potential single market. The advantages of harmonizing customs laws are obvious insofar as this removes trade barriers.... The application of EU rules and regulations would secure an effective functioning of any future free trade zone or unified economic area. Harmonization of regulations in the financial services sphere would help create a stable market in Russia, which would provide an incentive to attracting capital and stabilizing the capital flow. In conclusion, I would like to say that economic integration, accompanied by regulatory reform, would expedite Russia's economic growth.... I am sure that Russia and Russian business cannot afford not to adopt the same rules as are applied in all EU countries.[40]

Western economists by and large agree with this analysis.[41] Yet the Russians themselves are far from convinced. In essence, EU's attempts at liberalising and integrating the Russian economy and society are seen first and foremost as intrusions into the domestic affairs of the country with a view on discriminating Russian companies.[42] Some have gone as far as to argue that the main aim of the 'European project' is merely to exploit Russia's potential in order to reinvigorate its own ailing economy.[43]

The prevalence of these sentiments in the Russian debate has resulted in a growing weariness toward the logic of interaction propagated by the Union. This aversion takes several forms with similar traditional, sovereign undertones. First, the insistence of the Union as well as other European organisations, such as the Organization for Security and Co-operation in Europe (OSCE) and Council of Europe, on European norms and values is often seen as a thinly veiled attempt at hegemony and the use of double standards in judging Russia and other non-EU/European others in world politics.[44] In this respect, it is quite telling that in the recent years even the pro-Western and pro-reform liberal intelligentsia has started to view the EU policies as a systemic challenge aimed at preventing Russia from gaining full access to most important transnational structures and organisations.[45]

Second, the harmonisation of laws, even where permissible in principle, should only apply to certain relevant sectors, excluding the across-the-board harmonisation promoted by the Union that could be seen as detrimental to Russian sovereignty and statehood.[46] Third, the question of normative convergence is couched in terms of democratic legitimacy. Some Russian commentators have argued that the expectation of normative convergence makes Russia vulnerable to a potentially 'huge' democratic deficit as it is unilaterally forced to apply norms, rules and regulations without being given a chance to affect their essential content.[47] Fourth, the formation of a Common Economic Space with the Union, especially, is seen as potentially harmful and as undermining Russia's other economic projects in the post-Soviet space. Therefore, Russians insist that the process with the EU must be compatible and complementary to these other projects as well.[48]

Finally, European norms and standards are not only seen as a source of dilution of Russia's sovereignty, they are also increasingly seen as incompatible with and even harmful for Russia's own economic trajectory. The oil- and gas-led economic boom in Russia has resulted in a situation where Russians themselves have started to view their country as a more dynamic and successful economically than the European Union.[49] In this respect, an interesting document is the *The World Around Russia: 2017* scenario prepared at the influential Council on Foreign and Defense Policy (SVOP). In the document, the group of distinguished Russian scholars write how: 'A stagnant model of Europe's political development is not beneficial for Russia... Presently, it would be expedient for Russia to restore the balance between the political and economic-legal components of its relations with the EU at the level of equitable cooperation between independent agents of international relations.'[50]

Russian economists also point out that as the bulk of the Russian exports to the EU consists of energy and other raw materials that are already traded toll free, the actual short-term benefits of economic integration would be meagre while the potential costs for domestic manufacturers could be prohibitively high.[51]

One of the conclusions drawn from all this in Russia seems to be that it must look after its own interests regardless of the Union's attempts at normative hegemony or the weight of its institutions in framing common policies. This has manifested itself in the need to cultivate bilateral links with certain EU member states that cut across and undermine the common EU policies.[52] According to a foreign policy review prepared by the Russian Foreign Ministry, the insistence on the importance of bilateral relations with the EU member states is set to be emphasised even further in the future.[53]

Conclusion

This chapter has sought to explain Russia's rejection of the EU's ENP with a reference to a wider domestic context in Russia.[54] The essential finding of the analysis is that the ENP was rejected because its very logic – the Union's regional normative hegemony and the imposition of European norms and values in the process – was seen as incompatible with Russian ideas concerning the legitimate course of action internationally. In addition, Russia's growing weariness toward the idea of normative convergence also in the context of wider EU-Russia 'strategic partnership' seems to indicate that we are dealing with a more profound and growing rejection of the Union's normative hegemony than 'just' the rejection of one of its policy templates. In this respect, more is at stake than simply Moscow's hurt pride over being initially put in the same basket as Moldova and Morocco by the Union. In fact, the very logic of interaction based on certain shared ideals (European values) that the EU has sought to promote and cultivate during the post-Cold War era in Europe is being increasingly questioned by Russia. There is every indication that this trend that became so manifest during Putin's Presidency will be continued by his successor Dmitry Medvedev as well. For example, during his first foreign trip to Europe in June 2008, the new President stressed, while emphasising essential willingness to foster close cooperation with Europe, that Russia would reject all undertones of trying to impose any values or norms on the country.[55]

Having said this, one should note that at least so far Russia's actions have been mainly defensive ones: Moscow's insistence on equality and respect of its sovereignty has enabled it to ward off most the Union's normative hegemony but it has also highlighted the fact that Russia has been unable to come up with a set of ideas that would be competitive on the wider marketplace of ideas. This seems to be a recurring pattern in Russia's interaction with 'Europe': for not having been present at the creation of dominant modes of thought and institutions, Russia has been forced either to adapt its own constitution or resist that adaptation without being able to affect the essential content of these norms in any significant way.[56] In this respect, we may note that the problems the Union has faced with Russia tell us more about the inherent weaknesses of its own normative power than hint at Russia's vast potential in this respect. One of the interesting issues to be followed in the coming years is, however, whether Russia will be able to develop a coherent set of ideas – perhaps along the lines of 'sovereign democracy' currently being discussed in Russia – that would be able to challenge the Union's and wider West's normative power in the future.

What seems clear, however, is that these developments should be examined against the backdrop of wider constitution of international society. Here we should take note of the essential 'Westphalianness' of the current constitution of international society. In his magisterial overview of institutional change in world politics, Holsti has come to the conclusion that all the talk about 'erosion of sovereignty' and that we live in a 'post-Westphalian world' is not backed up by the empirical evidence. For him, the reverse seems to be the case with a 'good deal of the contemporary institutional context within which states pursue and defend their interests is recognizable in late seventeenth- and early eighteenth-century antecedents'.[57] In addition, one may also ask whether the possibilities of the Union's – and the wider West's – normative hegemony are actually diminishing and not increasing for the future. The recent and still emerging debate concerning the rise of economically successful but politically authoritarian powers seems to indicate that we might be witnessing an era where the hegemony of Western liberalism is eroding beyond repair.[58]

If this should be the case, then the EU could be left alone and increasingly marginalised with its normative approach to international relations. It would also mean that the Union's chances of tying Russia into its normative order in Europe will be severely circumscribed. This is so because Russia seems to have the option of approaching other power centres and normative agendas than the one represented by 'Europe' and the European Union. In this respect, Russia would seem to have the possibility of using the yet again increasingly Westphalian international society as a source of legitimacy when it is seeking to circumscribe and even subvert the Union's regional normative hegemony in Europe.

Notes

Statements of fact and opinion are those of the author and do not imply endorsement by the Government of Finland.

1. G. John Ikenberry (2001), *After Victory: Institutions, Strategic Restraint, and the Rebuilding of Order After Major Wars.* Princeton and Oxford: Princeton University Press.
2. Robert Kagan (2007), 'End of Dreams, Return of History', *Policy Review*, (August/September, available at http://www.hoover.org/publications/policyreview/8552512.html, last accessed 3 October 2007.
3. J. Samuel Barkin (1998), 'The Evolution of the Constitution of Sovereignty and the Emergence of Human Rights Norms', *Millennium: Journal of International Studies*, 27 (2), pp. 22952; Krasner (2001), 'Explaining Variation: Defaults, Coercion, Commitments', in Stephen D. Krasner (ed.), *Problematic Sovereignty: Contested Rules and Political Possibilities.* New York, NY: Columbia University Press, pp. 323–343; Reus-Smit (1997), 'The Constitutional Structure of International Society and the Nature of Fundamental Institutions', *International Organization*, 51 (4), pp. 555–589.
4. This section draws heavily from Hiski Haukkala (2010), *The EU–Russia Strategic Partnership: The Limits of Post-Sovereignty in International Relations.* London and New York: Routledge.
5. Vinod Aggarwal and Edward A. Fogarty (2004), 'Explaining Trends in EU Interregionalism', in Vinod Aggarwal and Edward A. Fogarty (eds), *EU Trade Strategies: Between Regionalism and Globalism*, . Basingstoke and New York, NY: Palgrave Macmillan, p. 231.
6. Karen E. Smith (1998), 'The Use of Political Conditionality in the EU's Relations with Third Countries: How Effective?' *European Foreign Affairs Review*, 3 (2), pp. 253–74; Richard Youngs (2001), 'European Union Democracy Promotion Policies: Ten Years On', *European Foreign Affairs Review*, 6 (3), pp. 355–73.
7. Kataryna Wolczuk (2004), *Integration without Europeanisation: Ukraine and its Policy towards the European Union.* EUI Working Papers, RSCAS 2004/15. Tuomas Forsberg and Graeme Herd (2005), 'The EU, Human Rights, and the Russo-Chechen Conflict', *Political Science Quarterly*, 120 (3), pp. 455–78.
8. Judith Kelley, (2006), 'New Wine in Old Wineskins: Promoting Political Reforms through the New European Neighbourhood Policy', *Journal of Common Market Studies*, 44 (1), pp. 29–55. Roland Dannreuther (2006), 'Developing the Alternative to Enlargement: The European Neighbourhood Policy', *European Foreign Affairs Review*, 11 (2), pp. 183–201.
9. Commission of the European Communities (2003), Communication from the Commission, *Wider Europe – Neighbourhood: A New Framework for Relations with our Eastern and Southern Neighbours* COM(2003) 104 final, Brussels,

174   *Hiski Haukkala*

11 March 2003, available at http://ec.europa.eu/world/enp/pdf/com03_104_en.pdf, last accessed 23 June 2008.

10. Since 2003 the Commission's blueprint has gone through several substantive transformations: Its name was changed from 'Wider Europe' to 'European Neighbourhood Policy'. The list of countries has also changed, as Russia – through its own insistence – was dropped from the initiative, whereas the countries of the Southern Caucasus (Armenia, Azerbaijan and Georgia) have been added to the list of 'neighbours'.

11. Commission of the European Communities (2004), Communication from the Commission, *European Neighbourhood Policy, Strategy Paper*, COM(2004) 373 final, p. 3, Brussels, 12 May 2004, available at http://ec.europa.eu/world/enp/pdf/strategy/strategy_paper_en.pdf, last accessed 23 June 2008.

12. Karen E. Smith (2005), 'The outsiders: The European neighbourhood policy', *International Affairs* (London), 81 (4), 757–73. Pertti Joenniemi and Chris Browning (2005), '"Ystävien piiri" Euroopan rajana – uuden naapuruuspolitiikan vaikutukset pohjoisessa', *Kosmopolis*, 35 (3), 6–19. Marius Vahl (2005) 'Lessons from the North for the EU's "Near Abroad"', in Christopher S. Browning (ed.), *Remaking Europe in the Margins: Northern Europe after the Enlargements*. Aldershot: Ashgate, pp. 51–67.

13. Federica Bicchi (2006), 'Our size fits all": normative power Europe and the Mediterranean', *Journal of European Public Policy*, 13 (2), pp. 286–303.

14. Margot Light (2003), 'In Search of an Identity: Russian Foreign Policy and the End of Ideology', *The Journal of Communist Studies and Transition Politics*, 19 (3), pp. 42–59; Bobo Lo, (2003), *Vladimir Putin and the Evolution of Russian Foreign Policy*. London: The Royal Institute of International Affairs and Blackwell.

15. Vladimir Chizhov (2004), 'European Union: A Partnership Strategy', *International Affairs* (Moscow), 50(6), pp. 79–87.

16. Kravchenko, Ivan (2007) 'The European Neighbourhood Policy', *International Affairs* (Moscow), 53 (1), pp. 43–49.

17. Ibid. p. 46.

18. Ibid. p. 49.

19. Vladimir Chizhov (2004), 'European Union: A Partnership Strategy', *International Affairs* (Moscow), 50 (6), p. 85.

20. For a discussion, see: Derek Averre (2005), 'Russia and the European Union: Convergence or Divergence?' *European Security*, 14 (2), pp. 175–202.

21. Vladimir Chizhov (2004) 'European Union: A Partnership Strategy', *International Affairs* (Moscow), 50 (6), p. 81.

22. Vladimir Chizhov (2006) Remarks at the 135th Bergedorf Round Table, 'Interests and Partners of German Foreign Policy', Berlin, 29 September–1 October 2006, available at http://www.koerber-stiftung.de/bg/recherche/pdf_protokoll/bnd_135_en_text.pdf, last accessed 23 June 2008. p. 90.

23. For a discussion with many illustrative Russian quotations, see: Derek Averre (2007), '"Sovereign democracy" and Russia's relations with the European Union', *Demokratizatsiya*, 15 (2), pp. 173–190.

24. Iit will be discussed in Haukkala (2010), *The EU–Russia Strategic Partnership: The Limits of Post-Sovereignty in International Relations*. London and New York: Routledge.

25. Michael Emerson (2005) 'EU-Russia Four Common Spaces and the Proliferation of the Fuzzy', *CEPS Policy Brief 71/May 2005*. Brussels: Centre for European Policy Studies. Katinka Barysch (2006), 'Is the Common Economic Space Doomed?' *The EU-Russia Review*, 2 (November 2006). Brussels: EU-Russia Centre, pp. 11–16.

26. Hiski Haukkala, (2003), 'What Went Right with the EU's Common Strategy on Russia', in Arkady Moshes (ed.), *Rethinking the Respective Strategies of Russia and the European Union*. Special FIIA–Carnegie Moscow Center Report. Helsinki and Moscow: The Finnish Institute of International Affairs and Carnegie Moscow Center, p. 75. Marc Maresceau, (2004), 'EU Enlargement and EU Common Strategies on Russia and Ukraine: An Ambigious Yet Unavoidable Connection', in Christophe Hillion (ed.), *EU Enlargement – A Legal Approach: Essays in European Law*. Oxford: Hart Publishing, p. 210.

27. Haukkala, (2010). See Note 24.

28. Advisory Council to the Minister of Foreign Affairs of Russia (2007), 'Russia in the Modern World', *International Affairs* (Moscow), 53 (2), p. 86, emphasis in the original.

29. Sergei Karaganov, (2005), 'Russia and the international order', in Dov Lynch (ed.), *What Russia sees*. Chaillot Paper 74, January. Paris: European Union Institute for Security Studies, pp. 23–43. Ibid., p. 32. Timofei Bordachev (2003), 'Strategy and Strategies', in Arkady Moshes (ed.), *Rethinking the Respective Strategies of Russia and the European Union*. Special FIIA–Carnegie Moscow Center Report. Helsinki and Moscow: The Finnish Institute of International Affairs and Carnegie Moscow Center, pp. 31–61.

30. Oleg Ziborov (2007), 'To Harmonize International Relations', *International Affairs* (Moscow), 53 (2), pp. 13–14.

31. Karaganov, Sergei et al (2005), 'Russia's European Strategy: A New Start', *Russia in Global Affairs*, 3 (3), pp. 72–85; Timofei Bordachev (2003), 'Strategy and Strategies', in Arkady Moshes (ed.), *Rethinking the Respective Strategies of Russia and the European Union*. Special FIIA–Carnegie Moscow Center Report. Helsinki and Moscow: The Finnish Institute of International Affairs and Carnegie Moscow Center, pp. 31–61. Timofei Bordachev and Arkady Moshes (2004), 'Is the Europeanization of Russia Over?' *Russia in Global Affairs*, 2 (2), pp. 90–102.

32. See 'Rossiya i Mir', 10 August 2007, available at http://www.levada.ru/press/2007081001.html, last accessed 26 September 2007.

33. Mikhail Maiorov (2007), 'On Moral Principles and National Interests', *International Affairs* (Moscow), 53 (2), p. 38.

34. Vladimir Putin, (2004). Address by President Vladimir Putin, Moscow, Kremlin, 4 September 2004, available at http://www.kremlin.ru/eng/speeches/2004/09/04/1958_type82912_76332.shtml, last accessed 25 September 2007.

35. Vladimir Chizhov (2004), 'European Union: A Partnership Strategy', *International Affairs* (Moscow), 50 (6), pp. 80–81.

36. Derek Averre, (2007) ' "Sovereign democracy" and Russia's relations with the European Union', *Demokratizatsiya*, 15 (2), p. 183.

37. Vladimir Chizhov, (2005), 'Russia – EU Cooperation: The Foreign Policy Dimension', *International Affairs* (Moscow), 51 (5), p. 137. Alexander Alekseev

(2001), 'Russia in European Politics', *International Affairs* (Moscow), 47(3), p. 41.

38. Vassily Likhachev, (2004), 'Russia and EU: Proficiency Essential', *Russia in Global Affairs*, 2 (2), p. 104.

39. Vasilii Likhachev (2000), 'Russia and the European Union: A Long-term View', *International Affairs* (Moscow), 46 (2), p. 122.

40. Richard Wright (2002), 'No State Has Ever Been Ruined By Commerce', remarks in 'The European Economic Area: Round Table Discussion', *International Affairs* (Moscow), 48 (4), pp. 181–82.

41. Stephen E. Hanson (2007), 'The WTO and Russian Politics', in NBR Special Report *Russia and the WTO: A Progress Report* 12 (March). Seattle, Washington: The National Bureua of Asian Research, pp. 7–12. Pekka Sutela (2005), *EU, Russia, and Common Economic Space*. BOFIT Online 3/2005. Helsinki: Bank of Finland, available at http://www.suomenpankki.fi/NR/rdonlyres/72D29959-BA8B-47D5-AA2B-DC4BA404E752/0/bon0305.pdf, last accessed 27 September 2007, esp. p. 28.

42. Heiko Pleines (2005) 'Russian Business Interests and the Enlarged European Union', *Post-Communist Economies*, 17 (3), p. 275.

43. Georgii Efimovich Skorov (2005), 'Rossiya-Evrosoyuz: Voprosi Strategicheskogo Partnerstva', *Mirovaya ekonomika i mezdunarodnye otnoseniya*, 3, p. 81.

44. Vladimir Chizhov, (2006), Remarks at the 135th Bergedorf Round Table, 'Interests and Partners of German Foreign Policy', Berlin, 29 September–1 October 2006, available at http://www.koerber-stiftung.de/bg/recherche/pdf_protokoll/bnd_135_en_text.pdf, last accessed 23 June 2008, p. 93.

45. Andrey Makarychev (2006), *Russia's Discursive Construction of Europe and Herself: Towards New Spatial Imagery*. EU-Russia: The Four Common Spaces Working Paper Series, 1–2. Nizhny Novgorod: Nizhny Novgorod Linguistic University, p. 7; see also Averre, Derek (2005) 'Russia and the European Union: Convergence or Divergence?' *European Security*, 14 (2), p. 180.

46. Ivan D. Ivanov (2002), Remarks in 'The European Economic Area: Round Table Discussion', *International Affairs* (Moscow), 48 (4), p. 184. Victor Khristenko (2004), 'Making Headway to Integration', *Russia in Global Affairs*, 2 (1), pp. 41, 46.

47. Timofei Bordachev (2003), 'Strategy and Strategies', in Arkady Moshes (ed.), *Rethinking the Respective Strategies of Russia and the European Union*. Special FIIA – Carnegie Moscow Center Report. Helsinki and Moscow: The Finnish Institute of International Affairs and Carnegie Moscow Center, pp. 52–53. Tatiana Romanova and Natalia Zaslavskaya (2004), 'EU-Russia: Towards the Four Spaces', *Baltic Defence Review*, 2 (12), p. 101.

48. Vladimir Chizhov (2006), Remarks at the 135th Bergedorf Round Table, 'Interests and Partners of German Foreign Policy', Berlin, 29 September–1 October 2006, available at http://www.koerber-stiftung.de/bg/recherche/pdf_protokoll/bnd_135_en_text.pdf, last accessed 23 June 2008. pp. 90, 92; Vladimir Putin (2003), Speech at a meeting with representatives of the European Round Table of Industrialists and the Round Table of Industrialists of Russia and the EU, the Kremlin,

Moscow, 2 December 2003. Available at http://2004.kremlin.ru/eng/text/speeches/2003/12/022100_56575.shtml, last accessed 26 June 2007. Vladimir Chizhov (2003), 'From St. Petersburg to Rome', *International Affairs* (Moscow), 49 (5), pp. 14–15.

49. Sergei Karaganov (2004), Remarks in 'Why Invent a New Model? Review of the discussion at the Russian Economic Forum', *Russia in Global Affairs*, 2 (3), p. 180.

50. SVOP (2007), *The World Around Russia: 2017. An Outlook for the Midterm Future*. Moscow: The Council on Foreign and Defense Policy, p. 112.

51. Vladimir Pankov (2007), 'Free Trade Between Russia and the EU: Pros and Cons', *Russia in Global Affairs*, 5 (2), pp. 113–123.

52. For a useful discussion of the trend, see: Timofei Bordachev (2005), 'Russia's European Problem: Eastward Enlargement of the EU and Moscow's Policy, 1993–2003', in Oksana Antonenko and Kathryn Pinnick (eds), *Russia and the European Union: Prospects for a New Relationship*. London and New York: Routledge and IISS, pp. 53–54.

53. Russian Foreign Ministry (2007), *Obzor vneshnei politiki Rossiiskoi Federatsii*, 27 March 2007, available at http://www.mid.ru/brp_4.nsf/sps/3647DA9774 8A106BC32572AB002AC4DD, last accessed 26 September 2007.

54. For a mirror analysis of the challenges posed to the Union by these processes, see: Hiski Haukkala (2008b), 'The Russian Challenge to EU Normative Power: The Case of European Neighbourhood Policy', *International Spectator* 43 (2), pp. 35–47.

55. Dmitri Medvedev (2008), Speech of Russian President Dmitry Medvedev at a Meeting with German Political, Parliamentary and Civic Leaders, Berlin, 5 June 2008.

56. Hiski Haukkala (2008a), 'A Norm-maker or a Norm-taker? The Changing Normative Parameters of Russia's Place in Europe', in Ted Hopf (ed.), *Russia's European Choice,*. Aldershot and New York: Palgrave Macmillan, pp. 35–56.

57. K. J. Holsti (2004), *Taming the Sovereigns: Institutional Change in World Politics*. Cambridge: Cambridge University Press, p. 302.

58. See, for example: Azar Gat (2007) 'The Return of Authoritarian Great Powers', *Foreign Affairs*, 86 (4), pp. 59–69; Robert Kagan, (2007), 'End of Dreams, Return of History', *Policy Review*, (August/September), available at http://www.hoover.org/publications/policyreview/8552512.html, last accessed 3 October 2007.

Part III

The European Neighbourhood Policy in Practice – Assessing Implementation and Impact

9
The ENP and the EU's Eastern Neighbours: Ukraine and Moldova as Test Cases

Gwendolyn Sasse

Introduction

The eastern neighbours of the enlarged EU have provided an important impetus for the conception and ongoing formulation of the European Neighbourhood Policy (ENP). Ukraine and, to some extent, Moldova have defined the shape and pace of the ENP. Both countries have declared EU membership their strategic objective, and they are trying to turn the ENP into a step toward that goal – against the initial intentions of the EU. Thus, Ukraine and Moldova are putting not only the overall scope of the policy to the test, but also the procedural similarity between the ENP dynamics and the accession process. This chapter tries to address the following, as yet underexplored, questions. Does the ENP shape the domestic politics of ENP countries? If so, how is the ENP framed, articulated and channelled?

Within the ENP the EU's conditionality is vague and in flux. Both the EU and the ENP countries are aware of this constellation. Therefore, the ENP hinges on a form of 'conditionality-lite'; it is 'light' on both ends of the power asymmetry.[1] The main explicit incentive within the ENP is the deepening of trade relations and a 'stake' in the internal market. The scope for policy, institutional and normative change under ENP conditionality is thus limited from the outset. Any lasting institutional, policy or behavioural 'lock-in' effect requires a deeper grounding in domestic politics than in the case of EU accession where political short cuts were available to the elites. The main interrelated functions of the ENP are twofold: mobilisation and socialisation. The ENP provides an external reference point which domestic actors in the ENP countries can choose to mobilise when it fits their agenda – a pro- or anti-EU agenda. The non-committal nature of the ENP and its unspecified end-point may enable domestic actors in ENP countries to politically sideline and de-legitimise an EU-oriented policy. Conversely, the inherent vagueness of the ENP process can make it easier for lukewarm or Eurosceptic actors in ENP countries to tune into the EU gradually and selectively. It might be hard to mobilise enthusiasm for EU integration and to coordinate reform policies effectively under the 'neighbourhood' concept, but it may be equally hard to use the ENP as a focal point of organised opposition or the formulation of an alternative to closer relations with the EU.

The ENP also provides a loose framework for socialisation. Compared to the cost-benefit analysis underlying EU accession, the ENP process allows for a wider range of responses and learning curves for the ENP countries and the EU itself. Many studies on the ENP refer to socialisation as the policy's main (or only) mechanism for policy transfer through closer cooperation within EU networks.[2] Socialisation is notoriously difficult to trace empirically. In the EU accession context it has proven hard to distinguish from the effects of conditionality.[3] The clearest evidence has come from the extension of normative power into policy areas outside the formal remit of conditionality.[4] The ENP provides a good arena for the study of the multiple layers and directions of socialisation. So far the predominant assumption has been that an accession candidate or ENP country undergoes a socialisation process. The ENP process clearly demonstrates the limitations of this one-sided understanding of socialisation. The EU itself and its various sub-sets of actors are as much part of the socialisation process as the actors and institutions in ENP countries.[5]

The EU's own assessment of the ENP has been upbeat, although the Commission has repeatedly acknowledged shortcomings.[6] In its recent overall assessment, the Commission singled out trade and economic integration, mobility and regional conflicts as the priority areas where the EU still needs to do more.[7] The Commission admitted persisting problems with the ENP's principles of differentiation and ownership and called for 'specific, time-bound and action-oriented' Action Plans, a 'clearer sequencing of measures', 'a realistic stock-taking of the extent of Action Plan implementation' and willingness to deepen relations with select partners where this is warranted and sought by the countries concerned'.[8] Ukraine and Moldova (as well as Morocco and Israel) were singled out as the ENP countries with which the EU intends to deepen its relations. The ongoing negotiations on Ukraine's enhanced agreement, an Association Agreement that will replace the Partnership and Cooperation Agreement (PCA), represent the most concrete step toward deepening relations within the ENP. Moldova's PCA is also up for renewal, but the negotiations have not started yet.[9]

The new idea of an Eastern Partnership, put on the EU's agenda by a Polish-Swedish proposal in May 2008 and taken forward by a Commission proposal in December 2008, reinforces the split between the Southern and Eastern dimension that has been inherent in the ENP since its inception.[10] Defined as an 'ambitious new chapter' and a 'step change' in the EU's relations with the six Eastern ENP countries (Armenia, Azerbaijan, Georgia, Moldova, Ukraine and potentially Belarus), the Eastern Partnership remains within the ENP framework and aims at rhetorically and substantially reinforcing the EU's commitment toward the Eastern neighbours in view of the more established 'Partnership for the Mediterranean' and the need of the EU to respond to the Georgian-Russian war of August 2008. It does so by increasing its financial assistance to the ENP envelope by €350 million in 2010–13, redeploying €250 million already allocated and singling out a number of 'flagship initiatves', such as an Integrated Border Management Programme, a facility for small and medium enterprises (SME), a range of different energy-related projects and cooperation on the prevention of and response to disasters).[11] The Eastern Partnership extends the prospect of an Association Agreement, currently only under negotiation with Ukraine, as the contractual focal point of closer relations with all the eastern ENP countries.

Ukraine: 'Procedural entrapment' in a membership perspective

The Parameters of EU-Ukrainian relations

The EU's enlargement of 2004 turned Ukraine into the EU's most important Eastern neighbour. Ukraine was the first post-Soviet state to sign a PCA with the EU in 1994, but it took the member states until 1998 to ratify it. In 1999 Ukraine became the second country after Russia with an EU Common Strategy, but this largely declaratory document added little to the substance of the relationship.[12] Until 2004 Ukraine's declared 'European choice' remained a pragmatic rhetorical device at the elite level that had little concrete resonance or meaning at the mass level.[13] The EU continuously bemoaned the patchy implementation of the PCA. Ukraine, in turn, complained about the EU's lack of commitment and, in particular, antidumping measures against its chemical and steel products.[14] The ENP and Ukraine's Action Plan (2005–2008) – the first one to be adopted under the ENP – have added a new momentum to EU-Ukrainian relations, though the expectations on both sides still diverge, as the metaphor of the 'politics of the half-open door' illustrates.[15]

The Commission's ENP Country Report on Ukraine of 2004 provided an overview of the country's key political, legal, social and economic developments.[16] This report provided the basis for the Action Plan drafted under President Leonid Kuchma, whose regime was subsequently toppled in the autumn of 2004. The long list of priority areas laid out in the Action Plan includes strengthening the stability and effectiveness of institutions guaranteeing democracy and the rule of law; enabling democratic elections, media freedom and freedom of expression; ensuring respect for the rights of persons belonging to national minorities; enhancing EU-Ukraine consultations on crisis management; cooperation in the field of disarmament, non-proliferation and regional security, including a solution for the Transnistria conflict; World Trade Organization (WTO) accession; the gradual removal of trade restrictions; improving the investment climate; tax reforms; a visa facilitation agreement; the gradual approximation of Ukrainian legislation, norms and standards with those of the EU; a dialogue on employment issues, including non-discrimination of migrant workers, and the full implementation of the Memorandum of Understanding on the closure of the Chernobyl nuclear power station.[17] A brief reference was made to the monitoring of these priorities through the bodies established under the PCA, without providing further details on benchmarks, timing and follow-up. Ukraine's Action Plan covers a period of three years (2005–2008) – initially, the EU had envisaged a five-year period. Allowing the timing of the Action Plan to coincide with the renewal date of the PCA created a procedural momentum for a new contractual relationship beyond 2008.

In the aftermath of the 'Orange Revolution' of 2004, the EU proved reluctant to renegotiate the Action Plan or reward Ukraine with a membership perspective. It simply added 'Ten Points' to the Action Plan to emphasise the EU's commitment to Ukraine's reform path, a speedy implementation of the Action Plan and an increase in financial assistance. One year after the adoption of the EU-Ukraine Action Plan, Benita Ferrero-Waldner, Commissioner for External Relations, singled out the Memorandum of Understanding on Energy Co-operation, the opening of negotiations on visa facilitation, the EU's granting of Market Economy Status to Ukraine and the EU Border Assistance Mission on the

Ukrainian-Moldovan border as the key achievements.[18] The emphasis remained on economic and technical issues – with the exception of the Transnistria conflict, which by the end of 2005 had been anchored more firmly on the EU's agenda, following Ukraine and Moldova's demonstration of political will for cooperation on border management issues.

Under President Viktor Yushchenko, EU and NATO integration became a cornerstone in foreign policy. The immediate post-Orange Revolution government under Prime Minister Yulia Tymoshenko formulated a 'Road Map' on the implementation of the ENP Action Plan in April 2005. This road map, reviewed annually, has remained the main attempt to streamline the measures required under the Action Plan and assign them to specific executive agencies. While many of the measures listed in the road map are still very general and leave ample room for discretion when it comes to measuring successful implementation,[19] they are a clear step beyond the generic nature of the Action Plans.[20]

Ukraine's 'Orange Revolution' was followed by an as yet inconclusive internal political struggle, which decreased the immediate pressure on the EU to enhance its relations with Ukraine. Ukraine's parliamentary elections in March 2006 could have renewed the 'orange coalition' of President Yushchenko, Yulia Tymoshenko and Socialist Party leader Oleksandr Moroz, but the coalition talks dragged on for months and brought Ukraine to the brink of a constitutional crisis. In August 2006 Yushchenko signed a coalition deal with Viktor Yanukovych, his former arch-rival in the 2004 Presidential elections. Although the controversial constitutional reform of 2006, agreed to in haste during the 'Orange Revolution', left the President in charge of the country's foreign and defence policy, it subordinated all the other ministries to the Prime Minister. In his capacity as Prime Minister, Yanukovych challenged the President's role in the sphere of foreign policy. This challenge culminated in his instruction to parliament to dismiss the pro-active, EU-oriented Foreign Minister, Borys Tarasyuk, in December 2006.

The deadlock between President and Prime Minister and the non-functioning of parliament motivated Yushchenko's call for pre-term elections in September 2007. The result reinforced Ukraine's political and regional divisions, but it revived an 'orange' coalition which saw Tymoshenko return to the post of Prime Minister and rule by the slimmest of margins. Despite the intense rivalry between Yushchenko and Tymoshenko – both are expected to run in the presidential elections in 2010 – there is a mutual agreement on relations with the EU. Somewhat surprisingly, Tymoshenko also joined Yushchenko in a big push for a NATO Membership Action Plan in the run-up to the NATO summit in Bucharest in April 2008.[21] By contrast, in the run-up to the 2007 parliamentary elections the foreign policy agenda of the two main contenders for the post of Prime Minister – Tymoshenko and Yanukovych – had looked rather similar. Yanukovych had led an anti-NATO campaign but proved supportive of a gradual deepening of relations with the EU, while Tymoshenko dropped her pro-NATO rhetoric in view of widespread negative public sentiment and uncertainty about NATO.

While the leadership's approach to the EU has not changed fundamentally, domestic instability, reaching new heights as a result of President Yushchenko's dissolution of parliament in September 2008, continuing uncertainty over yet another round of possible pre-term elections and the global financial crisis, distracts from the implementation of the ENP. Similarly, a recent information campaign about NATO, aiming to increase public support for it, has done little either to make the EU a focal point or to introduce clarity into the widely used phrase 'Euro-Atlantic integration' which conflates relations with the EU and NATO. In the run-up to the NATO summit in April 2008, the ENP enjoyed a somewhat greater presence in the public debate. It was presented as a proof of Ukraine's Western orientation and as a stepping stone toward NATO membership. This attitude is mirrored in an expert poll, conducted by the Razumkov Centre in June 2008: 33.3 per cent of the 100 government, media and non-governmental organisation (NGO) representatives polled believed that the Ukrainian executive's pro-active stance on the NATO Membership Plan in the run-up to the NATO summit had a positive effect on relations with the EU; another 33.3 per cent thought it had not influenced Ukraine's relations with the EU and 13.7 per cent spoke of a negative influence.[22] The previous eastern enlargements created a close association between EU and NATO membership and this linkage can be projected even more forcefully in the absence of concrete membership perspectives.

The war in Georgia in August 2008 highlighted the divisions within the Ukrainian foreign policy elite. President Yushchenko quickly positioned himself as one of Mikheil Saakashvili's most outspoken supporters, whereas Prime Minister Tymoshenko chose a more pragmatic approach in view of the pending negotiations over the Russian gas price. Yushchenko tried to use the momentum generated by the war and the visibility of the EU in the attempts at conflict management, to push for a Membership Action Plan (MAP) at the NATO summit in December 2008. However, the war in Georgia also brought the divisions inside the

EU to the fore, in particular with regard to the member states' relations with Russia and a shared concern about the security implications of Georgian or Ukrainian NATO membership in potential future conflicts in the region. At the NATO summit a new compromise was found by launching a process very similar to the MAP while postponing the critical issue of actual membership. The EU Eastern Partnership serves a similar purpose: it steps up the rhetorical emphasis on the southern Caucasus within the ENP, while limiting a spillover into discussions about EU or NATO membership. Thus, an event like the war in Georgia demonstrates how a loose policy framework like the ENP, which has little to offer in an acute emergency situation, increases the stakes and expectations tied to the EU and, in this case, has drawn the EU into a new arena of conflict management with ramifications for both internal EU and NATO politics.

Rhetoric and socialisation

Viktor Yanukovych, originally associated with a more sceptical stance on relations with the West, gradually adjusted his rhetoric in favour of the vaguely phrased 'European Choice'. In his capacity as Prime Minister he referred to his close cooperation with Yushchenko on EU-related issues and often emphasised sectoral reform under the EU-Ukraine Action Plan and a free trade zone with the EU.[23] In a speech in early December 2006 Yanukovych said that Ukraine could begin membership negotiations during his premiership (Ukrainian government, 2006).[24] During a visit to Brussels on 27 March 2007 Yanukovych said that the new Ukraine-EU Agreement replacing the PCA should clearly spell out reform priorities in recognition of the fact that only successive reform steps will bring both Ukraine and the EU closer to Ukraine's membership of the EU. He also acknowledged that a membership perspective would not be a promise of membership. He tried to ease both his own supporters and the EU into a more EU-oriented approach, which he described as an 'irreversible path' (Ukrainian government, 2007).[25] By the end of his premiership Yanukovych's official rhetoric had edged closer to the position of former Foreign Minister Borys Tarasyuk who had explicitly asked for a membership perspective to be added to the new enhanced agreement (Ukrainian Foreign Ministry, 2006).[26] Similarly, then parliamentary speaker Oleksandr Moroz (Socialist Party) expressed his hope that the new post-PCA agreement would make this perspective more explicit (Holos Ukrainy, 30 May 2007).[27] While Tarasyuk has actively tried to speed up Ukraine's closer integration with the EU and use the ENP as a platform for mobilisation – first as Foreign Minister, now as the chairman of the parliamentary committee dealing with EU matters – Yanukovych's rhetoric demonstrates a more gradual socialisation effect of the ENP process. There is a broad consensus in Ukraine's foreign policy establishment on closer relations with the EU, although differences remain in the emphasis, priorities and desired speed of change in these relations.[28]

Ukraine's most active pro-EU politicians and diplomats came through a transition from an initially deeply negative reaction to the ENP with its non-committal end point to a more pragmatic approach which recast the ENP as a platform for preparing for Ukraine's eventual accession. By the end of 2006 a duotone rhetoric had been firmly established. Some key Ukrainian actors, such as Roman Shpek, the head of the Ukrainian delegation in Brussels, were still calling the ENP 'an EU rather than a Ukrainian policy' and a 'cosmetic repair job' without a legal basis,[29] while others, such as Oleksandr Chalyi, then deputy head of the presidential secretariat, were calling for 'maximum pragmatism' in relations with the EU.[30] The new sense of pragmatism does not preclude references to Ukraine's overarching objective, and Shpek remains one of Ukraine's most vociferous officials pointing to the need to see the ENP and the negotiations about the new enhanced agreement as interim steps toward EU membership.[31] In September 2007 the Foreign Ministry sent Shpek to attend a high-level Foreign Ministers' meeting of EU member states and ENP countries in Brussels in an attempt to highlight Ukraine's wish to distance itself from other ENP countries.[32] This mixture of pragmatism and expectation was channelled into the ongoing negotiations about the enhanced agreement, now confirmed as an Association Agreement, which is due to be finalised in 2009.

The EU-Ukraine summit in September 2008 defined the new Ukraine's new agreement as an Association Agreement, thereby setting a new goalpost for other ENP countries to follow and inviting comparisons with the Europe Agreements in Central and Eastern Europe in the 1990s, which became the precursors of membership, or the Stabilisation and Association Agreements in the Western Balkans, which contain an explicit membership perspective. The focus of Ukraine's Association Agreement will be on 'deep free trade' and a long-term perspective for a visa-free regime between the EU and Ukraine, but avoids direct references to potential membership.[33]

Ukraine's foreign policy elite had hoped that this agreement would entail a deep free trade regime, a prospect for political association and, more unrealistically, an explicit membership perspective.[34] On the one hand, the drafting of this agreement has brought Ukraine's membership claim to the fore, but on the other, it has provided Ukraine-EU relations with a new incentive and focal point. The fact that Ukraine is the only ENP country currently negotiating an enhanced agreement is presented as proof of the country's special status within the ENP. In the run-up to the negotiations Yushchenko's presidential administration declared a 'European break-through', and this term still features in the public debate.[35] By projecting its expectations clearly and consistently, Ukraine's foreign policy elite has actively shaped the atmosphere of the negotiations. It is trying to capitalise on, what Hryhoriy Nemyria, the current Deputy Prime Minister in charge of EU affairs, called the 'constructive ambiguity' in EU-Ukrainian relations and the need to send signals 'through domestic actions'.[36] Ukrainian officials use the ENP's own emphasis on differentiation and co-ownership as an effective means of criticising any signs of EU unilateralism, such as the tone of the Commission's Communication of 2007 about the implementation of the ENP.[37]

Similarly, Ukraine's initial response to the Eastern Partnership had been lukewarm, as it appears to question Ukraine's role as the front runner among the eastern neighbours. Nevertheless, Nemyria described the Eastern Partnership as 'a step forward' and 'a new platform' which allows for the introduction of 'new mechanisms'. In particular, Nemyria singled out a new programme for institutional capacity-building in addition to Twinning and TAIEX and region-specific funding as the benefits of the new initiative.[38] Putting a positive spin on open-ended EU policy proposals has become part of Ukraine's strategy vis-à-vis the EU.

Socialisation and mobilisation through partial implementation

Even though there is an overall consensus on closer relations with the EU, the institutional rivalry between the President and the government and the dysfunctional relations between the government and parliament have undermined an effective implementation of the Action Plan. There is still no clear institutional framework for EU affairs in Ukraine's government apparatus. The initiative to take one of the measures in the road map forward is by and large left to individual officials in ministries.[39] Bureaucrats rather than politicians are the driving force behind ENP implementation. The socialisation and mobilisation of the bureaucracy is important, as the accession process in CEE has demonstrated, but in Ukraine these 'islands' lack central control. In the wake of the 'Orange Revolution' the position of Deputy Prime Minister for European Integration was created to coordinate Ukraine's relations with EU. Responsibilities for EU integration were divided between the then First Deputy Prime Minister Oleh Rybachuk, who was given the responsibility of drawing up a new National Strategy on European Integration for the implementation of the Action Plan and managing the Government Secretariat on European Integration, and then Foreign Minister Borys Tarasyuk, whose task it was to oversee Ukraine's international responsibilities vis-a-vis the EU (including the reform of the diplomatic service). No new ministry or governmental committee on European integration was established, but the intra-institutional reorganisation reflected a broader shift in Ukraine's overall orientation toward the EU. However, Ukraine's executive responsibility for EU matters remains split between many different actors, such as the President and the Prime Minister (or their respective Secretariats for European Integration) and several ministries, some of which are controlled by the President (Foreign Affairs) and others by the Prime Minister (Economics and Justice). Furthermore, the poor relations between the government and the parliament have hindered the adoption of *acquis*-related legislation, one of the main EU benchmarks for ENP progress.[40] In his current capacity as Deputy Prime Minister with a responsibility for European integration, Hryhoryi Nemyria routinely emphasises the need for streamlining the coordination of all issues related to EU integration, establishing clear hierarchies among the Action Plan priorities, spelling out their financial resources and time frames, and allowing for a more effective information flow between the administration and society.[41] He has also pointed to another practical problem, namely the lack of knowledge of the English language across the executive and administrative bodies. This language barrier hampers discussions about sectoral reform and legislative acts as well as the implementation of aid programmes.[42]

EU assessment of ENP implementation

The first ENP Progress Report on Ukraine of December 2006 stated that 'Ukraine consolidated a breakthrough in conducting a democratic election process that began with the Orange Revolution'.[43] However, the 'long pre- and post-election periods of political instability' and unresolved constitutional issues and limited cooperation with the Council of Europe's Venice Commission on these issues were highlighted. The cooperation between Ukraine and Moldova on the Transnistria issue, namely their commitment to the EU's Border Assistance Mission (EU BAM), was emphasised as an important step toward conflict resolution. The Report acknowledged that the WTO process had been enhanced, though 'concerns about loose monetary and fiscal policies' were recorded.[44] Some progress was noted in the areas of judicial reform and the fight against corruption, as well as substantial progress in the field of energy cooperation. The Report emphasised that EC financial assistance to Ukraine had doubled from €50 million in 2003 to €100 million in 2006 and was set to increase in 2007 with the new ENP financial instrument (ENPI).

The Commission's Progress Report for 2007 acknowledged that Ukraine 'continued to make progress in most areas', but pointed to a slower pace of economic reforms because of the political instability throughout 2007.[45] The major achievements listed were the launch of negotiations for an EU-Ukraine new enhanced agreement in February 2007, the finalisation of Ukraine's WTO entry, the entry into force in January 2008 of agreements on visa facilitation and readmission and the cooperation with the EU BAM, the mandate for which was prolonged by the Ukrainian and Moldovan governments until the end of November 2009.[46] The report voiced the expectation that in the long run EU BAM will contribute to the professionalisation of the customs, border guard and law enforcement services, and that inter-agency cooperation within and between Ukraine and Moldova will foster the rule of law in these agencies.[47] The exchange of customs information on the cross-border movement of goods was singled out as a tangible achievement to date.[48] The report noted that although the border between Ukraine and Moldova, in particular its Transnistrian section, 'is not properly controlled', illegal cross-border activities were 'more and more adequately combated'. Nevertheless, the Commission pointed out that because of inconsistencies in Ukrainian legislation and the high level of corruption, in particular in the judiciary, 'promising actions of law enforcement services are often wrecked'.[49] The whole report mentioned the conflict in Transnistria in only one sentence: 'overall, good progress has been made in the implementation of the cooperation for the settlement of the Transnistria conflict'.[50] EU BAM was presented as a contribution to conflict resolution as well as a wider instrument to address trafficking.

Under the new ENPI funding, Ukraine's allocation for 2007–2010 amounts to €494 million; the funding targets three priorities: 30 per cent is earmarked for democratic development and good governance (including public administration, judicial reform, human rights and civil society), another 30 per cent for regulatory reform and administrative capacity-building and 40 per cent for infrastructure development.[51] The 2007 allocation of €120 million was increased by €22 million from the EU's Governance Facility, a new instrument rewarding good performance, although the exact criteria according to which Ukraine scored high in view of the otherwise mildly critical remarks in the political sections of the Progress Report, remain opaque. The EC Governance Facility was created in 2007 to allow the EU to top up the ENPI allocations for one or two countries each year with a total of up to €50 million. This selective reward mechanism (for relative rather than absolute progress) is meant to send a political signal to the ENP countries, and it tops up democratic governance and rule of law priorities specified in a particular Action Plan.[52] In 2007 Ukraine and Morocco were the two countries awarded extra money under this facility. In the case of Ukraine, the democratic conduct of the elections, increased media freedom and attempts to tackle corruption appear to be the achievements the EU wants to build on with the financial top-up.

NGO assessment of ENP implementation

The interconnected socialisation and mobilisation dynamic of the ENP reaches beyond narrow foreign policy circles in the government, parliament and the administration. Ukraine's non-governmental sector is engaged in regular in-depth analyses of the progress achieved under the ENP. This non-governmental engagement with the ENP mirrors the shift in the official rhetoric from a negative assessment of the policy to an emphasis on the ENP as a policy-in-the-making, the potential of which Ukraine has yet to make use of.[53] The Razumkov Centre has gone furthest by publishing detailed reports on the implementation of the Action Plan. These reports are meant to provide an alternative assessment, to develop a more effective methodology for assessing implementation, to channel and strengthen the potential of third sector in keeping a check on state policy and to attract wider public attention to the issue of ENP implementation.[54] According to the 2008 Razumkov Centre report, 224 out of a total of 227 government actions over three years were in line with the Action Plan (217 completely, seven partly and three not implemented). Of the actions, 33 per cent are estimated to be fully implemented, 45 per cent partly and 22 per cent not implemented. The vast majority of actions are still at a preparatory stage, about 34 per cent have been addressed at decision-making level and 21 per cent have seen practical results through implementation.[55]

The Razumkov Centre sees its role as raising the legitimacy of EU integration through analysis, information and transparency.[56] These reports contrast the centre's own evaluation with the verdicts of the government and the EU.[57] Among the discrepancies in the latest report is the assessment of progress in the area of freedom of expression and a free media. While the EU and the Ukrainian government seem to have taken a broader view of improvements in this field, calling the changes 'significant', the Razumkov Centre goes through the planned legislative changes and finds them only partially or not implemented.[58] Likewise, the Razumkov Centre is more sceptical about the progress of structural economic reform.[59] On regional issues and conflict management all three assessments agree on 'significant' progress. The Razumkov Centre singles out the cooperation and regular information exchange with the office of the EU's Special Representative in Moldova.[60] In addition to EU BAM, the Razumkov Centre refers to the completion of the first phase of a new border management project (BOMMOLUK) and partial completion of the cooperation with the executive bodies in Moldova controlling border crossings. The border demarcation has been completed on the Ukrainian side, and partly completed on the Moldovan side.[61]

Expert polls conducted by the Razumkov Centre among about 100 representatives of national and regional government bodies, NGOs, research institutes and the media in 2006–2008 provide a good insight into trends among decision-makers and opinion-formers. Ukraine's EU membership has consistently been seen as a national interest by over 75–77 per cent of the experts polled.[62] The survey reflects a realisation that the speed of Ukraine's European integration had accelerated somewhat by June 2008: 64.7 per cent of those asked still think the speed is slow (down from 73.3 in 2007), but 27.5 per cent now think that Ukraine progresses at medium speed (up from 18.8 in 2007) and 2 per cent believe Ukraine is moving at high speed (up 1 from 2007, but down 1.8 from 2006).[63] The overall progress and speed of integration are remarkably evenly assessed across the regions of Ukraine.[64]

The overall impression of Ukraine's foreign policy direction cannot conceal scepticism about the ENP mechanisms as such. The percentage of those who see the Action Plan as a purely declaratory document has gone up from 26.9 per cent in 2006 (25.7 in 2007) to 34.3 in 2008; the share of those who think the Action Plan can act as a reform instrument has dropped from 61.4 per cent in 2007 to 54.9 in 2008, and the number of those who see the Action Plan as an effective instrument to get Ukraine closer to the EU's membership criteria has fallen from 13.5 per cent in 2006 to 4.9 in 2008.[65] The Presidency has consistently been seen as the institution influencing relations with the EU most positively. Despite a drop from 63.8 per cent in May 2005 to 43.5 in June 2008 (the biggest drop occurred from 2005 to 2006), Yushchenko is still strongly identified with EU-Ukrainian relations: in June 2008 only 12.4 per cent of the experts thought the government was the single most important actor shaping relations with the EU in a positive way (up from 4.3 per cent in 2005, with the biggest increase from 2007 to 2008, which indicates a more visible government presence in dealing with the EU).[66]

Moldova: a momentum for reform and conflict management

The parameters of EU-Moldovan relations

Moldova signed a PCA in 1994 that was ratified in 1998, but it repeatedly fell through the cracks of EU policy. It missed out on the symbolic value of a Common Strategy and was included only in the 1999 Stability Pact for South-Eastern Europe in 2001. With Romania and Russia being the two poles of Moldova's political orientation, the EU has only gradually emerged as a focal point. Moldova's 'Principal Directions of Foreign Policy' for 1998–2002 listed integration with the EU as a 'strategic objective'. Moldova's frozen conflict in Transnistria and the country's extremely low level of economic development[67] translated into expectations of a 'most superficial form of European integration' and comparisons were drawn with Belarus' lack of scope for closer relations with the EU.[68] However, a vague framework like the ENP paved the way for a more serious mutual engagement. The fact that membership is not on the cards for the time being seemed to be an advantage rather than an obstacle in the early stages of EU-Moldovan relations.

The 2001 election victory of the Communist Party, followed by the election of its leader Vladimir Voronin as president, did not convince the EU immediately of Moldova's declared EU orientation. However, when Voronin's attempt to cooperate with Moscow failed, his focus shifted to the EU. The parliamentary elections of March 2005, which according to the Organization for Security and Co-operation in Europe (OSCE) corresponded generally to democratic standards, did not bring any significant change in the political set-up of Moldova: the Communist Party saw its share of the vote reduced, but it still holds the majority in parliament. Parliament re-elected Voronin as president in April 2005. Parliamentary and presidential elections are scheduled for 2009, and although Voronin will not run again, he has shown an interest in making progress on the Transnistria issue before the elections.

The priority areas of the EU-Moldova Action plan, adopted in February 2005 for three years and subsequently renewed for a year, are: strengthening the stability and effectiveness of institutions guaranteeing democracy and the rule of law, including the 'effective protection of rights of persons belonging to national minorities'; democratic elections; freedom of the media and freedom of expression; reinforcing administrative and judicial capacity; resuming cooperation with the international financial institutions; poverty reduction; private-sector-led growth; improving the investment climate through structural reforms and anti-corruption measures; an efficient system of border management (including the Transnistrian 'sector'); working toward the EU granting Autonomous Trade Preferences by ensuring effective control of the origin of goods from Moldova; fighting organised crime and the trafficking in human beings; ensuring the efficient management of migratory flows with a view to a readmission agreement and a viable solution to the Transnistria conflict.[69] Compared to Ukraine's Action Plan, which Moldova used as a yardstick, the overall emphasis on political stability and security issues is more pronounced, although it was apparently the Moldovan side which insisted on including a separate chapter on Transnistria in the Action Plan.[70]

The indicative financial envelope under the National Indicative Programme for 2007–2010 is €209.7 million. The programme finances the implementation of three priorities: support for democratic development and good governance (25–35 per cent), regulatory reform and administrative capacity-building (15–20 per cent), and poverty reduction and economic growth (40–60 per cent). There is no special budget line for Transnistria-related issues, although all three priorities could be interpreted as being related to the conflict. The 2007 ENPI Annual Action Programme for Moldova envisages a budget of €40 million. EC assistance programmes have focused on integrated border management and improving border control and surveillance capacity in Moldova with a particular emphasis on the EU BAM operations on the Moldova-Ukraine border, the reform of the Moldovan social assistance system, technical assistance and twinning operations in view of the Action Plan and support for civil society, including in Transnistria.[71]

The Transnistria issue

The EU has only recently become a player in the Transnistria conflict. In February 2003 the Council imposed a travel ban on the Transnistrian leadership, which is still in place. Alongside the Council of Europe's Venice Commission, the EU also became an observer to the Joint

Constitutional Commission, which is trying to define a constitutional power-sharing arrangement. Moldova has indicated that it wants the EU to go beyond the role of an observer. The EU-Moldova Action Plan explicitly mentions 'shared responsibility in conflict prevention and conflict resolution' within the framework of the OSCE-led negotiation process.[72] The EU opened a European Commission delegation in Chisinau in October 2005, and an EU Special Representative (EUSR) to Moldova with a mandate for conflict resolution was appointed by the Council in March 2005.[73] The ENP and the EUSR have contributed to channelling the intermittent regional momentum for conflict management into regular contacts and talks.[74] However, the relationship between the EUSR, responsible to the Council, and the ENP, overseen by the Commission, remains unclear. The current EUSR, Kálmán Mizsei, is trying to make the case for channelling ENPI funding, overseen by the Commission, to Transnistria, in particular for civil society projects. The diplomatic efforts of the EUSR currently represent the EU's only direct contribution to conflict management. The EUSR is in close contact with all the key players and shuttles between Chisinau, Tiraspol and Brussels. His role resembles that of the OSCE High Commissioner on National Minorities in the 1990s. Similar to the position of the OSCE High Commissioner, a lot depends on the personality and pro-active mentality of the person filling the post of the EUSR. Brussels can provide a meeting place for political actors from Chisinau and Transnistria who tend to be reluctant to meet. On 14 May 2008, for example, the EUSR facilitated the first meeting in seven years between Moldova's parliamentary speaker, Marian Lupu, and his Transnistrian counterpart, Evgenii Shevchuk.[75] This meeting followed the first meeting in seven years between Voronin and Igor Smirnov, the Transnistrian leader in Transnistria on 11 April 2008. Moscow rather than the EU played a crucial role in brokering this meeting, but in the wake of this meeting the EU has facilitated further talks at different levels and in different locations: in June 2008, for example, Moldovan Prime Minister Zinaida Grecianii met her Russian counterpart Vladimir Putin in Moscow, where both sides reiterated the need to settle the Transnistria issue.[76]

The momentum to tackle the Transnistria issue has certainly been revived since the EU got itself directly and indirectly involved in the region through the ENP process and the EUSR. However, the impact of the ENP itself is less clear. Moreover, an enhanced role for the EU in Transnistria does not immediately change the dynamics of a frozen conflict, as the initial negative Transnistrian response and Transnistria's referendum of September 2006, which expressed overwhelming support for the course toward independence and 'free association' with Russia, demonstrated.[77] Over time, the EU's involvement in Transnistria could also expose the EU's limited conflict-resolution capacity resulting from the lack of a coherent EU foreign policy.

The ENP provides a new institutional focal point for Ukraine's more active engagement over Transnistria, namely through EU BAM. According to a bilateral agreement, Ukraine allows the transit of Moldovan goods through its territory only if they bear an official Moldovan customs stamp and, in return, Moldova facilitates access to official customs stamps for Transnistrian companies. The ENP context has also encouraged greater, though as yet intermittent, visibility of the Transnistria issue in the Ukrainian public debate. On 23 November 2007 the Ukrainian weekly *Zerkalo nedeli* carried an interview with the EUSR Kálmán Mizsei, which called the Transnistrian issue 'solvable' and emphasised Yushchenko's significant diplomatic efforts and the potential inherent in Voronin's call for confidence-building measures in Transnistria.

Voronin is trying to keep the momentum for conflict resolution going by projecting optimism about an impending solution to the conflict. He regularly ties this prospect to three factors: the EU's presence in Moldova, the new border control arrangements and the registration of economic entities from Transnistria in Moldova.[78] Unlike parts of the Ukrainian foreign policy elite, Voronin has distanced himself from a close linkage between NATO and EU integration and emphasises Moldova's neutrality.[79] The war in Georgia had a negative impact on the attempts at conflict management, making the Russian negotiating position more intractable again – at least temporarily.

Implementing the ENP: insufficient for socialisation and mobilisation?

Similarly to Ukraine, the implementation of Moldova's Action Plan involves a government road map. An overarching strategy document was drawn up in 2005 – the European Strategy of Moldova – based on specific ministerial suggestions. A National Commission for European Integration was established, chaired by the Prime Minister. The Moldovan government produces its own annual implementation reports which include a detailed breakdown of ministerial and parliamentary activities aimed at Action Plan implementation. The reports have been criticised for being too long, too self-congratulatory and for failing to distinguish between normal government activity and Action Plan implementation. The Ministry of Foreign Affairs was reorganised into the Ministry of Foreign Affairs and European Integration (MFAEI). The position of the Minister of Foreign Affairs and European Integration was raised to a deputy premiership, thus enhancing the institutional position of the MFAEI within the government and also enabling the ministry to coordinate with other state institutions in the implementation of the Action Plan for which the MFAEI has overall responsibility.[80] A department for European integration was set up within the MFAEI. It is divided into three directorates: political, economic cooperation and relations with South-Eastern Europe. Despite the reorganisation and enhanced standing of the MFAEI, the institutional capacity for dealing with EU issues in Moldova has remained weak, in particular in the so-called European integration departments in other ministries.

There is no special department in the MFAEI dealing with the Transnistrian conflict. This issue is pigeon-holed under the responsibility of the Ministry of Reintegration. Although this ministry is considered one of the most important ministries in Moldova and has the highest level of allocated budgetary funding, it has no official input into Action Plan implementation. The Deputy Minister of Reintegration, Ion Stavila, attends regular meetings with the representatives of the Commission delegation and the EUSR, but he does not see the Action Plan as falling within his remit: 'The Action Plans are an agreement between Moldova and the EU. The Transnistria question is excluded based on the assumption that it is an issue to be solved primarily by Moldova, Russia and Transnistria. The EU's role is limited mainly to that of observer.'[81]

NGO involvement in the ENP process has been slower off the mark than in Ukraine. Two coalitions of NGOs were set up to monitor the implementation of the Action Plan and governmental compliance with ENP goals: Euromonitor and Euroforum.[82] After a lacklustre start, these NGOs have been assuming an increasingly active role through their regular monitoring reports and by taking a public stance on specific issues, for example dual citizenship rights. There is some indication, however, that the ENP mechanisms are not sufficient to maintain the momentum for the constructive engagement of state and non-state actors with clear incentives and the parameters of the post-PCA agreement pending. Dissatisfaction on the part of the Moldovan government with the ENP process may also explain Moldova's recent attempts to further bilateral or regional partnerships, for example with Austria and Germany on cross-border crime, immigration and human trafficking as well as cooperation with the US (including military cooperation).[83]

EU assessment of ENP implementation

The Commission's 2006 ENP Progress Report on Moldova tries to spell out what initiatives have been taken by both the Moldovan institutions and the EU to deepen their relationship since the beginning of the ENP process. In particular, there is evidence of Moldova adopting a number of national strategies on issues emphasised in the Action Plan, such as a national anti-corruption strategy and the National Programme on Actions on Migration and Asylum, as well as legislation on sensitive issues such as trafficking and money-laundering. Moldova had demonstrated its political will to polish its international image by ratifying, for example, the European Convention on the Legal Status of Migrants and the Council of Europe Convention on Trafficking of Human Beings and by finally writing the death penalty out of its constitution.[84]

The Commission's 2007 Progress Report acknowledges Moldova's 'good progress in most areas during the reporting period'.[85] It singles out the 2007 local elections, the EU granting Moldova additional Autonomous Trade Preferences based on new procedures on control and certification of the origin of goods, the entry into force of visa facilitation and readmission agreements and the 'positive cooperation' with EU BAM as the major achievements in 2007.[86] On issues such as local government, judicial reform, anti-discrimination and trafficking, the Progress Report traces Moldova's attempts to implement various national strategies and action plans. It reads like an acknowledgement of the government's good intentions to address all of the issues in the Action Plan and align itself with the standards and practices of international legal norms and practices.

The Report comments separately on the 'cooperation for the settlement of the Transnistria conflict'. It mentions Moldova's close cooperation with the EU on all issues related to Transnistria and ongoing work 'to put into practice the proposals of the President of the Republic of Moldova on confidence-building measures'. It also concedes that the framework of the 5 + 2 talks (OSCE, Russia, Ukraine, Chisinau and Tiraspol + the US and EU as observers) remains 'frozen'. Moldovan legislation which makes it possible for economic operators from Transnistria to register in Chisinau and work on the basis of Moldovan laws and regulations, thereby gaining access to international and EU trade preferences, is singled out as an achievement.

Conclusion

This chapter has tried to go beyond a summary of EU policy developments. The inclusion of Ukrainian and Moldovan perspectives into the analysis underlines the importance of the domestic political context: it frames the ENP process and, in turn, is shaped by it. The ENP is built on 'conditionality-lite' – the incentives and the commitment on the side of the ENP country as well as the EU are vague and limited. By definition, the open-ended nature of the ENP rules out clear-cut effects. Instead, the ENP provides a rich empirical setting for the study of the processes of mobilisation and socialisation. By pointing to the overall potential or, conversely, the shortcomings of the policy, political and societal actors can use the ENP as an instrument to position themselves as pro- or anti-EU or, more generally, as pro- or anti-reform. Both Ukraine (Yanukovych) and Moldova (Voronin) have demonstrated how the openness of the ENP allows Eurosceptic actors to ease themselves and their supporters into a new line of argument. Over time, the predominant perceptions of the ENP appear to be moving through cycles of engagement and disengagement: in Ukraine, the foreign policy elite initially saw the ENP as a disappointment but chose to adopt an increasingly pragmatic approach, hoping to redefine the relationship over time. In Moldova, the ENP initially helped Moldovan politicians to gain a degree of international attention and credibility, but there is now evidence that as the ENP's vague perspective is beginning to sink in, the process has begun to store up dissatisfaction and potential disengagement from the implementation of the Action Plan.

With regard to socialisation, Ukraine and Moldova point to under-explored dimensions of this concept. First, socialisation is not a uni-directional process: it can weaken as much as strengthen EU-oriented foreign and domestic policies. Second, socialisation and mobilisation effects reach beyond the narrow circle of visible top-level politicians, but the links between the different layers of the political and administrative system, or between governmental and non-governmental actors can be hard to institutionalise. Third, socialisation can produce unintended consequences: the EU is trying to avoid a 'rhetorical entrapment'[87] in new enlargement promises, but it faces a 'procedural entrapment' in the functionalist underpinnings of the ENP process.[88] The logic of the ENP, in particular with regard to Ukraine and Moldova (and potentially Belarus), is such that in the case of consistent domestic reforms the EU will find it hard to deny these countries a membership perspective. Fourth, the ENP socialises the EU into a more visible role in foreign policy and conflict management and requires the mobilisation of adequate resources. The institutional and legal tensions in the EU's external relations are rendered more apparent within the ENP process, and the Transnistria conflict has emerged as a test case for improving cooperation between the Commission and the Council.

Ukraine and Moldova represent tough challenges for the EU: both countries are trying to redefine the ENP as a step toward membership. A better understanding of the ENP's interrelated dynamics of mobilisation and socialisation could underpin a more active and systematic interaction between the EU and the ENP countries in order to set and reach specific targets – at both the formulation and implementation stages. These targets are best thought of as resolving concrete problems rather than an overall approximation to the EU's norms and the *acquis communautaire*.

Notes

The research for this chapter has been supported by the EU's Specific Targeted Project MIRICO (Framework Six). Research assistance by Diana Isac and Olga Onuch and comments on earlier drafts by Claire Gordon, James Hughes and the participants of the workshop 'Much Ado About Nothing? The European Neighbourhood Policy since 2003' at the University of Nottingham (25–26 October 2007) are gratefully acknowledged.

1. G. Sasse (2008), 'The European Neighbourhood Policy: Conditionality Revisited for the EU's Eastern Neighbours', *Europe-Asia Studies*, 60 (2), pp. 295–316.
2. The EU's own information service highlights the importance of socialisation within the ENP with regard to confidence-building measures in the field of conflict resolution and, more generally, under people-to-people contacts (http://ec.europa.eu/world/enp/faq_en.htm).
3. F. Schimmelfennig and U. Sedelmeier (eds) (2005), *The Europeanization of Central and Eastern Europe*. Ithaca: Cornell University Press. J. Kelley (2006), 'International Actors on the Domestic Scene: Membership Conditionality and Socialization by International Institutions', *International Organization*, 58 (3), pp. 425–58.
4. R. Epstein (2008), 'The social context in conditionality: internationalizing finance in post-communist Europe', *Journal of European Public Policy*, 15 (6), pp. 880–98.
5. G. Sasse (2008), 'The European Neighbourhood Policy: Conditionality Revisited for the EU's Eastern Neighbours', *Europe-Asia Studies*, 60 (2), pp. 295–316.
6. Commission of the European Communities (2005a), *European Neighbourhood Policy: A Year of Progress*, IP/05/1467, 24 November, available at http://europa.eu/rapid/pressReleasesAction.do?reference=IP/05/1467; Commission of the European Communities (2005b), 'Communication to the Commission: Implementing and Promoting the European Neighbourhood Policy', Brussels, 22 November, SEC(2005) 1521.

7. Commission of the European Communities (2008a) Implementation of the European Neighbourhood Policy in 2007 COM(2008) 164, 3 April (http://ec.europa.eu/world/enp/pdf/progress2008/com08_164_en.pdf).

8. Ibid. pp. 8–9.

9. Unlike Ukraine, Moldova has downplayed the demand for a membership perspective in the post-PCA agreement, while focusing on a 'free visa regime' and 'a deep free trade zone' beyond the current Autonomous Trade Preferences (ibid.) and occasionally cross-referencing the prospect of association, which is discussed in the case of Ukraine (*AISmoldpres*, 25 June 2008). In the case of Morocco and Israel references have been made to an 'advanced status' and 'special status' respectively.

10. Commission of the European Communities (2008b), ENP Progress Report Ukraine COM(2008) 164, SEC(2008) 402, 3 April (http://ec.europa.eu/world/enp/pdf/progress2008/sec08_402_en.pdf).

11. Ibid.

12. G. Sasse (2002), 'The EU Common Strategy on Ukraine: A Response to Ukraine's "pro-European Choice"?' in A. Lewis (ed.), The EU & Ukraine. Neighbours, Friends, Partners? London: The Federal Trust, pp. 213–20.

13. M. Light, S. White and J. Löwenhardt (2000), 'A wider Europe: the view from Moscow and Kyiv', *International Affairs*, 76 (1), pp. 77–88.

14. For a discussion of the ambiguities surrounding Ukraine's legal approximation to the EU within the PCA framework, see: R. Petrov (2003), 'Recent Developments in the Adaptation of Ukrainian Legislation to EU Laws', *European Foreign Affairs Review*, 8 (1), pp. 125–141.

15. H. Timmermann (2003), 'Die EU und die "Neuen Nachbarn" Ukraine und Belarus', *SWP Studie* S41, October. Berlin: Stiftung Wissenschaft und Politik.

16. Commission of the European Communities (2004), European Neighbourhood Policy. Country Report Ukraine, COM (2004) 373 final (http://europa.eu.int/comm/world/enp/pdf/country/Ukraine_11_May_EN.pdf).

17. Commission of the European Communities (2004), *EU–Ukraine Action Plan*, pp. 3–4, available at http://ec.europa.eu/world/enp/pdf/action_plans/ukraine_enp_ap_final_en.pdf. In addition to the new ENP Action Plan, an EU Action Plan on Justice and Home Affairs with Ukraine has been in force since December 2001. The implementation of this mini-Action Plan is monitored by a detailed point-based scoreboard. As a result, the ENP Action Plan was brief on Justice and Home Affairs, although the two are gradually merging.

18. Commission of the European Communities (2005b), Communication to the Commission, *Implementing and Promoting the European Neighbourhood Policy*, Brussels, 22 November, SEC(2005) 1521.

19. Razumkov Centre (Ukrains'kyi tsentr ekonomichnykh i politychnykh doslidzhen' imeni Oleksandra Razumkova) (2007), *Natsional'na bezpeka i oborona*, No. 2 (86), Kyiv.

20. Ukrainian government (2005), *Plans for the implementation of the Action Plan*; available at http://www.kmu.gov.ua/control/uk/publish/article?&art_id=17977243&cat_id=1797724

21. The Ukrainian media coverage of NATO membership remained cautious to negative during this period. See, for example, 'ES chy NATO – zmina priorytetiv Ukrainy?', *Zerkalo nedeli*, 24 March 2008.

The ENP and the EU's Eastern Neighbours 203

22. Razumkov Centre (Ukrains'kyi tsentr ekonomichnykh i politychnykh doslidzhen' imeni Oleksandra Razumkova) (2008), *Natsional'na bezpeka i oborona*, No. 6 (100), Kyiv.
23. *Washington Post*, 5 October 2006.
24. Ukrainian government (2006), Speech by then Prime Minister Viktor Yanukovych, 14 December, available at http://www.kmu.gov.ua/control/en/publish/article?art_id=57281670&cat_id=2297108
25. Ukrainian government (2007), Speech by Viktor Yanukovych in Brussels, 27 March, available at http://www.kmu.gov.ua/control/uk/publish/article?art_id=72932732&cat_id=43255
26. Ukrainian Foreign Ministry (2006), Speech by Borys Tarasyuk, 8 February, available at http://www.oae.mfa.gov.ua/oae/en/news/detail/1608.htm
27. *Holos Ukrainy* (2007) 30 May.
28. Yanukovych, for example, combined his EU policy with rhetoric in favour of the Russia-championed Single Economic Space in the Former Soviet Union, an idea that contradicts the notion of free trade with the EU.
29. *Den'* (2006), 6 December; *Radio Svoboda* (2006) 14 December.
30. Mizhnarodnyi tsentr perspektyvnykh doslidzhen' (2006), *Visnyk tsentru*, No. 42, (346), 19 December.
31. *Interfaks-Ukraina* (2007), 23 January; *BBC Ukrainian Service*, (2007), 5 March; see also O. Derharchov (2007), *Pozytsiya Ukrainy shchodo Evropeiskoi polityky susidstva ta perspektyv spivpratsi z ES* (Kyiv: Friedrich Ebert Foundation: International Policy Analysis).
32. Radio Svoboda (2007), 3 September.
33. EU-Ukraine Summit, 2008.
34. The new agreement may well be called an 'Association Agreement' and thereby invite comparisons with the Stabilisation and Association Agreements in the Western Balkans that are defined as a step towards membership.
35. *UNIAN*, 9 March 2007.
36. Siruk, 24 February 2007.
37. Ukrainian Foreign Ministry (2008) Comment on the Communication of the European Commission, 3 May (http://www.mfa.gov.ua/mfa/ua/news/detail/11971.htm).
38. BBC Ukrainian Service, 10 December 2008.
39. K. Wolczuk (2007), 'Adjectival Europeanisation? The Impact of the European Neighbourhood Policy on Ukraine', Paper presented at the conference The Study of the ENP: Methodological, Theoretical and Empirical Challenges, Nottingham, 25–26 November 2007.
40. An exception to this was the eventual cooperation on legislation related to Ukraine's WTO accession in late 2006.
41. forpost, 26 June 2008.
42. Razumkov Centre (Ukrains'kyi tsentr ekonomichnykh i politychnykh doslidzhen' imeni Oleksandra Razumkova) (2008), *Natsional'na bezpeka i oborona*, 6 (100), p. 26.
43. Commission of the European Communities (2006c), ENP Progress Report Ukraine COM(2006) 726 final, SEC(2006) 1505/2, 4 December, p. 2, available at http://ec.europa.eu/world/enp/pdf/sec06_1505-2_en.pdf.
44. Ibid., p. 2.
45. Commission of the European Communities (2008b), ENP Progress Report Ukraine COM(2008) 164, SEC(2008) 402, 3 April, p. 2, available at http://ec.europa.eu/world/enp/pdf/progress2008/sec08_402_en.pdf.

204   *Gwendolyn Sasse*

46. Ibid.
47. Ibid., pp. 4, 6.
48. Ibid., p. 9.
49. Ibid., p. 4.
50. Ibid., p. 6.
51. ENPI, Ukraine, National Indicative Programme 2007–2010, p. 4.
52. European Community (2008), *Principles for the Implementation of a Governance Facility under ENPI*, available at http://ec.europa.eu/world/enp/pdf/governance_facility_en.pdf
53. Mizhnarodnyi tsentr perspektyvnykh doslidzhen', 2006; Mizhnarodnyi tsentr perspektyvnykh doslidzhen' et al 2007.
54. V. Chalyi (2007), 'Hromad'skyi monitoring – zaporuka efektyvnosti evrointehratsiinoho kursu Ukraini' in V. Chalyi (ed.), *Ukraina – ES : vid planu dii do posylenoi uhody*. Kyiv: Ukrains'kyi tsentr ekonomichnykh i politychnykh doslidzhen' imeni Oleksandra Razumkova & Instytut Evropy Universytety Tsyurikha, p. 6.
55. Ibid., p. 2.
56. Razumkov Centre (Ukrains'kyi tsentr ekonomichnykh i politychnykh doslidzhen' imeni Oleksandra Razumkova) (2008), *Natsional'na bezpeka i oborona*, 6 (100), p. 2.
57. Razumkov Centre, 2007; Razumkov Centre (Ukrains'kyi tsentr ekonomichnykh i politychnykh doslidzhen' imeni Oleksandra Razumkova) (2008), *Natsional'na bezpeka i oborona*, 6 (100).
58. Ibid., p. 7.
59. Ibid., pp. 9–10.
60. Razumkov Centre, 2007; Razumkov Centre (Ukrains'kyi tsentr ekonomichnykh i politychnykh doslidzhen' imeni Oleksandra Razumkova) (2008), *Natsional'na bezpeka i oborona*, p. 8.
61. Ibid., p. 9.
62. Ibid., p. 30.
63. Ibid., p. 31.
64. Ibid., p. 44.
65. Ibid., p. 32.
66. Ibid., p. 44.
67. National Statistics Office of the Republic of Moldova (2008), 'Main social and economic of the regions, counties and municipalities January–June 2008', available at http://www.statistica.md/publications/195/ro/Buletin_raional_2_2008.pdf.
68. J. Löwenhardt, R.J. Hill and M. Light (2001), 'A wider Europe: the view from Minsk and Chisinau', *International Affairs*, 77 (3), p. 606.
69. Commission of the European Communities (2004b), EU-Moldova Action Plan, 2004, pp. 3–4, available at http://ec.europa.eu/world/enp/pdf/action_plans/moldova_enp_ap_final_en.pdf.
70. S. Buscaneanu (2006), *How far is the European Neighbourhood Policy a substantial offer for Moldova?* Association for Participatory Democracy (ADEPT), Moldova, available at http://www.e-democracy.md/files/enp-moldova.pdf
71. Commission of the European Communities (2008), *ENP Progress Report Moldova* COM(2008)164, 3 April, p. 18. available at http://ec.europa.eu/world/enp/pdf/progress2008/sec08_399_en.pdf

72. Commission of the European Communities (2004b), EU-Moldova Action Plan, 2004, available at http://ec.europa.eu/world/enp/pdf/action_plans/moldova_enp_ap_final_en.pdf.

73. The EUSR's mandate includes i) strengthening the EU contribution to the resolution of conflict in Transnistria, ii) assisting in the preparation of EU contributions to the conflict resolution and iii) closely following the political developments in Moldova, including Transnistria, by developing and maintaining close contacts with the Moldovan government and other domestic actors.

74. This is even acknowledged by the usually reluctant Transnistrian leadership and its media. See, for example, *The Tiraspol Times*, 15 May 2008.

75. Similarly, Shevchuk attended a meeting in Brussels on human trafficking in Brussels with European, Moldovan and Transnistrian parliamentarians and NGOs on 15 May 2008 (Council of the European Union, 15 May 2008).

76. *AISmoldpres*, 20 June 2008.

77. Commission of the European Communities (2006d), ENP Progress Report Moldova COM(2006) 726 final, SEC(2006) 1506/2, 4 December, Brussels, p. 5, available at http://ec.europa.eu/world/enp/pdf/sec06_1506-2_en.pdf; M. Vahl and M. Emerson (2004), 'Moldova and the Transnistrian Conflict', in B. Coppetiers et al *Europeanization and Conflict Resolution: Case Studies from the European Periphery, Journal on Ethnopolitics and Minority Issues in Europe*, 1, chapter 4, available at http://www.ecmi.de/jemie/specialfocus.html.

78. *Kommersant*, 11 March 2008; *AISmoldpres*, 25 June 2008.

79. *Kommersant*, 11 March 2008.

80. N. Popescu (2005) 'The EU in Moldova: Settling Conflicts in the Neighbourhood', Occasional Paper 60. Paris: European Union Institute for Security Studies, available at http://www.iss.europa.eu/uploads/media/occ60.pdf.

81. Interview, Chisinau, July 2008.

82. E-democracy publishes a Euromonitor report every three months: http://www.e-democracy.md/en/re-ue/. Euroforum has set up working groups to monitor implementation of specific ENP Action Plan areas.

83. Interview with Victor Dragutan, Senior Advisor at the Ministry of Reintegration. The embassies of individual member states in Moldova tend to be better staffed and equipped and more responsive than the office of the Commission delegation in the country (Interview with Nicolae Negru, Editor of *Journal de Chishinau*, July 2008).

84. Commission of the European Communities (2006d), ENP Progress Report Moldova COM(2006) 726 final, SEC(2006) 1506/2, 4 December, available at http://ec.europa.eu/world/enp/pdf/sec06_1506-2_en.pdf.

85. Commission of the European Communities (2008), *ENP Progress Report Moldova* COM(2008)164, 3 April, p. 2, available at http://ec.europa.eu/world/enp/pdf/progress2008/sec08_399_en.pdf

86. Ibid.

87. F. Schimmelfennig (2001), 'The Community Trap: Liberal Norms, Rhetorical Action, and the Eastern Enlargement of the European Union', *International Organization*, 55 (1), pp. 47–80.

88. G. Sasse (2008), 'The European Neighbourhood Policy: Conditionality Revisited for the EU's Eastern Neighbours', *Europe-Asia Studies*, 60 (2), pp. 295–316.

10
The Impact of the ENP on EU-North Africa Relations: The Good, the Bad and the Ugly

Federica Bicchi

Introduction

EU-North Africa relations are a good test of the European Neighbourhood Policy (ENP) capacity to innovate positively on the previous state of affairs. Relations between the EU and Algeria, Morocco and Tunisia have a long history, whereas Libya has until recently thrived on its role of 'outsider'. The Euro-Mediterranean Partnership (EMP) has laid the basis for a new relationship with North African countries, with the usual exception of Libya. The ENP was meant to bring relations to a further stage, opening new avenues for cooperation. As a few years have lapsed, it is legitimate to ask whether the ENP has had an impact. Does the ENP stand for a positive contribution to the pattern of cooperation established by the EMP? Have the last few years witnessed a change of tack linked to the ENP? What are the areas of continuity and change between the EMP and the ENP? The aim of this chapter is to investigate these questions.

The chapter will focus on the three countries most concerned with ENP, namely Morocco, Tunisia and Algeria. I will explore relations between, on one hand, the EU and, on the other, these three countries. I will argue that with a broad generalisation, the state of the art can be summarised with the title of a Western movie, 'The Good, the Bad and the Ugly'. The EU's relations with Morocco (the Good) have thrived since the introduction of the ENP, Tunisia (the Bad) remains closed to any attempt to turn economic successes into political openings, while relations with Algeria (the Ugly) have experienced a series of ups and downs. Therefore, the ENP has not only emphasised bilateralism over region-building, but it has increased the distance between partners, as the 'regatta approach' was introduced. Moreover, it is becoming increasingly difficult to distinguish the end-goal of activities funded by the EU, as several display both a developmental goal and a security one.

This chapter starts by exploring the previous state of the relationships between the EU and North African countries, under the EMP. It then analyses the impact of the ENP on relations between the EU and each of these countries. It concludes by generalising across the three countries, and focusing on the advancement of bilateralism and the tightening link between development and security.

The EU and North Africa

The history of relations between the EU and North African countries has followed the ups and downs of Euro-Mediterranean ones more generally. The relationship can be generally divided in four stages.[1] At first, from the creation of the EEC to 1972, relations were on an ad hoc basis. Morocco and Tunisia signed a trade agreement in 1969, while Algeria did not formalise a trade regime. The second stage opened with the Global Mediterranean Policy, launched in 1972, which marked the 'invention' of the Mediterranean and brought the first systematisation of EEC relations with North African countries and with Mediterranean ones more generally. In fact, the North African countries were the first target of the discussion, when it started in 1970. They signed cooperation agreements in 1976, as well as Financial and Technical Protocols. After a lull during the 1980s, which marked a third stage in relations, a fourth stage opened at the end of the Cold War, with a long period of EU activism toward its Southern neighbours leading up to the launch of the ENP (and most recently, the Union for the Mediterranean, formally launched on 13 July 2008).

The real post-Cold War change came with the Euro-Mediterranean Partnership (EMP, or 'Barcelona Process,' as it has came to be known), which was formalised in 1995. Similarly to what happened in the early 1970s, the proposal first centred on a Euro-Maghreb Partnership, involving Algeria, Morocco and Tunisia. It later developed to include all the riparian Mediterranean countries, as well as Albania, Jordan, Mauritania and the Palestinian Authority. The EMP introduced several novelties, two of which are particularly interesting in relation to what would come later with the ENP: 1) an expanded agenda for discussion and 2) a multilayered and institutionalised dialogue.

The expanded agenda for discussion has made it possible to address virtually any topic at the periodical meetings. A look at the topics for ministerial meetings shows that topics range from economic affairs, to migration, culture and tourism, to name but a few. This variety of topics is unprecedented in relations between the EC/EU and its Southern neighbours. Traditionally, issues at stake have focused on economic relations, with a special interest in development. The Barcelona Process has broken with this tradition and has unleashed the possibility of addressing an agenda without firm limits.

Moreover, the dialogue in the EMP has included a variety of institutionalised channels for dialogue. It envisages not only the bilateral dimension of trade agreements and the unilateral dimension of EU aid provision, but also, and especially, the multilateral dimension that has periodically brought all the participants together. The importance of multilateralism has justified the view, best expressed by Adler and Crawford, that one of the main goals of the EMP has been region-building.[2] According to this argument, regardless of the reasons that have motivated the EU in its policy toward the area, the evidence is of a practice of regional security through partnership and mutual confidence. Region-building in the EMP has evolved from the example of European integration and of the Commission on Security and Cooperation in Europe (CSCE). From the former, it has taken the practice of free trade and common economics spaces, which in turn could lead to cooperation in other areas such as energy and transportation. From the latter comes the idea of a security dialogue fostered by periodical gatherings.

These two developments, however, created a trade off between, on the one hand, the depth with which topics could be addressed and, on the other, the emphasis on multilateralism. The sheer number of participants created difficulties in accommodating a variety of interests even before highly contentious issues such as Arab-Israeli relations, alternative models for economic development or frameworks for immigration management came into play. A common criticism has been that, in an attempt to please all participants, the Barcelona Process has focused too little on content, thus becoming a sort of 'UN of the Mediterranean'.

The ENP came into being against this background and, as we are going to see, it has heavily leaned away from multilateralism, but not necessarily in favour of deepened dialogue with all partners. Moreover, it is worth keeping in mind that the addition of the Southern neighbours, including North African countries, to the ENP was something of an afterthought, sanctioned by the dropping of the suffix 'new' in front of the initiative's name only in the second half of 2003. North African countries did not figure predominantly in the marketing of the initiative, either. Despite this low-key start, the ENP has grown into a reality, affecting relations between the EU and North African countries. Its impact, however, has varied dramatically from one country to the other, as we will now see.

Morocco, the good

The ENP has provided a quantitative and qualitative leap forward in relations between the EU and Morocco. This is the country among the North African ones to which the introduction of the ENP has made more of a difference. Cooperation now far exceeds the substance of meetings arranged under the provision of the EMP and of the Association Agreement. Morocco has been working extremely hard to improve on its relations with the EU and its efforts were recompensed with the granting of 'advanced status' on 13 October 2008.The differentiated approach of the ENP is 'precisely what Morocco has asked for' and relations have blossomed as a consequence. As we are going to see, this is a country that ticks all the boxes of the expected effects of the ENP and goes beyond what was originally expected from it.[3]

Relations between the EU and Morocco were already good under the EMP before the formulation of the ENP. Morocco was among the first partners to sign an Association Agreement in February 1996, which entered into force on 1 March 2000. The timetable for dismantling tariffs had 2003 as a starting date and ten years as a time frame. Partners initially 'agreed to disagree' on agriculture, with further negotiations being postponed to 2007 through a 'rendez-vous clause.' But this problem, which continues to mar relations between the EU and Morocco and to stay on the agenda for negotiations, is hardly limited to Morocco and has also remained a key issue with other countries.

Under MEDA, Morocco was the main recipient of funds. Over the period 1995–2003, it received c. €1.1 billion.[4] It has also been ahead of the other Mediterranean partners in terms of disbursement, with a rate of 65 per cent over the period 2000–2004.[5]

More generally, the country has been part of a number of institutional frameworks which, while not directly related to the EU, have given shape to Morocco's attempts to be as close to EU member states as possible. It is a member of the 5 + 5 group, which brings together countries of the Western Mediterranean. It is part of the *Union du Maghreb Arabe*, which has not been very active but is seen favourably by the EU. It is also a signatory of the Agadir Agreement, signed in 2004[6] by Morocco, Egypt, Jordan and Tunisia, which came about mainly in response to pressures from the EU to increase south-south cooperation and establish a free trade area among partners. In other words, Morocco's rebuffed applications to the EC in 1984 and again in 1987 have not turned away this country, which on the contrary has strived to find alternative ways to improve relations.

It comes as no surprise, therefore, that in terms of the ENP Morocco ticks all the boxes. Reports, Strategy Papers and Programmes have come out regularly and have generally been positive and operational. The Action Plan was approved at the Association Council in December 2004 and entered into force in July 2005. The Association Council has been very active. It has met once per year since the entry into force of the Association Agreement. In February 2003, the Association Council adopted a new structure, composed of six new sub commi-ttees: 1) Internal Market; 2) Industry, Trade and Services; 3) Transport, Environment and Energy; 4) Research and Innovation; 5) Agriculture and Fisheries (first meeting: 16 March 2005) and 6) Justice and Security. Later in that year, a new sub-committee on Human Rights, Democratisation and Governance was agreed, and working-group meetings on migration and social affairs were also held. There are currently ten committees.

The activism of the Association Council and its working bodies has not been limited to reviewing and managing the Association Agreement, but it has addressed ways to deepen it. In 2007 Morocco opened negotiations on the liberalisation of services and establishment. Moreover, in July 2007, at the Association Council in Brussels, it was agreed to set up an ad hoc working-group to consider changes to the current Association Agreement. Negotiations are under way and tackle the possibility of creating a so-called Deep Free Trade Area, entailing not only trade but also a rapprochement of domestic rules, such as on procurement and on sanitary standards, along the lines of what has been discussed with Ukraine. Smooth cooperation has been rewarded. For the period 2007–2010 Morocco has an envelope of €654 million, again the main beneficiary of the Mediterranean participants of the European Neighbourhood Policy Instrument (ENPI).

So far, the picture I have described of EU-Morocco relations has followed predictable lines, intensifying rather than innovating on a solid structure of cooperation. But there is more to it, because the substance and the forms of cooperation have ventured into new territories, which were not originally foreseen or received just a passing mention in the Action Plan. This is true both for new topics addressed and for institutional practices, as I am going to show.

First, in terms of subjects covered by the cooperation, the experience of Morocco gives meaning to the generally obscure ENP formula of 'a stake in the Single Market.' Aviation is a case in point. Morocco has concluded an Aviation Agreement with the EU, thus integrating its air transport into the European market, and it is in the process of doing so also for the energy and transport sectors. A 'Common Aviation Area' was established with the signature of the EU-Morocco Aviation Agreement on 12 December 2006. The Agreement entails opening of markets and regulatory convergence not only in economic terms but also for consumers' protection, safety standards and security issues. This Agreement is groundbreaking as in fact it goes beyond the 'open skies' agreement between the EU and the US. It entails harmonisation (or rather 'Europeanisation') of rules on flight safety and security, competition, state aid, consumer protection and protection of the environment. It also streamlines administrative procedures and, most importantly, has begun the removal of capacity restrictions between the EU and Morocco.

This Agreement, which might sound quite technical and abstract, has had an instant practical impact. Low-cost airlines have been quick to spring on the opportunity and new services were immediately created from a number of EU member states. To take an example, during the summer of 2008, there were 39 low-cost airline routes (on top of other air companies) reaching Marrakesh airport, which was extended in 2006 in order to be able to cope with an expected traffic of 3.8 million travellers per year. The new terminal of the airport, to be operational in 2009, will increase passengers' capacity to 6.5 million. That number will contribute to the expected goal of 10 million tourists per year to the country by 2010, fixed by Moroccan authorities, which nearly doubles the number of tourists who arrived in 2005. What the effect of this new load of tourists will be on the so-far selected cities of Marrakesh, Fex and Oujda is something that remains to be seen.[7] But to understand the political meaning of these developments, it is worth highlighting that the next country likely to conclude such an agreement is Israel, and toward this aim the Commission asked the Council for a negotiating mandate at the end of 2007. And low-cost airlines have already started to position themselves in what promises to be another rewarding market.

Another field in which Morocco is at the forefront of cooperation is in its enhanced political dialogue on the Common Foreign and

Security Policy (CFSP) and, most importantly, the European Security and Defence Policy (ESDP). Morocco participated in the EU-led operation Operation ALTHEA in Bosnia. The operation was decided on by the Council of the EU in July 2004 and launched in December 2004. It aimed to replace the Stabilisation Force (SFOR), which NATO decided to bring to a close, but it made use of NATO assets and capabilities, in agreement with the Berlin Plus Agreement. Morocco's contribution to the European Union Force (EUFOR) was 130 troops (out of 7000) based in Mostar together with the French contingent. Its contribution came to an end when EUFOR was scaled down in 2007. It was not the only non-EU country to participate to Operation ALTHEA, but it was the only Mediterranean one. As the operation was under the supervision of the Political and Security Committee in the Council of EU hierarchy, Morocco was de facto participating in an ESDP mission, sharing its costs, receiving classified information and putting its troops under the operational command of the EU. With the prospect of an 'advanced status', more possibilities for cooperation might emerge, for instance in Afghanistan.

It is worth mentioning another field of cooperation, if only because it has a long pedigree in terms of Euro-Mediterranean relations, namely rules of origin. Morocco is in the process of implementing the pan-Euro-Mediterranean origin cumulation system, which cumulates rules of origin across the Euro-Mediterranean area. In particular, a decision was taken at the Fifth meeting of the Association Council in November 2005 to open the door to such a practice in relation to clothing, once Morocco and Turkey had concluded an agreement on it.

Innovation is not limited to the substance of cooperation, but also involves the forms it takes. Morocco has been a very active country in setting up twinning projects. The first 'Justice, Freedom and Security' twinning initiative in the Mediterranean was launched here and involved training activities aimed at border control forces. The programme was then redirected to the management of border controls, providing financial support to a new emergency programme aimed at upgrading migration strategy as a whole, with a budget of approximately €67 million.[8] Between 2005 and 2007, there were 13 twinning projects funded under MEDA/ENPI, on subjects as diverse as maritime safety and administrative best practices.[9] A similar number is under consideration.

Moreover, cooperation on these projects has often flourished outside the formal institutional settings of the Association Committee, its subgroups and its working- groups. Contact between the parties on the ground has often developed in parallel with (when they have not antici-pated and precipitated it) the procedure elaborated by the Commission, which envisages a call for tender to select the European partner for a given objective. For instance, a twinning project on the application of a new Moroccan law on consumer protection was done directly through missions between the parties and the role of the sub-committee was to mention this possibility and then to 'congratulate for progress'.[10]

More areas for cooperation were mentioned in the advanced status road map agreed in October 2008. Not only it was agreed to open new dossiers for cooperation (most notably on the ESDP), but new institu-tional formats were also proposed, ranging from an EU-Morocco sum-mit to the participation of Morocco at the margins of some EU Council ministerial or working-group meetings.

Finally, Morocco has also innovated on the use of funds. It has been one of the first recipients, together with Ukraine, of EU funds disbursed under the new 'Governance Facility.'[11] This source of funding rewards ENP countries that display significant progress on priorities identified in the Action Plans in terms of democracy and human rights. It was allocated €50 million a year for 2007–2010. In 2007 Morocco received €28 million under this facility (thus bringing the overall amount of EU funds to Morocco for that year to €190 million). Recipient countries can then allocate this type of funds to any type of project and Morocco has earmarked funds for projects for reform of the public administration.

The only chapter that remains an incomplete success is on migra-tion, but not for lack of trying. There have been a number of issues on which cooperation between the EU and Morocco has worked well, such as the reform of border control management. While the EU has funded much of the progress, much has also come from bilateral cooperation with Spain. The EU has long been negotiating a readmission treaty with Morocco, but negotiations have reached an apparent dead end. Morocco adheres to all the fundamental objectives of the EU, but is unhappy about being (and being seen as) the policeman of the Mediterranean, accepting migrants originating from Africa when there is no tangible proof that they have transitted through Morocco, especially given the porous border between Morocco and Algeria. Moreover, Morocco refuses to give in without compensation on the visa chapter, which would lift some travel restrictions for Moroccans. But EU member states are also reluctant to grant concessions collectively, as they prefer to use them at the bilateral level.[12] Negotiations continue, although their urgency has diminished along with the decrease in illegal immigration across the Strait of Gibraltar thanks to cooperation between Morocco and Spain.

Everything considered, relations between the EU and Morocco have been very positive and the ENP has allowed expansion of the scope, the depth and especially the type of cooperation. This does not entail that everything is fine in absolute terms. The starting point for Morocco is a situation of limited economic development, a high rate of illiteracy (especially among women) and heavy reliance on agriculture. But measured against the previous background of EU-Moroccan relations under the EMP, the ENP has represented a quantitative and qualitative leap forward.

Tunisia, the bad

It might seem far-fetched to characterise Tunisia as the villain of the story. After an initial diffidence toward the perceived European bias of the ENP proposal, economic relations have been good and the two parties see eye to eye on most economic chapters. Economic exchanges are satisfactory, and at times even excellent, benefiting from the relatively advanced level of economic development in Tunisia and its outward driven model of economic development. Since 1 January 2008, for the first time in the history of Euro-Mediterranean relations, there is reciprocal free trade of industrial goods. Moreover, Tunisia is part of the *Union du Maghreb Arabe* and a signatory of the Agadir Agreement. Against this positive economic backdrop, the political dimension of the relationship is a non-starter. There is little political momentum attached to any form of cooperation. As the Country Report of 2004 put it in an understatement: 'Tunisia has decided to embark on cooperation in the areas of good governance and justice and home affairs on a very gradual basis only.'[13] The Action Plan is noticeably short on political issues, despite the dire situation on the ground, and it reflects the lack of a political process on the ground. The regime is founding its legitimacy on the provision of material goods in a nearly complete absence of political freedoms. The EU is de facto going along with this approach, but by doing so, it is relinquishing any attempt to have a policy beyond a foreign economic policy.

Beginning on the bright side, the ENP has allowed the EU and Tunisia to update and deepen the economic relationship created under the EMP. There has not been the same qualitative leap as in the case of Morocco, but opportunities have been created and exploited by both sides.

The Association Agreement, which was signed ahead of the Barcelona Conference on 12 April 1995, entered into force on 30 March 1998, the first to do so of the new generation of Agreements unleashed by the

EMP. The calendar for dismantling tariffs on industrial goods did not foresee any initial 'grace period' (differently from Morocco) and entailed a process over ten years, which has been respected. As a consequence, Tunisia can boast to be the first country to open its internal market to the competition of industrial goods coming from the EU, which is by itself a tremendous achievement given the state of the art in the area. The relevance of free trade in industrial goods must however be put into perspective, as the Tunisian economy is traditionally based on trade and it is a relatively open market, thus offering an easy platform for international trade and flows of international capital. In 2006, for instance, 54 per cent of gross domestic product (GDP) came from exports of good and services (compared to 33 per cent for Morocco).[14]

The Action Plan, which was adopted in July 2005 and entered into force in 2006, has worked as an update of the economic components of the Association Agreement. It specified deadlines, operationalised concepts and elaborated on practices that received only a mention or a hint in the Association Agreement. Moreover, Tunisia has embraced the Action Plan so closely that it has transferred its priorities into the Tunisian national development plan covering the period 2007–2016.

Agriculture is a sticky point for Tunisia as well as for its neighbours. Negotiations have started, but they have immediately run into difficulties on both sides. At the moment, all agricultural products are covered by tariffs, apart from specific quotas, such as on oil. The final goal is to reverse the situation and have free trade on everything, apart from specific quotas. But the forecast is for a few years of years of negotiations to approximate this result.[15]

Therefore, the picture in purely economic terms is relatively rosy. The ENP has produced a quantitative increase in economic relations, although not a qualitative one along the lines of what has happened with Morocco. But there are clear limitations to the economic success, and these fall all in the political camp. Indicators of these limitations are not only the absence of a real dialogue on human rights and democracy, but also the paucity of the dialogue on justice and home affairs.

The Association Committee did not meet between 2004 and 2007. The Subcommittee on Human Rights focused for a long time on rules and procedures and held no meetings at all between the end of 2006 and November 2007. The holding of a meeting at that date came as a deal for concessions on others fronts, including negotiations on agriculture and pharmaceuticals. Moreover, the Subcommittee on Justice and Security held its first meeting only in February 2008. It has mounted only a meagre agenda. As a matter of fact, there is no information on issues such as prisons or drug-related problems available at the EU level, while member states have a more privileged position in this respect.[16] This makes it all the more difficult to conduct a dialogue on these matters.

In terms of financial aid, too, Tunisia prefers to do without the help of the EU if that entails a degree of political influence on its domestic affairs. MEDA funds for the period 2000–2006 included a part on justice and home affairs which received an amount of €20 million. The initial amount proposed by the EU was more, but Tunisia wrote off nearly €6 million because of disagreements on the substance of the potential projects.[17]

Similarly, in the package of political concessions that marked the late months of 2007, Tunisia unblocked a set of non-governmental organisation (NGO) projects. But this was set out as a gesture of goodwill, without previous negotiations and without any intention to ease conditions on this front. Projects funded by the European Instrument for Democracy and Human Rights (previously the European Initiative for Democracy and Human Rights, EIDHR) have never got off the ground and microprojects, targeted at local NGOs, could not be launched in the current political climate.

It is thus striking to see how Tunisia has been able to separate the economic dimension of the ENP from the political one and set the tone of its relationship with the EU. Economic relations have flourished and are based on a very similar understanding of economic priorities for the country on the part of the EU and of the Tunisian regime. Whenever political tones have nuanced the economic dialogue, however, Tunisia has made it clear that it is ready to forego economic benefits if that entails opening a political dialogue. To do so, it has skilfully played on a 'third world' interpretation of human rights, by which the provision of political freedom would be useless without access to health care, housing, etc. Indices for material welfare are indeed relatively good in the country, especially in comparison to the other North African countries. Gross national income (GNI) per capita is US$2,970 per person (compared to US$2,160 in Morocco), illiteracy is relatively low at 25 per cent of the population aged 15+ (compared to 48 per cent in Morocco) and the percentage of the population owning the house it inhabits is very high.[18] Moreover, Tunisia has exploited traditional divisions among EU member states about how to address human rights and democracy concerns in the country, with Northern European countries (and especially the Scandinavian ones) preferring a more confrontational approach, whereas Southern European countries opt for a discussion behind closed doors.[19]

The question thus remains whether the ENP will avail the Tunisian interpretation of the opportunities it offers, and allow for a separation between economic and political affairs, or whether the implicit assumption of EU policy-makers, that economic progress will eventually spill over into the political domain, will come true. At the moment, the former prevails.

Algeria, the ugly

Algeria has been a difficult negotiating partner for the EU and at present, it has not yet formally developed all the documents and settings that characterise the ENP, despite always being mentioned among the countries included under the ENP. Since the cancellation of elections in 1992, the country has plunged into an extremely difficult domestic situation, which still drags on. Much of Algerian policy-makers' attention has thus focused on issues other than relations with the EU, and negotiations have suffered accordingly. As if the political situation was not enough, the economic context of Algeria is also a source of problems. The country is relatively rich, but the economic model that has guided Algeria's development presents several fundamental divergences from the EU. Not only there is a traditional presence of the state in the economy, but the importance of gas and oil over other commodities projects the country onto an international market of which the EU is only a part, although a substantial one. While the points of potential interest for cooperation are thus several, it has often been difficult to find the right tone and the ideal perspective to clinch a deal. It comes thus as no surprise that a number of reasons have prevented Algeria from formally participating in the ENP, while de facto it does.

The most important omission in the ENP context is the absence of an Action Plan for Algeria. There are several reasons for this. The Association Agreement was signed in 2002 and it entered into force only on 10 October 2005. There is thus little need, especially from Algeria's perspective, to update an Agreement which has just begun its implementation stage. On top of the timing, the implementation of the Agreement is going to be difficult, because it entails a complex transition to a market economy. An internal study by the Commission on the expected results of the Agreement's implementation showed that in its first stage, it is going to have a negative (and for certain sectors, very negative) impact on the Algerian economy.[20] Although the evaluation of the Commission focused on the benefits expected in the middle to long range, no swift application of the Agreement is in sight, as complex internal dynamics unfold as a consequence.

What there is, in lieu of the Action Plan, is a 'package' of issues on the agenda by mutual consent. Initially proposed by the Relex branch of the Commission, the 'package' includes issues that interest the EU (such as energy and readmission of migrants) and others that interest Algeria (such as visa facilities and World Trade Organization (WTO) accession). Moreover, several subcommittees were created in December 2007: Agriculture and Fisheries, Customs, Information Society (which will address issues such as research and education), Infrastructure (which includes energy), Justice and Home Affairs, Social Affairs and Trade. Some of these did meet before this date in the form of working-groups, most notably the one on Justice and Home Affairs and on Social Affairs. The glaring absence from this list is the Subcommittee on Human Rights. In the deal for the creation of sub-committees, it was decided to postpone the creation of this specific one although the decision specified that it will be created at a later date. The procedure in other Mediterranean countries has indeed been to create it later than the other subcommittees and Algeria clung to this precedent.

The absence of an Action Plan has not stopped relations, but has made them more irksome. The EU has been able to express its vision for Algeria and thus disburse funds for Algeria through the ENPI in the Strategy Paper and National Indicative Programme for the country, issued in 2006 and covering up to 2013 for the former and 2010 for the latter. Despite a desire on both sides to continue negotiations and pro-mote key chapters, such as energy, the climate for the implementation of provisions remains tightly linked to the contingent context prevai-ling at the time, with a number of provisos and precautions that cloud the smooth development of relations.

Negotiations thus continue, but from the point of view of the ENP they lack the political enthusiasm that characterises relations with Morocco and the neat format of relations with Tunisia. The unstable balance of Algerian domestic politics marks this country as the 'ugly' or, in less negative terms, the 'awkward' partner of the EU in North Africa.

The new agenda for EU-North Africa relations

The state of art relations between the EU and North African countries under the ENP has thus revealed a picture in which the ENP has had an impact in its brief lifespan, although a different one on each of the three countries. I captured this situation with reference to the Western movie 'The Good, the Bad and the Ugly,' as the three countries have developed in different directions. Morocco, here ironically defined as 'the good', has thrived on the opportunity to pursue a bilateral agenda with the EU and relations have flourished accordingly. Tunisia, while better placed in economic terms to benefit from relations with the EU, has progressed on the economic chapter but has maintained a low profile in political relations, because of its status as 'the villain' autocracy of North Africa. Algeria, 'the ugly', has continued to negotiate on a whole variety of chapters, but relations remain troublesome.

Looking at the overall picture that emerges from this overview and focusing on the commonalities rather than on differences, it is possible to argue that three broad issues characterise the new agenda of EU-North Africa relations, as set by the ENP.

First, this overview confirms that bilateralism has increased in importance over region- building. There is nothing new in this. Del Sarto and Schumacher have described how the collapse of the peace process and the enlargement process of the EU already undermined the region-building dimension within the EMP. They also stressed how the ENP replaced the principle of regionality with differentiated bilateralism.[21] Similarly, Pace highlighted the tension between, on the one hand, the EMP and its 'regionalist strategy' and, on the other, the ENP and its 'normative bilateral basis'.[22] Moreover, North African countries are traditionally not interested in regionalism. It is thus not surprising that the implementation of the ENP has brought about an increase in bilateralism. The Union for the Mediterranean, which signalled a new development in the Barcelona Process, does emphasise regional and sub-regional projects. It remains to be seen, however, whether they will take involve North African countries and if so, whether the ensuing dynamics will counter the strong bilateral appeal of the ENP.

Second, following on from the increase in bilateralism, the ENP has entailed an increased distance among the three North African countries themselves in their relationship with the EU. The 'regatta approach' has led to North African countries sailing at different speeds, as the ENP has created a different pace and a different political momentum for cooperation. The attempt to keep a common agenda for all EMP participants has given way to the possibility of deepening issues of interest for some countries but not for others, and this in turn has led to the deepening of relations with Morocco, a sluggish political dialogue with Tunisia and a set of fits and starts with Algeria. Like the three characters in the movie, the three countries are locked in a regional context because of their geographical location. But their political and economic choices, as well as the EU power of attraction, are not bringing them together in a common political-economic setting.

Finally, I will offer a last point to the debate about the future of EU-North African relations. This essay has focused predominantly on the cooperation initiated under the EMP and on the impact of the ENP on it. But it is clear that 11 September and the increasing securitisation of European external affairs have affected the quality of that cooperation as relations thickened. As described by Joffé, the EU has progressively securitised its relations with North African countries.[23] This process, which started with the Tampere Summit in 1999, accelerated dramatically after 11 September 2001. The most substantial change has occurred in relations with Morocco, which has expanded its relations with the EU in such a substantial way. Algeria has participated in this trend, while Tunisia has remained at the margins of it. The draft EU Action Plan against terrorism[24] defined Morocco and Algeria as priority countries for counter-terrorism, receiving technical assistance to build their counter-terrorism capacity. In 2006, the EU thus launched a programme to support the fight against terrorism in these two countries, whereas Tunisia has received some funding, but on a lesser scale. In a bold institutional innovation, the reception of assistance is coordinated between member states, the Commission and the UN, and there has been a concrete attempt to bring into line national budgets and the EU budget.[25]

One of the key issues in the near future for EU-North African relations, therefore, will be how partners will frame activities that can potentially fall under either chapter of their cooperation: development and fight against terrorism. There are activities that are 'dual use' as they might respond to both needs. For instance, the Action Plan for Morocco mentions, as a medium-term priority to strengthen democracy and rule of law, the modernisation of prison administration, 'in particular the elements dealing with training, reintegration and protection of prisoners' rights'. The draft EU Action Plan against Terrorism casts a different light on the same activity, highlighting the importance of the fight against radicalisation in prisons as 'part of a wider programme of counter-terrorism technical assistance for Morocco'.

While the quantity and the quality of cooperation with the EU will thus depend largely on the decisions made in North African capitals, the overarching EU concern with security is bound also to affect the ENP.

Notes

1. F. Bicchi (2007), *European Foreign Policy Making toward the Mediterranean*. New York/Basingstoke: Palgrave Macmillan.
2. E. Adler and B. Crawford (2006), 'Normative Power: The European Practice of Region Building and the Case of the Euro-Mediterranean Partnership (EMP)', in E. Adler, F. Bicchi, B. Crawford and R. Del Sarto (eds), *The Convergence of Civilizations. Constructing the Mediterranean Region*. Toronto: University of Toronto Press. For a different argument in a similar vein, see: M. Pace (2007), 'Norm shifting from EMP to ENP: the EU as a norm entrepreneur in the south?' *Cambridge Review of International Affairs*, 20 (4), pp. 659–75.
3. Commission of the European Communities (2004a), Commission Staff Working Paper. Country Report Morocco {COM(2004)373 final}, Brussels, 12 May 2004, SEC(2004)569, p. 5.
4. Commission of the European Communities (2004a), Commission Staff Working Paper. Country Report Morocco {COM(2004)373 final}, Brussels, 12 May 2004, SEC(2004)569, p. 4. €342 million were devoted to structural adjustment facilities, in the form of budgetary aid to support the implementation of reforms in fields such as finance, health, education, water management, transport.
5. Commission of the European Communities (2004a), Commission Staff Working Paper. Country Report Morocco {COM(2004)373 final}, Brussels, 12 May 2004, SEC(2004)569, p. 4.
6. The Agreement has not yet entered into force and it has been largely superseded by the progress made on the Greater Arab Free Trade Area.
7. In Marrakesh, 90 per cent of the medina is now owned by foreigners. Carole Cadwalladr, 'Is this the end of "abroad"?' *The Observer*, 26 November 2006.
8. ENP Progress Report, Morocco, 4 December 2006.
9. See Archive of funding opportunities for Morocco, on the European Commission EuropeAid website.
10. Interview, Commission Official, RELEX, Brussels 30 January 2008.
11. Whereas a minority of EU member states voiced some concern about Ukraine, Morocco's case was unanimously supported. Interview, Commission Official, EuropeAid, Brussels, 29 January 2008.
12. Interview, Commission Official, RELEX, Brussels, 29 January, 2008.
13. Commission of the EuropeanCommunities (2004b), *Commission Staff Working Paper. Country Report Tunisia* {COM(2004)373 final}. Brussels, 12 May 2004, SEC(2004)570, p. 4.
14. Source: World Bank Database, 2006.
15. Interview, Commission Official, RELEX, Brussels, 29 January 2008.
16. Interview, Commission Official, RELEX, Brussels, 30 January, 2008.
17. Ibid.
18. Source: World Bank Database, 2006.
19. Interview, Commission Official, RELEX, Brussels, 27 January, 2008.
20. Interview, Commission Official, RELEX, Brussels, 29 January, 2008.
21. R. Del Sarto and T. Schumacher (2005), 'From EMP to ENP: What's at Stake with the European Neighbourhood Policy towards the Southern Mediterranean?' *European Foreign Affairs Review*, 10 (1).

22. M. Pace (2007), 'Norm shifting from EMP to ENP: the EU as a norm entrepreneur in the south?' *Cambridge Review of International Affairs*, 20 (4), pp. 659–75.
23. G. Joffé (2008), 'The European Union, Democracy and Counter-Terrorism in the Maghreb', *Journal of Common Market Studies*, 46 (1), pp 147–71.
24. The Action Plan is classified. This version was made public by Statewatch.
25. Counter-Terrorism Coordinator, Council of the EU (2007), *Second annual review of the implementation of the Strategy for Combating Radicalisation and Recruitment*, Brussels, 23 November 2007, p. 5.

11
The ENP and the Southern Caucasus: Meeting the Expectations?

Narine Ghazaryan

Introduction

The European Neighbourhood Policy (ENP) was developed as a response to the new political environment created by the last two rounds of European Union enlargement and as a potential means to solve the 'inclusion-exclusion dilemma.'[1] It is a unique policy which unites separate geographical and political regions within one single framework of the EU's external relations. The most striking feature of the ENP within the EU's foreign policy is this regional dimension. The main criterion for countries to be involved in the ENP is their geographical location: that is, the neighbourhood of the Union. The ENP covers such regions as Eastern Europe, the Southern Caucasus and the Mediterranean, with each of which the EU previously had a separate framework of cooperation.[2]

The Southern Caucasus, comprising Armenia, Georgia and Azerbaijan, is one of the regions embraced within the policy because of its strategic location and its vicinity to the Union, which became immediate after the accession of Romania and Bulgaria in 2007 (Georgia shares maritime border with these countries). In spite of its size, tensions between the constituent countries of this region have remained high since the break-up of the Soviet Union. Thus, while the region continues to attract the interest of various foreign powers eager to establish their dominance, at a regional level rivalries have developed between the Caucasian states themselves, as well as between territories within these states.[3]

Although the EU was present in the Southern Caucasus from the beginning of 1990s it lacked a comprehensive policy toward the region.[4]

The framework for cooperation with the countries of the Southern Caucasus which preceded the ENP, the Partnership and Cooperation Agreements (PCAs), had limited success through a lack of incentive and political will on both sides.[5] Although the introduction of the ENP offered opportunities to develop a relationship further with these countries, nevertheless, its unclear incentives and ambiguous mechanisms raised concerns as to its ultimate success. To help reinvigorate the ENP, the Eastern Partnership was initiated in June 2008, to include Ukraine, Moldova, Georgia, Armenian, Azerbaijan and potentially Belarus.

This paper explores the history and current state of the EU's relations with the Southern Caucasus and considers the interests that the Union is pursuing in the region. It describes the inclusion of the Southern Caucasian countries in the ENP and the main challenges to be addressed, and it considers the security concerns of the Union within the ENP, taking into account the conflicts within the region which were considered to be 'frozen' until 2008. Finally, the paper addresses the expectations of the EU and of Armenia, Georgia and Azerbaijan within the ENP and the newly emerging Eastern Partnership.

The EU and the Southern Caucasus

The relationship between the EU and the Southern Caucasus can generally be divided into two stages. The first stage includes the establishment of bilateral relations between the parties and a rather reluctant attitude by the Union, marked by an absence of a coordinated policy towards the region, which persisted until the end of the 1990s. The beginning of the new millennium marked the second stage of the relationship, when the Union acknowledged its interests and expressed a willingness to engage more actively and to develop a comprehensive policy towards the region. This period mainly reflects the security concerns of the EU and primarily relates to the ENP.

The EU's strategy toward the Southern Caucasus before the launch of the ENP

The relationship between the European Union and the countries of the Southern Caucasus is less than two decades old. The European Community (EC) entered into external relations with this region in the late 1980s and in the beginning of the 1990s. This was influenced by such dramatic events as the fall of Berlin Wall in 1989, the collapse and fragmentation of Soviet Union in 1991 and the birth of independent states.

There is a presumption that the Southern Caucasus does not constitute a region and that it is just a 'cliché' created during the Soviet era.[6] The term 'South Caucasus' was chosen as an alternative to 'Transcaucasus' in order to separate it nominally from Russia, from whose perspective it was considered to be 'Transcaucasus', that is, beyond the Caucasus.[7] In fact, relations between all three states do not leave any doubt as to the absence of regional cooperation or identity in general. As Lynch identifies, there is no regional dialogue and an atmosphere of suspicion and insecurity is sustained by a complete lack of trust.[8] This absence of regional cohesion is accurately reflected in the EU's dealings with the Southern Caucasus before the ENP. As noted by Lynch, the Union's initial relations with these countries through the PCAs were a part of a general approach to the countries of the 'former Soviet Union', which was a regional category itself for the EU.[9] In addition the EU has been rather reluctant to intervene in the problems of the Southern Caucasus. The armed conflicts in Nagorno-Karabakh, Abkhazia and Southern Ossetia received little attention from the Union, which was more preoccupied with the doorstep conflicts of the Balkans.[10]

Nevertheless, bilateral relationships with the three Caucasian countries were established through PCAs, set up with the countries of former Soviet Union (with the exception of Baltic states) as an alternative to Europe Agreements (EAs). The PCAs with Armenia, Georgia and Azerbaijan were concluded in 1996, two years after Russia, Ukraine, Kazakhstan and the Kyrgyz Republic and closely followed by Moldova and Belarus, and entered into force in 1999. Contrasting with the EAs, the preambles of the PCAs do not provide for 'the process of European integration' or the 'objective of membership'; they contain vague notions of gradual rapprochement and a wider area of cooperation between Europe and its neighbouring regions.[11] Thus, by establishing different frameworks for cooperation, the Union drew a dividing line,[12] which it is now keen to erase with the ENP. More importantly, the PCAs established a political dialogue between the Union and the Caucasus states and provided for a very wide range of issues for cooperation.[13]

A cursory examination of the content and scope of the PCAs with Armenia, Georgia and Azerbaijan reveals little difference, beyond the name of the country signing the agreement. The PCAs with all three countries are largely identical, with little to differentiate between them. They did not reflect the concerns of any individual countries and were not meant to address any challenges they faced at the time,[14] when they had all already gone through the first years of independence and dealt with different problems with the transition of their economies, as well as several conflicts concerning all three of them.

Although the PCAs were drafted in similar fashion to the EAs, there were important features which gave the emerging relationship an entirely different character. Both types of agreement established a political dialogue, although their aims differed substantially: dialogue established by the EAs was used for the pre-accession process, whereas that provided by the PCAs, in particular with South Caucasian countries, aimed at accompanying and consolidating the *rapprochement* between the parties, as well as supporting the political and economic changes taking place in these countries. Although the Preambles of the PCAs provided for a 'political conditionality' clause, analogous with the EAs, this did not have the same effect, since the membership incentive was much more powerful than just establishing a wider area of cooperation between the Union and the relevant country.[15] The institutions provided by the PCAs generally reflect those established by the EAs, although these are referred to as 'cooperation' instead of 'association'.[16] However, the major difference, affecting the nature of the whole agreement, is the power of the Association Council to make binding decisions for the purpose of attaining the objectives of the EA.[17] The Cooperation Council established within a PCA is not entitled to take decisions imposing obligations on the signatories, diminishing the importance of this institution.

As noted above, the lack of incentive and eagerness by both sides to implement the PCAs was central in the failure to achieve the aims of the Agreements. The partnership established was 'a label on a mere trade agreement', where the parties failed to develop the PCA.[18] However, the inclusion of the PCAs within the ENP leaves a hope for certain success of the PCAs, at least as a sound basis for developing future partnership.

The Southern Caucasus and the EU in the new century

It is only since the beginning of this century that the EU's attitude toward the Caucasian region has shifted. The General Affairs Council of February 2001 acknowledged the EU's eagerness to engage with the region more actively, in particular with a view to contributing towards conflict prevention and post-conflict rehabilitation.[19] The change of attitude was evidenced with more active involvement by the EU in the problems of the region (e.g., through support for border control in Georgia and establishing a rule of law mission in the country) and with the appointment of a Special Representative of the EU to the Southern Caucasus in 2003.[20]

This shift of attention was conditioned by a number of strategic and geopolitical assumptions. In particular, the main importance of the Southern Caucasus for the EU stems from the Union's strong dependence on Russian energy and Mediterranean oil supplies and its need to search for alternative solutions. Azerbaijan is a significant exporter of oil from the Caspian basin, while Georgia and Armenia are important in particular as an alternative transit route for energy supply from the East to the Western market.

The EU's interests in South Caucasus are not easy to pursue since this region is influenced by other political actors including Russia, the US, Turkey and Iran. It should be pointed out that although the Southern Caucasus is referred to as 'region' in relations with foreign actors, none of the latter cooperates with the three countries as a region: rather, each of the international actors, including the EU, has different relations and cooperation level with each of the countries.

The EU established a closer political cooperation with Georgia after the so-called 'Rose Revolution' in 2003, where a new Georgian government started to seek closer cooperation with the US, NATO and the EU. In particular, it launched a European Security and Defence Policy (ESDP) mission and employed the Commission's Rapid Reaction mechanism to support the post-revolution democratic processes. The Commission developed close cooperation with other actors in the region, namely the Organization for Security and Co-operation in Europe (OSCE) and the UN, and financed a number of projects aimed at confidence-building and economic development in Georgia.

Relations with Azerbaijan and Armenia are less developed. The EU has not been engaged in the resolution of the Nagorno-Karabakh conflict and has not developed any special projects with the countries, although the Union is a significant trade partner for both Armenia and Azerbaijan, and the latter is the EU's largest trade partner in the region.[21] The EU signed a Memorandum of Understanding in 2006 on the strategic energy partnership with Azerbaijan and expressed its interest in the so-called 'Trans-caspian gas project' aimed at exploitation of gas sources of the Caspian region involving Azerbaijan and Turkmenistan.[22]

Russia's role in the region is crucial, since it considers these territories as its historical zone of influence. In particular it is Armenia's most important ally, especially in the field of military cooperation, where Russia has two military bases in the country. Armenia considers Russia as its main security guarantor because of the threats from Azerbaijan related to the disputed territories of Nagorno-Karabakh and economic isolation stemming from the close ties and cooperation between Georgia, Azerbaijan and Turkey. Moreover, the country has strong dependence on energy supplies from Russia. It was hoped that the opening of a gas pipe from Iran on 19 March 2007 would make Armenia less dependent on Russia. These expectations were, nevertheless, crushed when a large share in the project was sold to the Russian Gazprom.[23]

Cooperation between Russia and Azerbaijan intensified after the first state visit in 2001 by President Putin, with the exploitation of energy resources in the Caspian Sea, as well as military cooperation when Azerbaijan participated in Russian-organised naval exercises in the Caspian in 2002.[24] However, in comparison with Armenia, Azerbaijan seems to seek recognition as an independent political actor in the region by relying on its natural resources. The call from the Minister of Foreign Affairs of Azerbaijan to the EU in the beginning of 2007 to seek an alternative route for energy supplies through Azerbaijan is evidence to this policy.

Russia's relations with Georgia since the 'Rose Revolution' in 2003 continued to deteriorate, with Russia relying heavily on the policy of using economic sanctions and visa restrictions. The situation was exacerbated by the secessionist movements in Abkhazia and South Ossetia, allegedly supported by Russia, reaching their peak in 2008. The proclamation of independence by Kosovo and its subsequent recognition by the US and most of the member states of the EU was widely criticised by Russia, which was willing to demonstrate the negative consequences of this precedent in South Ossetia and Abkhazia. Later on, Russia, considering the promise of membership to Georgia and Ukraine at the NATO Bucharest Summit in April 2008, 'stepped into manipulation' of both regions.[25] These developments led to the August 2008 war which will be referred to below.

US interests in the region most notably centre on its energy resources, its geographic position and the presence of the moderate Muslim state of Azerbaijan,[26] which is important in view of the foreign policy of the US in the broader region during recent years. In addition, Azerbaijan proved to be an important strategic partner in the war on terror, sending troops to Afghanistan and Iraq as well as granting permission to US military forces to use its territory. Building close political ties with Georgia gave the US an opportunity to create a counterbalance to Russian dominance in the region. Relations between the US and Armenia are conditioned by the strong Armenian lobby[27] through the US Congress. As a result the aid received by Armenia from the US is the highest per capita among all the former Soviet republics.[28]

Other regional powers such as Iran and Turkey also play an important role. While Turkey is actively cooperating with Azerbaijan and Georgia, it has not had any diplomatic relationship with Armenia. Bearing in mind the blockade of Armenia from West and East by Turkey and Azerbaijan, it is clear that Armenia would be very willing to strengthen political and economic ties with its southern neighbour, Iran. First, of all Iran serves as an alternative to Armenia's main export route through Georgia. Secondly, Iranian cooperation is very important for Armenia in the terms of diversifying energy supplies. Nevertheless, Armenia's close cooperation with Iran is not without risks, not only from the perspective of Russia, but also bearing in mind the relationship of Iran with the US.[29]

There are currently considered to be two non-official alliances within the Caucasian region.[30] On the one side there is Azerbaijan, Georgia and Turkey backed up by the US in support of exploration and transportation of Caspian oil avoiding Russia; on the other Armenia has sided with Russia and Iran in an attempt to guarantee its security and avoid economic blockade. In this 'crowded scene',[31] where the interests of different players are often overlapping and conflicting, the EU had the task of developing a policy which allowed it to play a stronger and distinct role, maintain its interests in the region and simultaneously appeal to local expectations. The inclusion of the Southern Caucasus in the ENP was the first step in this direction.

The ENP in the Southern Caucasus

Despite the fact that at the General Affairs Council of 26 February 2001 the EU acknowledged its willingness to play a more active role in the Southern Caucasus region, the countries of Southern Caucasus were not initially included in the ENP. One explanation for this may be the absence of any advocates for the region among the member states of the Union. Thus, the Communication on Wider Europe confined the list of European Union neighbours to Russia, Western newly independent states (NIS) and the Southern Mediterranean. However, following a recommendation made by the Commission, this omission was corrected on 14 June 2004 by the Council in the ENP Strategy

Paper, which offered Armenia, Azerbaijan and Georgia the opportunity to participate in the ENP. This inclusion was motivated by a number of factors. First, the European Security Strategy (ESS) Paper identified that the Union should take a 'stronger and more active interest in the region' because of the presence of several conflicts there.[32] This particular factor will be considered in more detail below. Second, an EU Special Representative for the South Caucasus was appointed in July 2003. In addition, certain events in the countries of the Southern Caucasus also influenced the position of the European Commission and Parliament on the inclusion of the region,[33] in particular, the 'Rose Revolution' in Georgia in November 2003 and the 2003 parliamentary and presidential elections in Armenia and Azerbaijan.

Following the inclusion of Georgia, Armenia and Azerbaijan in the ENP, Action Plans were signed with each of the countries on 14 November 2006 on the basis of respective Country Reports prepared by the Commission.[34] The APs are political documents establishing the strategic objectives of cooperation between each country and the EU for a period of five years. They are intended to ensure that the PCAs are implemented, building ties in new areas, as well as to encourage and support further integration of the South Caucasian countries into European economic and social structures.[35]

Despite the 'soft law' status of APs, progress in their implementation was supposed to serve as a basis for the further development of cooperation leading to the conclusion of a neighbourhood agreement. New Article 7a EU, as amended by the Lisbon Treaty, provides for an opportunity to conclude specific agreements with neighbouring countries which may contain reciprocal rights and obligations, as well as the possibility of undertaking activities jointly.[36] A neighbourhood agreement was not signed with any of the South Caucasian countries before they were supplanted by the initiation of the Eastern Partnership.

The scope of the ENP as a policy is very broad and it embraces a long list of issues spread within different pillars of the EU's constitutional structure. It represents an attempt at fusing those three pillars within one policy framework.[37]

The Action Plans with Georgia, Armenia and Azerbaijan outline certain priority areas for cooperation and establish further actions specifying or complementing the priority areas. The main priority areas for cooperation are the same for each country. These include strengthening democratic institutions, respect for human rights and fundamental freedoms, economic development, improvement of investment and business climate, further convergence of economic legislation and administrative practice. Encouragingly, all three Action Plans call for enhanced efforts in the field of regional policy, thus requiring the countries concerned to continue their efforts with their neighbours to resolve regional issues and to promote reconciliation, as well as to participate in regional initiatives in different fields.

Another common priority area is the energy sector. While in the case of Georgia and Azerbaijan the focus is on bilateral cooperation, according to the Action Plan with Armenia cooperation in this field will focus on development of an internal energy strategy, including an early decommissioning of the Medzamor Nuclear Power Plant.[38] Thus, the problem of Armenian isolation from its neighbours in terms of cooperation in the energy sector was not addressed in any of the Action Plans.

Security concerns within the ENP agenda

Objectives of the ENP and the Southern Caucasus

The inclusion of the Southern Caucasian region in the ENP, as noted above, is linked to fact that security is placed high on the ENP agenda. The elaboration and development of the ENP was certainly affected by the tragic events of the 1990s and later events which marked the beginning of the new century. The numerous wars of former Yugoslavia demonstrated the limits of the EU's political impact, especially as the conflict took place on the European continent. Moreover, the events of 11 September 2001,[39] military operations by NATO in Afghanistan and, later on, the invasion and occupation of Iraq have reinforced the importance of global security on the agenda of the international community, including the European Union. The shortcomings of EU foreign policy became clear when the position taken by member states over the war in Iraq exemplified the absence of cohesion in the foreign policy of the Union.[40]

It is clear that the objectives of the ENP focus on the security concerns of the Union. The ideas of promoting stability and prosperity, enhancing relationships based on shared values and avoiding new dividing lines[41] should be considered to serve one single purpose, which is guaranteeing the security of the Union – security which might be threatened by immediate neighbours, or by the neighbours of neighbours. The fact that security concerns were laid in the basis of the policy is clear from the joint Solana/Patten letter of 7 August 2002, when the idea of the ENP was officially mooted for the first time: '...there are a number of overriding objectives for our neighborhood policy: stability, prosperity, shared values and the rule of law along our borders are all fundamental for our own security. Failure in any of these areas will lead to increased risks of negative spill-over on the Union.'[42] Similarly, Commissioner Ferrero-Waldner noted that the question of borders is not merely a matter of defining them but 'because they are key to many of our citizens' urgent concerns-security, migration and economic growth'.[43]

It is notable that the launch and development of the ENP took place in parallel with the ESS initiated in 2003 and intending to express the role of the Union as a major player able to respond to global security challenges, especially in its neighbourhood.[44] The link between the ENP and the ESS is obvious in case of the South Caucasian region, where the ENP Strategy Paper directly referred to the ESS on the matter of inclusion of Georgia, Armenia and Azerbaijan within the policy.[45]

The linkages between these two policies are clear from the introduction to the ENP Strategy Paper, which explicitly provides that the new policy 'will also support efforts to realise the objectives of the European Security Strategy'.[46] The ESS in its turn gave important meaning to the idea of 'building security in the neighbourhood' when declaring that: 'we need to extend the benefits of economic and political cooperation to our neighbours in the East while tackling political problems there'.[47] This is particularly important since the last two enlargements have bought the Union even closer to the conflicts in the Southern Caucasus as well as to the greatest problem in the Middle East, which is the Arab/ Israeli conflict. Thus, the EU's task is to make a particular contribution to stability and good governance in the immediate neighbourhood and 'to promote a ring of well governed countries to the East of the European Union and on the borders of the Mediterranean with whom we can enjoy close and cooperative relations.'[48]

Considering this provision as regards the neighbourhood of the Union, it is obvious that this is not accidental, since all the regions covered by the ENP face serious problems with security. In particular, most of the conflicts precipitated by the break-up of the Soviet Union took place in the Southern Caucasus. It should be noted that these mainly arose from the divisive border lines drawn between the Soviet republics at the beginning of the twentieth century. While the armed conflicts in South Ossetia and Abkhazia were considered as internal to Georgia, the Nagorno-Karabakh conflict is mainly between Armenia and Azerbaijan, since the Karabakhi part does not officially take part in the negotiating process. This conflict is the one which makes regional cooperation practically impossible. All of these conflicts were considered to be 'frozen', until the August 2008 war between Russia and Georgia demonstrated the explosive nature of the South Ossetian and Abkhazian conflicts. Although there were ongoing negotiations over the status of these territories within different international frameworks for over a decade, none of the parties involved was ready for serious compromises.

Because of the general reluctance of the EU to address the problems of the region in the previous decade, at the time they were taking place the conflicts received little attention from the EU, whose role was limited to humanitarian assistance. Nevertheless, the changes in the international and regional circumstances required more active engagement with real and potentially destabilising threats, such as illegal migration, regional arm races, environmental problems[49] and drug trafficking. Consequently a more active involvement by the Union in relation to these conflicts materialised at the second stage of the relations with the three Caucasian republics. While initial measures were rather uncoordinated,[50] the appointment of the Special Representative was aimed at coordinating the Union's activities in the region and developing a comprehensive policy.

The mandate of the Special Representative has gradually changed since the first appointment. Initially it included activities contributing to the prevention of conflicts and preparing the return of peace to the region. The Special Representative was also meant to assist in conflict resolution, although rather than giving a separate role for the Union, this was aimed at supporting the UN Secretary-General and his Special Representative for Georgia, the Group of Friends of the UN Secretary General for Georgia, the OSCE Minsk Group and the conflict-resolution mechanism for South Ossetia under aegis of the OSCE.[51] However, the more proactive attitude of the Union to the region has resulted in the change of the Special Representative's mandate. Currently it includes assisting in creating the conditions for progress on settlement of conflicts, as well as contributing to the settlement of conflicts and facilitating the implementation of such settlements in close coordination with the existing frameworks.[52] Nevertheless, this development did not result in influential participation by the EU in the conflict-resolution processes.

Although the Union did not participate in establishing peace in the region, it had enough power – and still has in case of Nagorno-Karabakh conflict – to participate in the resolution of conflicts by motivating the dialogue between the parties through the ENP. Currently it seems that such an opportunity has been lost as regards the South Ossetian and Abkhazian conflicts.

August 2008 war

As mentioned above, the deterioration of relations between Russia and Georgia was echoed in Abkhazia and South Ossetia. The increased Russian military presence in Abkhazia and the downing of a Georgian unmanned aircraft, as well as armed incidents in South Ossetia in July and at the beginning of August 2008 which left several dead and injured led to rather tragic events.[53] Close to midnight on 7 August 2008, a senior Georgian military official announced that Tbilisi had decided to restore 'constitutional order' in South Ossetia. After a night of large-scale military offensives supported by artillery which resulted in the swift advance of Georgian forces, Russian forces got involved in the conflict. Russia justified its intervention by accusing Georgia of 'genocide' against Ossetian people and its right to protect its own citizens.[54]

The military activities escalated subsequently with Abkhaz forces heading to the Kodori gorge, the only part of their territory still under Georgian control, forcing the escape of Georgians and with Russians troops crossing the Georgian border, occupying Georgian military bases and destroying infrastructure.[55] In the following days, Russian units sank several Georgian naval vessels in the port of Poti, and blew up a vital railway bridge linking Tbilisi and the west of the country.[56] The importance of terminating the hostilities was recognised internationally, but it was the EU which was in a position of mediating between the parties. Thus, mediation by the EU Council President Nicolas Sarkozy produced a six-point ceasefire document on 12 August. As part of the ceasefire agreement, Georgia undertook to sign a non-resumption of hostilities agreement, which South Ossetians and Abkhazians had been demanding before the outbreak of fighting.[57]

The diplomatic intervention by the EU Presidency showed that with 'dynamic leadership' the EU can play a significant role in the region's politics.[58] Member states have subsequently approved the ceasefire during an emergency session of Foreign Ministers Council.[59] Nevertheless, the limited extent of the actions at the EU's disposal was more than evident when the Council was deciding on possible sanctions against Russia. The member states split into two, with the Baltic and Eastern European states calling for a very tough response to Russia, and most of the old member states, with due respect to their dependence on Russia, calling on a more careful approach.[60] The maximum response by the EU was the suspension of signing a new agreement with Russia until the complete withdrawal of Russian troops from Georgian territory.[61] EU observers were deployed to the areas adjacent to South Ossetia and Abkhazia after the Russian troops pulled out in the October 2008.

Its diplomatic intervention clearly demonstrated the importance of Southern Caucasus for the EU, particularly compared to the beginning of 1990s. At the same time the events of August 2008 proved that the ENP was not sufficient to guarantee the security of the EU and its neighbours.

Meeting expectations?

Meeting expectations through the ENP

The ENP marked a new stage in the development of the relationship of the EU with the countries of the Southern Caucasus. On the one hand, it provided the necessary framework for the partners to pursue their mutual interests and meet their expectations. On the other hand, the ambiguities embedded within the policy and its mechanisms raised concerns as to its ultimate success in meeting these expectations.

The expectations of the parties are different. While the EU is mostly concerned with security, the expectations of Caucasian countries are greater, given the EU's 'high status' among them.[62] In particular, these countries are very willing to integrate with the European Union, including through membership.[63] Further integration with the EU should be possible, provided the Eastern partners succeed in establishing independence from Russia. As the Georgian conflict illustrated, in spite of four years of engagement through the ENP, the EU still did not have sufficient presence in the region, and lacked dialogue with Russia on their common neighbours.

Expectations as regards membership were rejected by the inclusion of these countries in the ENP. This echoes a general problem with the expectations of the EU's neighbouring countries, since the ENP seemed to solve the 'inclusion-exclusion' dilemma solely from the perspective of the Union. However, the ENP was drafted to offer a 'next best' scenario, with certain features aimed at bringing these countries as close as possible to the Union both politically and economically.

The most important and contradictory element is the positive conditionality borrowed from the enlargement experience. Although this was supposed to bring a dynamic nature to the relationship between the parties, as opposed to the PCA's static nature,[64] one of the main drawbacks of the policy was the credibility problem of the incentives on offer. These incentives were not precisely defined, and the language of the policy changed from document to document. It was not clear what the Union was offering by a 'stake in the internal market' or 'everything but institutions', or what this means.[65] The only clear aspect of the offer was the exclusion of a membership perspective. In particular the incentives were too vague, and 'too little' is on offer by the Union in order to encourage reforms in each aspect of internal life of neighbouring countries, such as strengthening of democracy and economic reforms.[66] Moreover the absence of a membership perspective looked rather odd, given that the Union intended to apply the same pre-accession requirements to these ENP partners as to aspirant members, thus sending 'contradictory signals' to its neighbouring countries.[67] Ultimately, the Union failed to draw a distinction between its status as a 'potential end goal' for its neighbours and as a vehicle for reforms for these countries.[68]

Another element of the ENP, the principle of joint ownership, was introduced by the Strategy Paper on the ENP. It assumed that the EU would not impose priorities or conditions on its partners, and that APs would take into account a clear recognition of mutual interests in addressing a set of priority issues.[69] It should be noted that, considering the principle of joint ownership in the light of conditionality, certain contradictions arise. Conditionality assumes that there are certain requirements set up from the very beginning, whereby the party establishing the requirements is monitoring the fulfilment of the obligation by the other party. In addition, imposing certain requirements from the very start of the partnership process by one cooperating party to another, without considering the internal readiness of the neighbouring country, reinforces the ownership of the process and raises doubts as to its joint nature. Moreover, there is a contradiction between the intentions of these two principles, which according to Kelley is conditioned with the dilemma of credibility experienced within the enlargement process.[70] Thus, joint ownership does not sit easily with the unequal conditions implied by conditionality.[71] Rather, joint ownership will be possible only within the limits created by the requirements imposed by unequal conditionality.

Moreover, the principle of joint ownership was not followed throughout the whole process of policy formulation. The neighbours did not affect the process of setting the agenda. The objectives and means of the policy are the same for all partners, and the partner countries can have a vote only where they are consulted in the elaboration of Action Plans.[72] Although certain commentators consider this practice as contrasting with the Commission's Progress Reports and the Accession Partnership documents in the context of enlargement, where it is the EU alone which judges and recommends reforms within the candidate countries,[73] as noted by Haukkala and Moshes, it seems that the Union still tries to control the process as much as possible.[74] The wording of the Commission's Wider Europe Communication, according to which the Council should establish the Action Plans and accompanying benchmarks based on proposals from the Commission and wherever possible with prior discussion with the cooperating countries, adds credence to this view.

The principle of joint ownership is linked to the other basic principle of the ENP, which is differentiation. This principle should be welcomed, at least in the context of the countries of the Southern Caucasus. It assumes that, based on the common set of issues corresponding to the objectives of the ENP, the drafting of Action Plans and the priorities agreed with each partner will depend on the particular circumstances of that country.[75] Differentiation is a promising basis for cooperation, since depending on its motivation and commitment a country can achieve a higher level of integration in the absence of meeting a common goal established for all the countries involved in the policy.[76] However, it is exactly this aspect of differentiation which, instead of supporting the principle of joint ownership, is more likely to 'create new dividing lines and undermining rather than supporting the principle of joint ownership'.[77] This is because, like conditionality, it will lead the level of integration to differ from country to country, thus preventing the ENP from being a coherent policy for all the countries engaged, in particular for countries of the Southern Caucasus. The implications of this principle were obvious at the development stage of the ENP when it was already possible to classify the neighbours involved depending on their ambitions within the policy.[78]

It can be concluded that, by adding the principles of joint ownership and differentiation, the EU has tried to adapt the pre-accession policy to the ENP as much as possible. However, these principles do not sit well with the main principle of conditionality borrowed from the enlargement experience. Nevertheless, the greatest tension generally comes from the question of using the enlargement policy when membership was not on offer. This aspect of the ENP calls into question the legitimacy of demanding similar commitments from both those countries who are eventually offered membership and those who are offered just a 'stake in the internal market'.[79]

New expectations through the Eastern Partnership

The imperfections of the ENP, as well as the attempt at fusing radically different regions and countries within the same cooperation pattern and the articulation of the idea of 'Mediterranean Union' since 2007, led to structural changes in the ENP as predicted by Missiroli.[80] The Eastern Partnership was endorsed at the European Council in June 2008, with the initiative of Sweden and Poland. It will include Ukraine, Moldova, Armenia, Azerbaijan, Georgia and possibly Belarus.

The Conclusions of the European Council in June 2008 referred to the Eastern Partnership as an 'eastern dimension to the ENP'.[81] Whether this implied a regional split in existing policy, or accorded cooperation between the EU and its 'European' neighbours with a new direction was left for elaboration by the European Commission by the spring of 2009. However, because of the Georgian war the Extraordinary European Council of 1 September instructed the Commission to present a proposal earlier. Consequently, the Commission drafted a communiqué for the Eastern Partnership which was published on 3 December 2008. According to the proposal the European Partnership will give the ENP 'a new Eastern dimension' which will politically and economically go substantially beyond what has been available under the ENP.[82] As set out in the Commission's communiqué, the initiative was launched at an 'Eastern Partnership Summit' in June 2009.

At the outset the Eastern Partnership seems to be promising. The draft communiqué proposes signing Association Agreements which will not per se amount to a promise of a membership perspective. At the same time, the conclusion of these Agreements 'will be without prejudice to the partners' 'European aspirations'.[83] While the ENP was rather unclear with its incentives, the Eastern Partnership aims to establish 'a single deep and comprehensive Free Trade Area, providing the basis for the development of a common internal market, such as the European Economic Area'. If the model of the European Economic Area (EEA) is reproduced in the Eastern neighbourhood, this will significantly meet the expectations of neighbours to become a part of European family and to secure the EU's presence in the region. As in case of EEA countries, the Eastern Partners will have to adopt the entire *acquis communautaire*, as well as to accept the rulings of the European Court of Justice. In the long term one aim of the Eastern Partnership will be the creation of a visa free travel regime; however initially it will be aimed at speeding up the existing visa regime and establishing Common Application Centres.[84] Another positive development is the increase of financial assistance from €6 per head currently to €12 by 2013 and subsequent to €20 by 2020.

While the recognition of the 'Europeanness' of Eastern neighbours and the developments mentioned above should be welcomed, the Eastern Partnership simultaneously raises certain concerns. First of all, it brings new confusion as regards the ENP. The Eastern Partnership acknowledges the European identity of Eastern partners and their 'European aspirations', which doesn't seem to be natural development of the ENP; rather, it can be considered as a reorientation in policy toward these countries. Although the promise of a free trade area based on the model of the EEA could be seen as a clarification to the unclear incentives offered by the ENP, it nevertheless questions the aptness of the principles of the ENP, in particular those of joint ownership and differentiation. In addition, a rather confusing statement is included in the Preamble of the communiqué, according to which the Eastern Partnership is 'complementary to the relations between the EU and Russia that include a dialogue on our common neighborhood.' The inclusion of dialogue on common neighbourhood in relations between Russia and the EU should be welcomed since it presents an opportunity to guarantee that their mutual interests are not incompatible. However, positing the Eastern Partnership as complementary to the partnership with Russia assumes that the development of Eastern Partnership will depend on Russia to certain extent. This is particularly relevant in the context of the expectations of Eastern partners, most of which are seeking greater independence from Russia.

Conclusion

Relations between the EU and the Southern Caucasus have undergone a number of major developments over the last two decades. The 1990s were characterised by an unwillingness on the part of the EU to engage with the region and its problems. The need to establish relations with Georgia, Armenia and Azerbaijan resulted in the PCAs merely repeating each other and largely remaining on paper.

The inclusion of the Southern Caucasian countries within the ENP marked a new stage in the relationship between the EU and them. Although the ENP offered new mechanisms for bringing the parties closer together both politically and economically, it nevertheless comprised certain problematic issues discussed above. By drawing on the enlargement experience while at the same time rejecting the membership perspective, the Union, without precisely defining the 'carrot' on offer, could not rely on its 'high status' among these countries and motivate them to make the necessary steps for possible integration, whether within the region itself or with the Union. These factors, together with the developments mentioned above, necessitated a policy rethink toward the Eastern neighbourhood, including the Southern Caucasus, which led to the Eastern Partnership initiative.

The Eastern Partnership brings Ukraine, Moldova, Belarus and the countries of the South Caucasian countries together as a wider region. It can be considered as negative development that the South Caucasian countries are merged with other countries which will take the focus away from the region. Despite the appointment of a Special Representative for the Southern Caucasus and the inclusion of all three countries simultaneously in the ENP, this did not succeed in promoting regional dialogue and cooperation. In addition, in not taking part in the negotiation process of the Nagorno-Karabakh conflict, the EU lacked the ability to assist in tackling the major obstacle to regionalism. However, the inclusion of the Southern Caucasus in a wider Eastern region of European neighbours and the creation of the Eastern Partnership should be welcomed.

The Eastern Partnership clarifies and widens the incentives for cooperation, bringing forward creation of a free trade area based on the model of the EEA. Moreover, it provides for possibility of signing Association Agreements with respective countries. In this respect, the Eastern Partnership expresses the readiness of the EU to commit to its Eastern neighbours in real terms, whereas the ENP was primarily about the commitments of the EU's neighbours, set against unclear incentives.

While the substance of the Eastern Partnership is still to be fully realised, certain general implications should be pointed out. The Eastern Partnership is an advance on the EU's total reluctance to engage with Southern Caucasus in 1990s. However, unless the Eastern Partnership compensates for the shortcomings of the ENP and provides mechanisms for achieving what it promises, it might compromise the EU's credibility in the region. In addition, while the ENP disregarded the role of other actors in the region, in particular that of Russia, the Eastern Partnership recognises the necessity of a dialogue with others. However, the EU's cooperation with its Eastern partners will remain complementary, rather than in competition, to its relations with Russia. This means that the development of the Eastern Partnership will only go so far as it will not complicate Russia's interests. This will be significantly different to what the Eastern partners expect from the EU.

It is promising that the EU is no longer willing to disregard the Southern Caucasus region or its problems any longer. However, much more commitment will be required from the EU in order to assert its presence in the region and to pursue its own interests while simultaneously meeting the expectations of its neighbours.

Notes

1. K.E. Smith (2005) 'Engagement and Conditionality: Incompatible or Mutually Reinforcing?' in R. Youngs, M. Emerson, K.E. Smith and R. Whitman (eds), *New Terms of Engagement*. London: The Foreign Policy Centre and British Council, p. 28.
2. The countries involved in the ENP are Algeria, Egypt, Israel, Jordan, Lebanon, Libya, Morocco, the Palestinian Authority, Syria and Tunisia as comprising Mediterranean region; the countries of Eastern Europe are Ukraine, Belarus and Moldova and the South Caucasian states, that is Armenia, Georgia and Azerbaijan. http://ec.europa.eu/world/enp/partners/index_en.htm.
3. S. Jones (1995), 'Georgia: The Caucasian context', *Caspian Crossroads*, 1 (2 Spring), available at http://ourworld.compuserve.com/homepages/usazerb/123.htm (5 July 2001). There is a departure from the author's classification, where he identifies the first rivalry as among the regional hegemons, that is Russia, Turkey and Iran. For the purposes of this paper, the first rivalry is widened also to include other international players in the region, such as the US.
4. This included the technical and humanitarian aid provided to the region through ECHO and TACIS, later on EIDHR programmes.
5. European Communities (1999a), Partnership and Cooperation Agreement between the European Communities and their Member States, of the one part, and the Republic of Armenia, of the other, *Official Journal* 1999 L 239/3; European Communities (1999b), Partnership and Cooperation Agreement between the European Communities and their Member States, of the one part, and the Republic of Azerbaijan, of the other, *Official Journal* 1999 L 246/3; European Communities (1999c), Partnership and Cooperation Agreement between the European Communities and their Member States, of the one part, and the Republic of Georgia, of the other, *Official Journal* 1999 L 205/3.
6. Heinrich Böll Foundation, 'Regional Preconditions for the Development of an Integrated European Policy Towards the South Caucasus', Documentation of the Conference at the Heinrich Böll Foundation, Tbilisi, June 2004, pp. 12–13.
7. N. Sabanadze (2002), 'International Involvement in the South Caucasus', ECMI Working Paper 15. Flensburg: European Centre for Minority Issues.
8. D. Lynch (2003b), 'A Regional Insecurity Dynamic' in 'The South Caucasus: A Challenge for the EU', Chaillot Paper 65. Paris: EU Institute for Security Studies, p. 10.

9. D. Lynch (2003c), 'The EU: Towards a Strategy' in 'The South Caucasus: A Challenge for the EU', Chaillot Paper 65. Paris: EU Institute for Security Studies, p. 179.
10. Bruno Coppieters (2003), 'An EU Special Representative to a New Periphery' in 'The South Caucasus: A Challenge for the EU', Chaillot Paper 65. Paris: EU Institute for Security Studies3, p. 169. The Nagorno-Karabakh conflict erupted in 1998 as a movement for independence for Nagorno-Karabakh Autonomous Region from the Republic of Azerbaijan which has later escalated into an armed conflict between Armenia and Azerbaijan. Peace Agreement was concluded on 16 May between Armenia, Azerbaijan, Nagorno-Karabakh and Russia in Moscow. De facto Nagorno-Karabakh is an independent republic, as to its de jure status, there are ongoing negotiations within the OSCE Minsk Group, which, however, have not led to any significant solution. Abkhazia had the status of an autonomous republic within Soviet Georgia. Following Georgia's declaration of independence, armed conflict began in August 1992 when Georgian troops were deployed to Abkhazia. Large-scale hostilities ended after the Abkhaz side broke the ceasefire agreement of 27 July 1993 and captured the Abkhaz capital city of Sukhumi on 27 September. Most of the Georgian population of Abkhazia fled or was forcibly expelled as a result of the conflict. On 14 May 1994 an *Agreement on a Cease-Fire and Separation of Forces* was signed, and the UN Observer Mission in Georgia was established to monitor compliance with the ceasefire. South Ossetia enjoyed the status of an autonomous region within Georgia. On 10 November 1989, the South Ossetian Supreme Soviet approved a decision to unite South Ossetia with the North Ossetian ASSR, part of Russia. A day later, the Georgian parliament revoked the decision and abolished South Ossetian autonomy. Violent conflict broke out toward the end of 1991, but in 1992 Georgia was forced to accept a ceasefire to avoid a large-scale confrontation with Russia. The ceasefire is monitored by the OSCE mission in Georgia.
11. S. Peers (1995), 'From Cold War to Lukewarm Embrace: the European Union's Agreements with the CIS states', 44 *International and Comparative Law Quarterly*, 44, p. 831.
12. M. Maresceau and E. Montaguti (1995), 'The Relations between the European Union and Central and Eastern Europe: A Legal Appraisal' 32 *Common Market Law Review*, 32, p. 1328.
13. They include political dialogue, trade in goods; provisions on business and investment; payments and capital; competition; intellectual, industrial and commercial property protection; legislative cooperation; economic cooperation; cultural cooperation; financial cooperation and institutional, general and fiscal provisions.
14. R. Balfour (2007), 'Promoting Human Rights and Democracy in the EU's Neighbourhood; Tools, Strategies and Dilemmas' in R. Balfour and A. Missiroli, *Reassessing the European Neighbourhood Policy*, EPC Issue Paper 54 (June), available at http://www.epc.eu/en/pub.asp?TYP=TEWN&LV=187&see=y&t=&PG=TEWN/EN/detailpub&l=12&AI=852 , last accessed 15 October 2007.
15. Thus, the Preamble stipulates that 'convinced of the paramount importance of the rule and respect for human rights, particularly those of minorities,

the establishment of a multiparty system with free democratic elections and economic liberalization aimed at setting up a market economy.'

16. For example European Council (date) Europe Agreement establishing an association between the European Communities and their Member States, of the one part, and the Republic of Latvia, of the other part, Title X.

17. Ibid., Article 112.

18. C. Hillion (1998), 'Partnership and Cooperation Agreements between the European Union and the New Independent States of the Ex-Soviet Union', *European Foreign Affairs Review*, 3, pp. 419–20.

19. General Affairs Council, Brussels, 26–27 February 2001.

20. Mr Helkki Talvitie was appointed as a Special Representative for the Southern Caucasus in 2003 by Council Joint Action 2003/496/CFSP of 7 July 2003 concerning the appointment of an EU Special Representative for the South Caucasus, *Official Journal* 2003 L 169/74.

21. E. Nuriyev (2007), 'EU Policy in the South Caucasus: A View from Azerbaijan', CEPS Working Document 272 (July), p. 13.

22. K. Geropoulos (2008), 'EU bets on Turkmenistan for Trans-Caspian pipeline', *New Europe*, 2 June; E. Nuriyev (2007), 'EU Policy in the South Caucasus: A View from Azerbaijan', CEPS Working Document 272 (July), pp. 9, 13.

23. R. Giragosian (2006), 'Shadow Dancing: Armenia's Courtship with Independence', *Armenian Diaspora*, 15 December. http://www.armenianow.com/?action=viewArticle&AID=1903.

24. Supra note 8, at p. 18.

25. NATO (2008), Bucharest Summit Declaration, Issued by the Heads of State and Government participating in the meeting of the North Atlantic Council in Bucharest on 3 April 2008, NATO Press Release (2008)049; International Crisis Group (2008b), 'Russia v Georgia: The Fallout', Europe Report No 195 (22 August), p. 11.

26. Ibid., p. 16.

27. Please provide text to note cue 26.

28. B. Shaffer (2003), 'US Policy' in 'The South Caucasus: A Challenge for the EU', Chaillot Paper 65. Paris: EU Institute for Security Studies, Paris, p. 59.

29. Sanctions were imposed by Bush administration on certain Armenian companies which were accused of helping Iran to obtain materials for the production of weapons of mass destruction in 2002.

30. Supra note 7, at p. 23.

31. S. Cornell (2004), 'Europe and the Caucasus: In Search for A Purpose', Central Asia-Caucasus Institute Analyst (6 February). http://www.cacianalyst.org.

32. As was identified in The European Security Strategy Paper, adopted by the European Council in December 2003.

33. European Parliament (2004) Resolution 'EU Policy towards the South Caucasus (2003/2225(INI)) (26 February).

34. ENP Action Plans with Georgia, Armenia and Azerbaijan. http://ec.europa.eu/world/enp/documents_en.htm.

35. ENP Action Plan Georgia, p. 2.

36. European Union (2007), Treaty of Lisbon amending the Treaty on European Union and the Treaty establishing the European Community (2007/C 306/01), *Official Journal of the European Union*, English Edition, C 306, Volume 50, 17 December 2007.

37. M. Cremona and C. Hillion (2006), 'L'Union fait la force? Potential and limitations of the ENP as an integrated EU foreign and security policy', in A. Copsey and N. Mayhew (eds), *European Neighbourhood Policy: The Case of Europe*, Sussex European Institute, SEI Seminar Papers Series 1, p. 20.
38. Action Plan Georgia, Priority Area 8; Action Plan Azerbaijan, Priority Area 8; Action Plan Armenia, Priority Area 6.
39. M. Cremona and C. Hillion (2006), 'L'Union fait la force? Potential and limitations of the ENP as an integrated EU foreign and security policy', in A. Copsey and N. Mayhew (eds), *European Neighbourhood Policy: The Case of Europe, Sussex European Institute*, SEI Seminar Papers Series 1, p. 23.
40. R. Dannreuther (2006), 'Developing the Alternative to Enlargement: The European Neighbourhood Policy', *European Foreign Affairs Review* 11, p. 183.
41. Commission of the European Communities (2003), Communication from the Commission, *Wider Europe – Neighbourhood: A New Framework for Relations with our Eastern and Southern Neighbours* COM(2003) 104 final, Brussels, 11 March 2003; Commission of the European Communities (2004), Communication from the Commission, *European Neighbourhood Policy, Strategy Paper*, COM(2004) 373 final, Brussels, 12 May 2004.
42. Joint letter by EU Commissioner Chris Patten and the EU High Representative for the Common Foreign and Security Policy on Wider Europe. 7 August 2002, available at http://www.europa.eu.int/comm/world/enp/pdf/_0130163334_001_en.pdf.
43. B. Ferrero-Waldner (2006), Guest Editorial: 'The European Neighbourhood Policy: The EU's Newest Foreign Policy Instrument', *European Foreign Affairs Review* 11, p. 139.
44. European Council (2003), 'A Secure Europe in a Better World' European Security Strategy Paper, Brussels, 12 December 2003.
45. May ENP Strategy Paper, supra note 33, at p. 10.
46. Amichai Magen (2006), 'The Shadow of Enlargement: Can the European Neighbourhood Policy Achieve Compliance, Centre on Democracy, Development and the Rule of Law', Stanford Institute for International Studies, Working Papers, 68 (August), p. 400.
47. European Security Strategy Paper, supra note 36, at p. 8.
48. ENP Strategy Paper, supra note 33, at p. 6.
49. Supra note 25.
50. European Council (2001), Council Joint Action 2001/759/CFSP of 29 October 2001 regarding a contribution from the European Union to the conflict settlement process in South Ossetia, *Official Journal* 2001 L 286/4; European Council (2003a) Joint Action 2003/473/CFSP of 25 June 2003 regarding a contribution of the European Union to the conflict settlement process in Georgia/South Ossetia, *Official Journal* 2003 L 157/72.
51. European Council (2003b) Council Joint Action 2003/496/CFSP of 7 July 2003 concerning the appointment of an EU Special Representative for the South Caucasus, *Official Journal* 2003 L 169/74; European Council (2003c), Council Joint Action 2003/872/CFSP of 8 December 2003, *OJ* 2003 L 326/44.
52. European Council (2006), Council Joint Action 2006/121/CFSP of 20 February 2006 appointing the European Union Special Representative for the South Caucasus, *Official Journal* 2006 L 49/14.

53. International Crisis Group (2008a), 'Georgia and Russia: Clashing over Abkhazia', Europe Report 193 (5 June), p. 4; International Crisis Group (2008b), 'Russia v Georgia: The Fallout', Europe Report 195 (22 August), p. 2.

54. Although Russia claimed that over 2000 civilians have been killed in South Ossetia, the Human Rights Watch expressed its concerns over the lack of accurate information. *The Guardian* (2008), 'Russia exaggerating South Ossetian death toll, says human rights group' (August 13).

55. Абхазские вооруженные силы начали операцию в Кодорском ущелье, *Россия в Глобальной Политике*, 12.08.2008, available at http://www.globalaffairs. ru/news/10106.html; 'Российские войска уходят из грузинского города Гори', *Reuters Россия и Страны СНГ*, 19.08.2008, available at http://ru.reuters.com/ article/topNews/idRUZVE94087020080819?pageNumber=1&virtualBran dChannel=0; 'Russian jets attack Georgian town', BBC News, 09.08.2008, available at http://news.bbc.co.uk/1/hi/7550804.stm

56. International Crisis Group (2008b), 'Russia v Georgia: The Fallout', Europe Report 195, (22 August), p. 3.

57. Ibid., p. 9.

58. Ibid., p. 21.

59. European Council (2008), 'Council Conclusions on the situation in Georgia', 13 August 2008.

60. *EU Observer* (2008b), 'EU Shies Away from Strong Action Against Russia' (1September), available at http://euobserver.com/?aid=26667; *EU Observer* (2008a), 'EU Diplomats keen to avoid Russia controversy' 13 August), available at http://euobserver.com/?aid=26605.

61. *BBC News* (2008), 'EU suspends talks on Russia pact' (1 September). Available at http://news.bbc.co.uk/1/hi/word/europe/7592541.stm *EU Observer* (2008c),'EU Secures Deal on Russia Withdrawal'(9 September), available at http://euobserver.com/?aid=26708.

62. A. Labedzka (2006), 'The Southern Caucasus', in Blockmans and Lazowski (ed.), *The European Union and Its Neighbours: A Legal Appraisal of the EU's Policies of Stabilisation, Partnership and Integration.* The Hague: T.M.C. Asser Press., p. 611.

63. In his interview with a German Internet magazine 'Der SPIEGEL' in July 2007 the Armenian president was realistic as regards the membership perspective, but he confirmed the willingness of Armenia to undertake necessary actions to ensure that cooperation with European Union reaches a higher level. The vast majority of the Georgian population see membership of the Union as a future perspective (*EUobserver*, 19 May 2006).

64. Dov Lynch (2003a), 'The New Eastern Dimension of the Enlarged EU', in J. Batt, D. Lynch, A. Missiroli, M. Ortega and D. Triantaphyllon, 'Partners and Neighbours: A CFSP for A Wider Europe', Chaillot Paper 64, EU Institute for Security Studies , p. 44.

65. Wider Europe Communication, supra note 5; R. Prodi (2002), 'A Wider Europe-A Proximity Policy as the Key to Stability', Speech to the Sixth ECSA-World Conference, 2002, Brussels 5–6 December, Speech/02/619.

66. C.J. Hill and M.H. Smith (eds) (2005), *International relations and the European Union*. Oxford: Oxford University Press, p. 287–88.

67. Supra note 31, p. 39.
68. A. Missiroli (2003), 'The EU and its Changing Neighbourhoods: Stabilisation, Integration and Partnership', in J. Batt, D. Lynch, A. Missiroli, M. Ortega and D. Triantaphyllon, 'Partners and Neighbours: A CFSP For A Wider Europe', Chaillot Paper 64. Paris. European Union Institute for Security Studies, p. 27.
69. ENP Strategy Paper, supra note 33, at p. 8.
70. J. Kelley (2006), 'New Wine in Old Wineskins: Policy Learning and Adaptation in the New European Neighbourhood Policy', *Journal of Common Market Studies* 44, p. 36.
71. Supra note 31, at p. 40.
72. Hiski Haukkala (2003), 'A Hole in the Wall? Dimensionalism and EU's New Neighbourhood Policy', The Finnish Institute of International Affairs, UPI Working Papers 41, pp. 18–19.
73. N. Tocci (2006), 'Democracy and Human Rights in the ENP', Paper prepared for the EUI Workshop, 1–2 December.
74. Supra note 59, pp. 18–19.
75. ENP Strategy Paper, supra note 33, at p. 8.
76. H. Haukkala and A. Moshes (2004), 'Beyond "Big Bang": the challenges of the EU's neighbourhood policy in the East'. Helsinki: Finnish Institute of International Affairs, p. 52.
77. Supra note 31, pp. 40–41.
78. In M. Emerson, G. Noutcheva and N. Popescu (2007), 'European Neighbourhood Policy Two Years on: Time indeed for an 'ENP Plus', CEPS Policy Briefs, 126 (21 March), these countries are classified as willing, passive, reluctant and excluded partners.
79. E. Tulmets (2006), 'Is a Soft Method of Coordination Best Adapted to the context of EU's neighbourhood', Paper prepared for the EUI workshop, 1–2 December 2006.
80. A. Missiroli (2007), 'The ENP Three Years on: Where From-and Where Next?', European Policy Centre, Policy Brief, March 2007.
81. Presidency Conclusions, Brussels European Council 19/20 June 2008, p. 19.
82. Commission of the European Communities (2008), Press Releases Rapid, Top News from the European Commission, 24 November to 21 December 2008.
83. *EU Observer* (2008), 'Brussels to Recognise 'European Aspirations' of Post-Soviet States' (24 November).
84. Ibid.

12
The ENP and the Middle East

Carlos Echeverría Jesús

Introduction

This chapter outlines the modest impact of the European Neighbourhood Policy (ENP) in the Middle East region. The chapter describes how the ENP is a departure from the previous EU policy toward the region and examines the potential for the policy to facilitate a more ambitious role for the EU in the Middle East.

The chapter begins by outlining the ENP and the context in which it was born from a Middle East perspective, before addressing specific issues currently affecting the Near and Middle East and the role presently played by the EU, and exploring the prospects for the ENP to provide the EU with the means for a more ambitious role.

Before turning to the Middle East it would be useful to clarify the definition of the Mediterranean adopted in this chapter. The Mediterranean is not a unified space but essentially a meeting point or border of different powers, cultures and religions. The latter is of particular importance, given that all the monotheistic religions originated within the proximities of the Middle East and the Mediterranean. At a time when the EU is seeking stability and cooperation in the Middle East the different conflicts affecting the region seem to be both intractable and multidimensional: Palestinian internal divisions, the complexities in the Israeli political arena, the attitude of the Syrian government and the security situation in Lebanon.

The ENP and the Middle East

In 2004, the ENP was adopted by the EU to support its partners' political, economic and social reform processes and to deepen bilateral relations with them.[1] Through the ENP, the EU is promising close partnership in order to facilitate growth and modernisation in the partner countries. The EU recognises that the need for political and economic interdependence with its neighbouring regions provides the Union with a duty to create an enlarged area of political stability and functioning rule of law. The ENP introduces a reordering of priorities resulting from greater EU coherence and a clearer collective sense of EU interests. It offers the prospect of a 'stake in the EU's internal market' to those countries that make concrete progress in demonstrating shared values and effective implementation of political, economic and institutional reforms.

The ENP brings together disparate countries and regions – Eastern Europe, a number of Middle Eastern countries, North Africa and the Southern Caucasus. In geographical terms, it involves countries with whom the EU shares land or marine borders. It builds upon existing relationships (Partnership and Cooperation and Association Agreements and the Euro-Mediterranean Partnership (EMP)) and currently offers privileged political and economic relations to 16 countries.[2] Cooperation under the ENP is based on a mutual commitment to common values: democracy and human rights, rule of law, good governance, market economy principles and sustainable development.

For two decades the European Community's approach to the Middle East centred on bilateral relations with selected states and the Palestinian body, and on an embryonic political and diplomatic approach to the region as a whole, initiated with the Venice Declaration (1980). Since the beginning of the Middle East Peace Process (MEPP) in Madrid in October 1991, the EU has become an increasingly important actor, assuming the role of chair of the Working Group on Regional Cooperation, and as a member of the Quartet since 2003, together with the US, Russian and the UN. The Quartet is an innovative international mediating instrument for dealing with the Middle East, and the EU is one of its pillars.

Support from the different actors approaching the Middle East in the last two decades, including the EU and its member countries, has been relatively limited vis-à-vis peace efforts and democratisation. In most recent years, engagement has been limited in response to an increasing reluctance to contemplate far-reaching democratisation on the part of countries such as the Palestinian Authority or Egypt, where Islamists have been becoming increasingly important political actors. At the same time, the war in Iraq initiated in March 2003 has served to weaken diplomatic efforts, because of divisions among member states. In addition, the European vision of the Middle East (and North Africa) is clouded by perceptions of persistent tensions and conflicts, regular upsurges of terrorist activity, domestic political tensions in some countries, lack of political openness, increasing popularity of more or less radicalised Islamist movements, fast demographic and labour force expansion, slow economic growth, high unemployment and stagnating incomes.[3] In this context, without the membership perspective that only Turkey enjoys in the enlarged region, ENP partners from the Middle Eastern countries may not be as motivated to undertake domestic reforms.

The ENP approach and the position of the Middle East countries in the global context

The first proposals for the formulation of a new neighbourhood policy, put forward in 2002, considered only a number of eastern European countries – a British initiative only included Belarus, Ukraine and Moldova.[4]

The March 2003 Communication of the Commission on the ENP names 14 countries as neighbouring countries and partners to the project of creating a new framework of relations. These were Belarus, Moldova, Russia and Ukraine in the European continent, together with Algeria, Egypt, Jordan, Israel, Lebanon, Morocco, the Palestinian Authority, Syria and Tunisia – all already participants in the Barcelona Process – and Libya in the Mediterranean basin.[5] Turkey was not included in the ENP framework because candidacy to EU makes it ineligible.

Four months later, in the July 2003 Communication on the Neighbourhood Instrument, the prospective members Rumania and Bulgaria (who were to subsequently join the EU on 1 January 2007) and the Balkan countries were associated with the ENP programme.

In the Security Strategy *A Secure Europe in a Better World*, released in Brussels on 12 December 2003, the 'ring' of special interest for the EU was extended to include the Southern Caucasus countries (Armenia, Azerbaijan and Georgia).[6] Subsequently, in the European Commission's Strategy Paper on the ENP of 12 May 2004, the Southern Caucasus were added among the ENP partner countries, but Bulgaria and Romania were dropped because of their advances in the negotiation process for membership of the Union. By 2008 the ENP included 16 partners, the initial 13 (Russia is not now included), plus the three Southern Caucasus countries. The nature of the ENP has thus been heavily influenced by the politics of Eastern enlargement.

In its *Strengthening the ENP* Strategy Paper and Progress Reports in December 2006, the Commission reported that ENP was already working and that most neighbours had made progress on political and economic reforms. However, in light of the continuing challenges which these partners and the EU face, and the fact that they feel the costs of their reforms now while the benefits only come later, the Commission proposed that the EU should provide more incentives to support partners' reforms and to convince those that were still hesitant. These incentives were to include:

- increased dialogue and cooperation on cross-cutting issues such as energy, transport, environment, research, border management, migration, etc;
- more people-to-people contacts;
- the possibility of participating in relevant European Commission agencies and programmes;
- the enhancement of regional cooperation between partners;
- increased political and foreign policy cooperation including more involvement in conflict-settlement efforts; and
- increased funding opportunities in the form of a Neighbourhood Investment Fund and a Governance Facility.

This increasing role of the ENP has raised concerns as to its consequences for the pre-existing EMP framework.[7] The involvement of Egypt, Israel, Jordan, Lebanon, the Palestinian Authority and Syria in the ENP in principle permits the EU to develop a 'Middle East connection'. The EU's bilateral links with each of these countries are crucial for assuring the Union's presence in the region, even if that presence is limited given that not all of the countries of the Middle East are included in the ENP and there is no global approach to the region.

The example of the EU's approach in the east, based on existing Black Sea cooperation, demonstrates that it can develop a regional approach, provided conditions are favourable. However, this is not the case for the Middle East area.[8] In its December 2006 report on the ENP the Commission made proposals for strengthening the ENP in the region, including a more active role for the EU in conflict-settlement efforts. The problem is that the protracted conflicts that have beset the Middle East for the last 60 years are the single most important obstacle to political and economic reform in the region. The duration of these conflicts has allowed the region's security problems, including terrorism, the proliferation of weapons and the existence of refugees to multiply, reinforcing the negative perceptions of various political actors.

The future of the Middle East as a region in the new ENP era

The ENP may be a good approach for parts of the EU's neighbourhood, but it is addressed to very different actors and regions than those of the Middle East. In the Middle East, the MEPP created an attractive scenario for the 1990s but it has become problematic in recent years. The breaking out in September 2000 of the 'Al Aqsa Intifada' and the repercussions of this in the region cast a shadow on the political panorama. At that time, France decided, with the support of Arab states, to withdraw the Peace and Stability Charter from the agenda of the IV Ministers for Foreign Affairs Conference of the Barcelona Process, held in Marseilles on 15–16 November 2000. In addition, Syria and Lebanon did not attend the meeting, the political dialogue was frozen and conflicts intensified in the region. The emerging tension challenged the consensus that had prevailed since 1995: that, in spite of its drawbacks, the Barcelona Process constituted an essential and unique framework for the overall configuration of North-South relations in the Mediterranean.

At the level of the bilateral Israel–Syria relationship, in the period from 2000 to 2007 Syria continued to back Hezbollah and Hamas actions against Israel and the latter attacked Syrian positions three times. The first attacks were in Lebanon, in April and July 2001, in retaliation for attacks on Israel Defense Forces (IDF) positions by Hezbollah, killing almost 20 Syrian soldiers. The second was in October 2003, when Israeli aircraft launched an air raid against the People's Front for the Liberation of Palestine's (PFLP) Ayn al-Sahib training camp in Syria and flew over President Bashar al-Assad's palace. The third was one year later, when in September 2007 Israel attacked what it designated as a 'nuclear facility' in Dayr al-Zawr.

Concerning the Israeli and Palestinian conflict: in August 2005, Israel pulled its settlers and soldiers from the Gaza Strip but violence continued, increasing after the electoral victory of Hamas in the January 2006 Palestinian general election. The control of Gaza Strip by Hamas and the July 2006 Hezbollah attack on an Israeli patrol increased insecurity in the area. Since the war between Israel and Hezbollah an international – mainly European – international force of almost 15,000 peacekeeping soldiers has been installed in Southern Lebanon.

In addition, Syria is also suffering direct effects of the war in Iraq, with almost 2 million Iraqi refugees living in Syria. Given this scenario, where the most pessimistic are now announcing the approach of a new civil war in Lebanon, a fair and lasting global solution to the Middle East conflicts seems to be very unlikely, and the ENP is obliged to be limited to the country-by-country level.

What the Mediterranean and Middle East partners ask themselves, and ask the EU Commission, is whether the ENP will gradually replace the EMP, or transform it at a certain stage into a sub-region in a framework in which the Mediterranean is not the centre of gravity.[9] The Mediterranean partners find themselves implementing, at the same time, the Association Agreements approved under the EMP, the Action Plan in the context of the ENP and the Work Programmes, also within the EMP.

Moreover, the Middle East as a whole is not included in the ENP framework and only a number of countries belonging to the Near and the Middle East do participate at the bilateral level. In addition, the EU does not have a comprehensive approach to the Middle East. Even when the Commission addresses the issue of the ENP it rarely cites the Middle East and when it does is always in generic terms (e.g. Commissioner Ferrero-Waldner talked about a November 2007 meeting on energy involving the EU, its countries and the ENP partners including those from Africa and the Middle East).[10] In sum, the EU is fully bilateral in its emphasis and does not have a vision of how regional peace can be made possible, for instance by linking Israel and Arab conflicts to a comprehensive approach involving actors such as Iran, Iraq or the Jihadist Salafist terrorism.

In historical terms, the faltering MEPP impacted negatively on the Barcelona Process, and the EU's Common Foreign and Security Policy (CFSP) and the European Security and Defence Policy (ESDP) are marked by member states' disagreements and therefore vary in their strength and impact on the Middle East. Regrettably, international negotiations have so far failed to resolve the conflicts affecting the Middle Eastern region. For instance, the Middle East peace conference convened by the US on 27 November 2007 in Annapolis brought together a number of weak leaders from the region and the role of the EU was marginal.[11] Actors have called for more political involvement from the Quartet and its members.[12]

In strategic terms, if the EU and the US are able to craft common Middle Eastern policies, then the ENP stands a good chance of success. One problem is that up to now the role of the EU and the US has decreased in the Middle East in recent years. Another is that the ENP overlaps with US interests in Europe's peripheries. This is perhaps most notable in the Middle East where the EU has been able to match the US initiative for a so-called Broader Middle East and North Africa, maintains the EMP and has developed negotiations with Iran since 2002 on the nuclear issue.

Developments in the Palestinian Authority's territories are blocking the implementation of the ENP. For the time being, the only EU political, economic or financial involvement is focused on the dialogue with President Mahmoud Abbas, as the legitimate President of all Palestinians, and on providing humanitarian assistance to both the West Bank and Gaza.[13] The deterioration of EU-Palestinian bilateral relations has been deepened through three steps: first, when in January 2006 Hamas won the Palestinian elections; later when in February 2007 Saudis sponsored the Mecca Agreement between Abbas and the Hamas Prime Minister Ismail Haniyeh that was boycotted by the Quartet and finally in June 2007 when Hamas seized Gaza in a showdown with Abbas forces.

Concerning Israel, the ENP enabled the EU to establish more symmetrical relations with this state. In addition, the ENP has provided the EU with a chance to support the Fouad Siniora's Lebanese government at a time when both sides of the Atlantic were in opposition to Syria and in favour of political change in Lebanon. In sum, it seems that the ENP is improving relations between the EU and Israel and is doing more to meet Israel's demands vis-à-vis the Palestinian Authority. In the aftermath of the Hamas election victory in January 2006 and deterioration of the region, the EU fully supported the Presidency of Abbas and avoided contacts with the Government of Hamas, and has tried more recently to provide political impetus to the international peace conference held in Annapolis on 27 November 2007.

In the near future the ENP could be instrumental in enabling the EU to use its bilateral relations with Middle Eastern actors to bolster its role. The EU or a number of EU countries are already supporting security missions in the area – for example, the EU Monitoring Team at the Gaza border and the contribution of more than 7000 troops to the 15,000 UN Interim Force in Lebanon (UNIFIL)[14] – and Brussels keeps strong contacts with all the main actors in the region. With Syria as the last country to sign an Association Agreement with the EU in the Barcelona Process' framework, Damascus and Brussels have now agreed on the Country Strategy Paper, opening the door for full relations in the ENP context and for the EU to deal with political and diplomatic matters at the bilateral level, with potentially wider regional implications.[15]

The fact that the ENP does not include other relevant Middle Eastern countries such as Iraq, Iran or the Gulf Cooperation Countries (GCC) does reduce its effectiveness in terms of acting as a political and diplomatic instrument for a regional approach. However, it permits the Union to approach important actors such as Egypt, Jordan, Israel, Lebanon, the Palestinian Authority's Presidency and Syria, if the political will exists. Expectations emerged with the November 2007 peace talks and the EU considered the ENP instrumental for supporting the involvement of the most important actors of the Near East. Finally, the global process has not been resumed and the ENP remains instrumental only for channelling relations on a country-by-country basis.

Conclusion

This chapter has argued that the ENP represents a new approach in the EU's relations with its neighbours in general and with a number of Middle Eastern countries in particular. The EU has benefited from the ENP in articulating specific goals and interests. The ENP uses proven methodology that has already helped the EU to support transition in Central and South-Eastern Europe and incentives to promote democratic and economic reforms, supporting countries' own efforts. According to the ENP's principles, the new framework offers a wide spectrum of partners the prospect of an increasingly close relationship with the EU, involving a significant degree of economic integration and a deepening of political cooperation.

The ENP complements the multilateral Barcelona Process and its transition toward the Union for the Mediterranean in 2008, which continues to be a key element of EU relations with the Mediterranean countries. With many of the same general objectives, the aim of the ENP is then to support its partners' political, economic and social reform processes and to deepen bilateral relations with them. It does not aim either to develop relations at a regional level, for instance with the complex Middle East, or to deal with frameworks such as the MEPP and others. The EU does not have a comprehensive approach to the Middle East, and this makes its position vulnerable to the almost inevitable conflict in the region. Nevertheless, the ENP permits the EU to maintain a presence in the region in addition to various other approaches, including the CFSP (participation in the Quartet), the ESDP (participation in the Gaza border monitoring and support for the Palestinian police) and the roles played by a number of individual EU countries (such as the military contribution of France, Italy and Spain to the UN

Interim Force in Lebanon – UNIFIL II – in Southern Lebanon). Once the Lisbon EU Summit agreed on the new Treaty for the EU, on 19 October 2007, the issue of becoming more involved in international issues in general and in the Middle East in particular has again been an open question among the EU member countries. The question for future debate is whether deeper EU engagement in the Middle East could help to transform this region into a peaceful and prosperous scene. In parallel, the ENP, while weak on multilateralism, is doing its job maintaining a safer bilateral framework in which each country can adapt its level of ambition in its relations with the Union with the rhythm of the implementation of agreed internal reforms. Ultimately, the ENP is and will remain more focused on producing national change than on promoting regional transformation and integration.

Notes

1. Commission of the European Communities (2003), Communication from the Commission, *Wider Europe – Neighbourhood: A New Framework for Relations with our Eastern and Southern Neighbours* COM(2003) 104 final, Brussels, 11 March 2003, available at <http://ec.europa.eu/world/enp/pdf/com03_104_en.pdf>.
2. Algeria, Armenia, Azerbaijan, Belarus, Egypt, Georgia, Israel, Jordan, Lebanon, Libya, Moldova, Morocco, the Palestinian Authority, Syria, Tunisia and Ukraine.
3. This negative perception has been reinforced by the contents of the four Reports on the Arab World written by a group of Arab experts by command of the United Nations Development Programme (UNDP). See them at <www.undp.org>.
4. Andreas Marchetti (2006), 'The European Neighbourhood Policy. Foreign Policy at the EU's Periphery', Bonn: Center for European Integration Studies-Discussion Paper C 158, p. 6.
5. In 2008 the Barcelona Process evolved toward the Union for the Mediterranean, a French proposal that has become a 'communitarised' framework which is including the Barcelona Process' heritage and an additional step in practical terms providing specific projects. See Council of the European Union: Barcelona Process: Union for the Mediterranean Ministerial Conference. Marseille, 3–4 November 2008. Final declaration Press-EN 15187 (Presse 314), Marseille, 4 November 2008.
6. Council of the European Union, *A Secure Europe in a Better World. European Security Strategy*. Brussels, 12 December 2003. http://www.consilium.europa. eu/uedocs/cmsUpload/78367.pdf. Last accessed 10 November 2009.
7. See Azzam Mahjoub (2005), 'La politique européenne de voisinage: un dépassement du partenariat euro-méditerranéen', *Politique Étrangère*, 3, pp. 535–44; Michael Emerson and Gergana Noutcheva, 'From Barcelona Process to Neighbourhood Policy: Assessments and Open Issues', *CEPS Working Paper 220* (2005); Elisabeth Johansson-Nogués (2005), 'A ring of friends? The implementation of European Neighbourhood Policy for the Mediterranean' *Mediterranean Politics*, 9 (2), pp. 240–47.

8. See *Black Sea Synergy – bringing the region closer to the EU IP/2007/486*, quoted in *Strengthening the ENP*, Rapid Press Releases MEMO/07/336, Brussels, 30 August 2007, in <http://europa.eu/rapid/>.
9. See the statement of the Egyptian Ambassador Nehad Abdel Latif at the International Conference 'Working Together. Strengthening the ENP', held in Brussels on 3 September 2007.
10. Benita Ferrero-Waldner: 'Opening Speech' at the Brussels ENP Conference, 3 September 2007.
11. Harvey Sicharman (2007), 'Annapolis: Three-Ring Diplomacy', 6 December 2007, Foreign Policy Research Institute E-Notes at <www.fpri.org>.
12. See the statement of the Egytian Ambassador Nehad Abdel Latif evoking the continuing Arab-Israeli conflict and the unresolved Palestinian Problem, as well as instability in the region as a whole. He also addressed the urgent necessity of a cultural dialogue particularly in the light of the increasing manifestations of discrimination, intolerance and defamation of religions.
13. Benita Ferrero-Waldner, Commissioner for External Relations and European Neighbourhood Policy, on the current developments in the Palestine Territory Brussels, 15 June 2007, at <http://europa.eu/rapid/>.
14. See the visit of the Foreign Ministers of France, Italy and Spain to Lebanon on 20 October 2007, in 'Líbano. España, Italia y Francia intentan desbloquear la crisis', *El País*, 21 October 2007, p. 10.
15. ENP Instrument, *Syrian Arab Republic, Strategy Paper 2007–2013 and National Indicative Programme 2007–2010*, at <http:/ec.europa.eu/world/enp/pdf/country/enpi_csp_nip_syria_en.pdf>.

Conclusion

13
The ENP in Future Perspective

Antonio Missiroli

Introduction

There is no doubt that the enlarged European Union needs an effective and coherent common policy to deal with its numerous 'neighbours' – old and new. And there is no doubt either that remarkable efforts have been put into developing what is officially called European Neighbourhood Policy (ENP), implemented since 2004.

The main question is: does the existing ENP meet the expectations, needs and demands of a desirable common policy toward the EU's (old and new) bordering and adjacent countries or areas? It is a legitimate question to ask, since coming to a shared assessment of what needs to be done in common – and how – vis-à-vis the immediate periphery of the Union is a key factor for shaping both internal cohesion and external influence.

This paper aims to analyse the way in which the ENP has developed over the past four years, assessing its intrinsic potential as well as its inbuilt weaknesses, and exploring what directions it may take in the future – factoring in also the new institutional architecture that the new Lisbon Treaty (if and when implemented) would create in the domain of 'foreign policy' at large.

Where from...

When the 'Big Bang' enlargement to eight Central European and two Mediterranean countries materialised in late 2002, the British and the Scandinavians in particular started pushing for a common initiative aimed at the new Eastern periphery of the Union – as South-Eastern Europe was already involved in the Stabilisation and Association Process and would soon be given (at the Thessaloniki European Council of June 2003) a specific EU membership perspective.

In December 2002, the same Copenhagen European Council that finalised the 'Big Bang' endorsed the initiative but – on the insistence of the Southern EU members – included in it also the Mediterranean countries that, until then, had been involved in the so-called Barcelona Process, that is the Euro-Mediterranean Conference launched in 1995.

This resulted in the 'Wider Europe' Communication released by the Commission in March 2003. In June 2004, a few months after the 'Rose Revolution' in Tbilisi, the initiative was further extended to the South Caucasus republics of Armenia, Azerbaijan and Georgia – much as they still lie some 1000 km away from the nearest EU member (Romania) – and was also rebranded as 'European Neighbourhood Policy'. As such, it was more clearly separated from any EU accession prospect.

On the whole, the ENP was expected to deal with 17 neighbours – the 'Outer Seventeen', to paraphrase the famous definition of the seven initial members of the European Free Trade Association (EFTA) created in the late 1950s to counter the newly founded six-strong European Economic Community.

The main 'neighbour' of the EU, however, was not included: Russia declined to be incorporated into the scheme and opted for developing bilateral cooperation with the Union on an allegedly more 'equal' basis, although it was open to accepting similar policies and actions as those implemented with other countries involved in the scheme.

Ever since, the ENP has gradually absorbed the existing Technical Assistance for the Commonwealth of Independent States (TACIS) and MEDA programmes – for the East and South, respectively – and defined benchmarks and 'priorities for action' against which to evaluate the disbursement of funds. Yet the initial Council decision of putting apples and oranges – Eastern Europe and Southern non-Europe – in the same policy basket has remained.[1]

Other internal nuances affected the overall EU approach. Then Commission President Romano Prodi, for instance, mentioned the goal of building 'a ring of friends' around the enlarged EU. Both Commissioner for External Relations Chris Patten and High Representative for the Common Foreign and Security Policy (CFSP) Javier Solana spoke rather of 'a ring of well-governed countries'. The difference (a country may be considered as a 'friend' while not being particularly 'well-governed') was not to be missed.

Moreover, the new scheme allowed the 'recycling' of – in the best sense of the term – a number of Commission officials that had been intensely and successfully involved in preparing the 'Big Bang': between 2003 and 2004, in fact, they were gradually transferred from DG Enlargement to a dedicated new unit in DG Relex. In the autumn of 2004, with the new Commission taking office, Benita Ferrero-Waldner's brief was renamed 'External Relations *and* European Neighbourhood Policy' – thus giving the ENP a specific slot in the overall spectrum of EU actions, and the Commissioner a new mandate that could be preserved even in the event of creation of the 'EU Minister for Foreign Affairs' foreseen by the Lisbon Treaty (due to enter into force on 1 November 2006).

Such a transfer was, per se, a positive development. Applying to the 'neighbours' (old and new) a similar logic to the one that had driven the 'Big Bang' – a common 'template' based on conditionality, but potentially different speeds for all the countries involved based on compliance – could indeed give more teeth and consistency to the traditional Community policies based on financial assistance to foster stability.

Enlargement, however, differs from the ENP in a number of different ways. To start with, candidates for accession can be chosen, whereas geographic neighbours cannot. Also, relations with future members are profoundly uneven (as the EU basically dictates the terms for the accession negotiations), unlike those with simple neighbours, who are not (or not necessarily) *demandeurs*. Lastly, enlargement is based on a *finalité* of which the ENP is entirely deprived.

Lack of coherence

The initial steps of the new policy were not exactly encouraging. For instance, the 'priorities for action' elaborated in December 2004 for the first seven ENP Action Plans (aimed at Ukraine, Moldova, Jordan, the Palestinian Authority, Israel, Tunisia and Morocco) amounted to a long shopping list of very diverse items without any visible hierarchy.

Furthermore, some of the commitments made by the EU in this framework – such as trade liberalisation and a 'stake' in the internal market – lacked credibility. The Union has been conspicuously reluctant to open up its agricultural and labour markets, while the 'neighbours' have been mostly unable (and sometimes also unwilling) to implement single market legislation and meet the required standards.

More generally, the Eastern European countries – starting with Ukraine, especially after the 'Orange Revolution' of the autumn of 2004 – complained that the ENP did not entail an accession prospect. The Mediterranean countries, in turn, complained that it overlapped with and rivalled the Barcelona Process, although the Euro-Mediterranean

Partnership is a multilateral forum, while the ENP is essentially a bilateral framework between the EU and each individual neighbour.

Finally, bilateral agreements with the EU were already in force at the onset of the ENP: Partnership and Cooperation Agreements with the Eastern and South Caucasus countries, and Euro-Med Association Agreements with Israel, Egypt and Lebanon. The new Action Plans came to intersect with these, generating delays and ultimately affecting the overall perception of the new policy.

On the whole, the ENP seems to suffer (still) from being *neither enlargement nor foreign policy* proper. It cannot exercise conditionality as effectively as the former, nor does it bring to bear all the political tools and levers of the latter. At the same time, it enshrines elements of both.

On top of that, the persistent ambiguity over the ultimate 'borders' of the Union (particularly resented by the Eastern neighbours) and the tension between East and South (and their respective mentors) – that have led some analysts to compare the ENP to a 'Twix' bar – have ended up weakening, rather than strengthening, the ENP and its 'transformative' potential.

A first balance sheet

The first two years of full implementation of the ENP came to an end in December 2006, along with the 1999–2006 EU budget. Sixteen countries had been involved – six from Eastern Europe and the South Caucasus, ten from the Mediterranean – and 11 Action Plans had been put in place, including those for the Southern Caucasus and Lebanon.

The priorities for action had been streamlined and ranked, but they remained quite diverse. Among the top four for both the Eastern and the Mediterranean countries, in fact, the only priority that recurred in all of the Action Plans was the 'improvement of the investment and business climate' – which, admittedly, reflected the EU's self-interest.

Among the others, the fight against corruption was paramount with the Eastern countries, the fight against terrorism with the Southern ones. The former were expected to 'develop' democracy, the latter to 'encourage' it. And while conflict resolution was crucial in the East and the Caucasus, developing transport and infrastructure was essential in the Mediterranean.

This also highlighted the growing diversity of goals attached to the ENP, some of which do not fall within the remit of the Commission, let alone DG Relex proper. Combating (or just containing) the spread of terrorism and weapons of mass destruction (WMD), solving 'frozen' conflicts in border or contested regions, stemming (or just controlling) illegal immigration, securing energy supply: these are all issues that can hardly be addressed effectively in the context and with the instruments of only the ENP. Indeed, they seriously risk overloading it.

Still, some of the 'neighbours' have done quite well: Morocco, Jordan and Ukraine in particular – that is, those who were already convinced of the merits of reform – plus of course Israel, which was and still is a special case anyway.[2] By contrast, others had shown little progress (Tunisia and Egypt being the most relevant cases in point), while Belarus and Libya remained problem countries and Algeria hard to engage, according to the Commission's own assessment made in the Communication of 4 December 2006 that launched the new 'ENP-plus'.[3]

It is a fact, however, that the Action Plans are now better defined and tailored to the specific characteristics of each recipient country, although this makes the original idea of a common 'template' more elusive. The practice of linking funding to performance also represents undeniable progress, especially if one looks at the poor record of the MEDA programme. Yet any objective impact assessment of the ENP proper on the various countries' performances remains problematic: at best, it has contributed to reinforcing existing progress, but it has failed to make a difference where no progress was discernible.

The resources

Meanwhile, with the new seven-year EU budget, the overall financial endowment has improved: the new European Neighbourhood and Partnership Instrument (ENPI), replacing both TACIS and MEDA, amounts to roughly €12 billion for the period 2007–2013, with a real increase of 30 per cent over the previous period. In addition, the European Investment Bank has earmarked special lending programmes.

Still, the new endowment lies below the initial requests of the Commission in the 2005 budget negotiations; it now incorporates headings that were previously included elsewhere in the EU budget; and ENPI money (rather than the dedicated Stability Instrument) has already been used for the reconstruction of Lebanon, thus reducing the actual availability of cash.

More generally, the overall population of the countries covered by Action Plans is well above 120 million: as a result, per capita allocations remain modest, especially considering the breadth of policy areas to cover.

The EU can certainly do better. But how much is enough?

If one takes the entire set of policy goals attached to the ENP, €12 billion over seven years – plus a dedicated staff of 30-odd officials in the Commission (not including those who are only tangentially involved in it) – represent a pittance indeed. However, if one takes a more limited view of the scope of specific actions (and also considers the declining resources that the member states devote to their own neighbours), the current endowment may be seen as an acceptable point of departure. Still, it would seem desirable that the 2008–2009 budget review made more resources available to the ENP.

Finally, while the ENPI cake is marginally bigger, its shares have slightly changed: 62 per cent now goes to the South (it was 70 pre-2007) and 38 to the East (30 per cent previously), although the difference is much less pronounced in per capita terms. Internal disputes over regional allocations, however, have not abated: while the so-called 'Club Med' keeps fighting its corner, the now more numerous Central European EU members demand extra resources for their own neighbours.

And it is not only a matter of money. When the then incoming German Presidency announced, at the end of 2006, that it would promote a new *Ostpolitik* for the whole Union, the Southern EU members reacted by encouraging the ensuing Portuguese presidency to rebalance that toward the South. For its part Slovenia, which presided over the Union in the first half of 2008, was more balanced – being, in fact, both a Mediterranean and a Central European country.

But differences exist also inside each 'geopolitical' coalition, so to speak: Germany's vision of an EU *Ostpolitik* does not necessarily coincide with Poland's; Finland and Denmark share many views, bar how to deal with Russia in the Caucasus; France and Spain are often at odds over Morocco – and so are the UK and Italy over Libya.

Last but certainly not least, a fundamental question needs to be addressed at some stage in the future: what is in it for our neighbours? Arguably, not enough: it is difficult to reject entirely the charge that the ENP seems primarily designed to meet the interests of EU members, also in terms of internal balance, and that it tends to present the recipients with a take-it-or-leave-it list of requests and conditional offers (bar eventual EU accession) that may fall on deaf ears. Trade is perhaps the most relevant case in point – and one that, significantly, does not lie within the remit of DG Relex: when it comes to opening the Union's market to South Mediterranean tomatoes or Georgian wine, in fact, the overall EU approach shows all its limits.

...and where to

To start with, why not make the distinction between East and South more explicit, turn the 'Twix' bar into a 'Kit Kat' and envisage more distinct 'templates' – or rather (*sub-*) *regional clusters* – for the Union's neighbours?

The key differentiation would be between European and non-European ones, but additional distinctions may also prove useful.

To start with, Ukraine and Moldova (plus Belarus, whenever the conditions are ripe) can be put into a slightly different box from the South Caucasus countries, namely one more similar to that reserved for the Western Balkan countries – with the new Black Sea 'space' and the fledgling GUAM framework (Georgia, Ukraine, Armenia and Moldova) connecting them all. For the three Caucasus republics, indeed, much will also depend Turkey's future, as their 'neighbour-ness' to the EU is in part a variable of Ankara's accession prospects. All these countries are, incidentally, members of the Council of Europe and therefore share a commitment to common values and principles, which provides an additional rationale for their inclusion in a distinct cluster.

The priorities for action would thus be roughly the same for all these 'Eastern EU neighbours', and so would the relevant incentives and rewards offered by the EU. These could prove more solid in the realm of trade, as is already the case with Ukraine (and perhaps soon Georgia), where concessions are easier for the EU to make bilaterally than multilaterally.

The second main cluster would be for the *non-European* neighbours. Here, too, a common set of priorities, incentives and rewards would be in place, but while the Barcelona-related ambition of a Mediterranean 'free trade area by 2010' should be abandoned once and for all, more realistic and balanced goals should be set regarding trade on the one hand and good governance, managed migration and the fight against terrorism on the other. For instance, is the *acquis* an appropriate term of reference for countries with no prospect or intention of joining the EU ever? And how compatible are, at least in the short term, the calls for internal liberalisation and those for tighter controls on illegal migration and prevention of terrorist activities?

Within this second broad cluster, the Maghreb/North Africa region presents peculiar challenges that only partially overlap with those of the Mashrek/Middle East proper – and this should be taken into account, too. In other words, two or even three sub-clusters (also considering

Israel's special position) may deserve to be devised, in order also to combine the country-specific approach that has gained ground over time with a credible sub-regional approach in which cross-border issues can also be addressed more effectively and comprehensively.

At the same time, differentiation based on performance should remain, and the greater commonality among these 'Southern neighbours' could make it easier to enforce peer pressure and best practice.

Such geographical 'clusters' could also turn out to be the most appropriate framework in which to place, in perspective, two recent major policy initiatives to revamp the ENP: the Union for the Mediterranean, proposed by France in mid-2007 and finalised in the autumn of 2008 at a summit in Marseille; and the Eastern Partnership, jointly launched by Poland and Sweden in May 2008 and set to be finalised by early 2009.

The latter represents in many ways a response to the former. And, taken together, they reproduce the geopolitical dualism (or cleavage) that lies at the heart of the ENP. While differences are discernible between their respective formats (in terms of the status of non-EU players, overall institutional set-up and practical goals), they both tap into the same reservoir of instruments. And each aims at concentrating the minds of EU policy-makers (and interested member states) on a specific sub-set of neighbours by taking them as a group. This could indeed be used to achieve much needed differentiation inside the ENP but without generating too much fragmentation and 'ad-hoc-ery'.

On top of that, the Eastern Partnership proper may end up profiting from the shockwaves of the August 2008 conflict in Georgia. In fact, the potential stabilising role of the EU (also in comparison with NATO) in the wider area that lies between the enlarged Union and Russia has been emphasised by recent developments, to the extent that even traditionally enlargement-sceptic countries (including France) have started considering the possibility of opening up an accession perspective for Ukraine, however far on the horizon. This could in turn speed up a de facto decoupling of Eastern Europe (arguably including the South Caucasus) from the Southern/Mediterranean neighbours, thus creating a dedicated policy 'space' for the Eastern Partnership in which a degree of *finalité* could eventually be brought to bear.

As a result, some elements of sub-regional cooperation and integration inside each main cluster could become part of the overarching ENP 'template', and also increase the incentives and rewards that the EU could apply. Policy consistency, in other words, should be coupled with a better balance between *conditionality* and *reciprocity*, that is between the interests of the EU and those of the neighbours themselves – lacking which, the ENP seriously risks not being 'bought' by its main recipients.

Moreover, and more specifically, all EU neighbours could thus acquire new incentives to align themselves to CFSP decisions; could gain special access to European Security and Defence Policy (ESDP) bodies and missions, well beyond the current generic one as 'third countries', and could even participate directly in some EU specialised agencies – especially those that matter most for an effective neighbour-hood policy, starting with Frontex.

New treaty, new Commission, new policy?

Finding new and more effective incentives for the neighbours and ways to 'deepen' the ENP has indeed been the key priority for the Commission – and the Union at large – over the past two years, as showed by a series of Presidency Reports (June 2007) and Commission Communications (March 2008) on its implementation and further development.

This proves once again that the ENP remains very much a work in progress, and in part also a misnomer: it does not deal with *Europe's* but rather with the EU's 'near abroad'; it does not apply to a *single* neighbourhood; and it is not a *policy* in its own right but rather a set of instruments searching for their most appropriate rationale and set-up. In a way, it is still tied to the traditional approach of a 'civilian power', with all its advantages but also its intrinsic limitations.

In retrospect, it can also be argued that the ENP is the product of a peculiar time in the European integration process and the development of its external policies, coming as it did at the end of the 'Big Bang' enlargement (which prompted a reassessment of the Union's borders and programmes) and at the beginning of a mounting confronta-tion between the Council and the Commission over their respective competences in 'foreign' policy.

As a result, it has been conditioned as much by intra-EU bureaucratic politics as by the different geopolitical priorities of the member states (for which it has become a quintessential catalyst), let alone the linger-ing uncertainty over the future of enlargement itself. Institutionally, it has basically coincided with the mandate of the Barroso Commission (2004–2009) and, in particular, with the tenure of Commissioner Ferrero-Waldner. Yet things are likely to change with the appointment of a new Commission – arguably in the autumn of 2009 – especially if the new provisions enshrined in the Lisbon Treaty (ever) enter into force.

The new treaty, in fact, is expected also to have a significant impact on the ENP as we know it. This is not so much the case with the article (I-57) devoted to 'the EU and its neighbours', which says next to nothing. What matters instead is the whole new architecture to be built with the creation of the double-hatted 'High Representative of the Union for Foreign Affairs and Security Policy', supported by a European External Action Service (EAS), let alone the acquisition of a single legal personality for the Union as such.

In this respect, of course, important details still have to be thrashed out regarding the implementation of such new architecture: some are expected to be sorted out toward the end of the ratification process (whenever this happens, if at all), others are more likely to go through a trial and testing period of a few years (possibly until 2013/14, when both the current EU budget and the next Commission expire), at the end of which the whole 'foreign policy' set-up of the enlarged Union may look quite different from the current one.[4]

In this transitional phase, in fact, the ENP is expected to fall under the supervision of the new High Representative (HR), who will also be one of the Vice-Presidents (VP) of the Commission. However, the HR/VP's overall job description and workload appear unmanageable already. As a result, some specific common policies could remain under the *operational* responsibility of a dedicated Commissioner and/or Council Special Representative.

A degree of 'double-hatting' could indeed help to address some of the structural weaknesses of the ENP. This is hardly possible in the framework of the current treaty, but it would become mandatory – at least at the top – with the new one. What is more, it would impose better coordination (and possibly integration), that is between the separate geographical desks of, respectively, the Commission and the Council Secretariat, *possibly within the framework of the new External Action Service*; and it could extend also below the level of the HR/VP proper, with cascading effects on the whole foreign policy machinery, including the EU Delegations in third countries.

Accordingly, the management of a more integrated and better targeted ENP, capable of bringing to bear all the tools at the disposal of the Union across its 'pillars', could be trusted to more than just one Commissioner, and supervising the regional policies for each of the clusters mentioned above (or others, of course). And the need to devise and share out credible portfolios for a growing number of Commissioners could contribute to making this happen: if there has been a Commissioner for Multilingualism, it should not be taboo to consider having one for the Union for the Mediterranean (possibly alongside Development) and one for the Eastern Partnership (possibly alongside Enlargement), especially if the next college is organised in policy-based sub-groups coordinated by a 'senior' Commissioner or Vice-President.

The Santer Commission (1994–99) did already operate on the basis of a geographical division of competences among members of the college. That experience did not prove particularly successful then, because it was also coupled with a further division of functional competencies (involving, i.e. trade and humanitarian aid) that dispersed rather than concentrated minds and resources. After that, while a dedicated DG for Enlargement was created, coordination among the Commissioners in charge of external policies remained difficult and patchy. Yet the Lisbon Treaty's overall architecture could prevent that from happening again and generate more coordination and consistency across the board.

In principle, and in perspective, a degree of cross-pillar 'contamination' should be considered a positive development, contributing as it would to a more coherent and 'joined-up' common policy toward the Union's neighbours that would include (and bind) not just the Community/Union as such, but also the individual member states.

This would be much harder to put in place *without* the Lisbon Treaty. While some distribution of geographical portfolios among Commissioners would still be conceivable, the absence of a common 'roof' and coordination across pillars could turn this into a liability rather than an asset. Indeed, this is a typical case in which only new legal obligations may be able to overcome the lack of political will and institutional incentives to improving policy formulation and implementation. Still, a degree of internal hierarchisation coupled with some geographical division of labour could only benefit the overall effectiveness of the Commission in external relations, building on the experience made with the Prodi Commission (1999–2004) under the coordination of Chris Patten.

Regardless of what may happen with the Lisbon Treaty, in other words, the formation and internal set-up of the next European Commission will represent a big opportunity to rethink and relaunch the Union's approach to the outside world, starting with its neighbouring areas. In fact, as it stands now (and despite the progress made since its inception), the ENP displays and epitomises all the essential features of the current

EU policy-making system in external and foreign policy – for good and, especially, for ill.

Notes

1. For initial assessments see J. Batt, D. Lynch, A. Missiroli, M. Ortega and D. Triantaphyllon (2003), 'Partners and Neighbours: A CFSP for a Wider Europe', Chaillot Paper 64, Paris, EUISS; K.E. Smith (2004), 'The Outsiders: The European Neighbourhood Policy', *International Affairs*, 81 (4), pp. 757–73.
2. See R. Del Sarto (2007), 'Wording and Meaning(s): EU-Israeli Political Cooperation. According to the ENP Action Plan', *Mediterranean Politics*, 12 (1), pp. 59–75.
3. For an independent evaluation country by country see M. Emerson, G. Noutcheva and N. Popescu (2007), 'European Neighbourhood Policy Two Years On: Time Indeed For an "ENP-plus"', CEPS Policy Brief 126 (March). For a more 'horizontal' one, see R. Balfour and A. Missiroli (2007), 'Reassessing the European Neighbourhood Policy', EPC Issue Paper 54 (June).
4. For a first assessment, see G. Avery, A. Missiroli, J. Howorth, D. Rijks, S. Duke, R. Whitman, et al (2007), 'The EU Foreign Service: How to Build a More Effective Common Policy', Working Paper 28 (November). Brussels, EPC; B. Crowe (2008), 'The European External Action Service: Roadmap for Success', *Chatham House Report*. London: Royal Institute of International Affairs.

Index